CONSTANTINE

CONSTANTINE

History, historiography and legend

Edited by Samuel N. C. Lieu and Dominic Montserrat

London and New York

First published 1998
by Routledge
11 New Fetter Lane, London EC4P 4EE

Simultaneously published in the USA and Canada
by Routledge
29 West 35th Street, New York, NY 10001

Typeset in Garamond by
J&L Composition Ltd, Filey, North Yorkshire
Printed and bound in Great Britain by
Creative Print and Design (Wales), Ebbw Vale

British Library Cataloguing in Publication Data
A catalogue record for this book is available
from the British Library

Library of Congress Cataloging in Publication Data
Constantine: history, historiography and legend/edited by
Samuel N. C. Lieu and Dominic Montserrat. p. cm.
Includes bibliographical references and index.
1. Constantine I, Emperor of Rome, d. 337. 2. Emperors–Rome–Biography.
3. Rome–History–Constantine I, the Great, 306-337–Historiography.
4. Religion and state–Rome–History. 5. Legends, Christian–Rome.
I. Lieu, Samuel N. C. II. Montserrat, Dominic
DG315. C65 1998
937′.08′092–dc21   97–45571

ISBN 0-415-10747-4

CONTENTS

CONTENTS

CONTRIBUTORS

Timothy Barnes is Professor of Classics at the University of Toronto, where he has taught since 1970. He has published widely on the history, literature and religions of the Roman Empire between Tertullian and Augustine. He has recently completed a book entitled *Representation and Historical Reality in Ammianus Marcellinus*.

Averil Cameron is Warden of Keble College, Oxford.

Stuart G. Hall retired from the chair of Ecclesiastical History at King's College London in 1990, and now serves as a priest in the Scottish Episcopal Church. His publications include an edition of *Melito of Sardis On Pascha and Fragments* (1979), *Doctrine and Practice in the Early Church* (1991) and *Gregory of Nyssa: Homilies on Ecclesiastes* (1993). Since 1977 he has been editor of Early Church material for the *Theologische Realenzyklopädie*, to which he has also contributed articles, including one on Constantine.

Bill Leadbetter was Education Officer at the Museum of Ancient Cultures, Macquarie University and is now at Edith Cowan University, Perth, Western Australia.

Samuel Lieu is Professor of Ancient History and Director of the Ancient History Documentary Research Centre at Macquarie University, NSW, Australia. He previously held a personal Chair at Warwick University, UK, and was Director of the Centre for Research in East Roman Studies. He is currently co-Director of the international Corpus Fontium Manichaeorum project which is sponsored by UNESCO.

Stephen Mitchell is Professor at the University of Wales Swansea

LIST OF CONTRIBUTORS

and chairman of the University of Wales Institute of Classics and Ancient History. He is the author of *Anatolia: Land, Men and Gods in Asia Minor* (Oxford 1993) and *Cremna in Pisidia: An Ancient City in Peace and War* (London 1995).

Dominic Montserrat is Lecturer in Classics and Ancient History at the University of Warwick. He is the author of *Sex and Society in Graeco-Roman Egypt* (Columbia University Press 1996). This is his second collaboration with Sam Lieu on the historiography of Constantine, the first being *From Constantine to Julian: Pagan and Byzantine Views* (London 1996).

Jane Stevenson is Research Fellow in the Centre for British and Comparative Cultural Studies at the University of Warwick. She was previously at Sheffield University, and Pembroke College, Cambridge. Her most recent book is *The Laterculus Malalianus and the School of Archbishop Theodore* (Cambridge 1995). She is currently working on *Early Modern Women Poets: An Oxford Anthology*, and on Latin poetry by women.

Roger Tomlin is the University Lecturer in Late Roman History at the University of Oxford and a Fellow of Wolfson College. He is also interested in the Roman army, Roman epigraphy, and oriental rugs. He is joint editor of *The Roman Inscriptions of Britain* and has published the Roman curse tablets from Bath as *Tabellae Sulis* (1988).

Terry Wilfong is currently Assistant Professor in the Department of Near Eastern Studies and Assistant Curator of the Kelsey Museum, University of Michigan, and editor of *Bulletin of the American Society of Papyrologists*. He received a PhD in Egyptology from the University of Chicago in 1994, and has lectured and published extensively on ancient, Graeco-Roman and Late Antique Egypt.

Anna Wilson is a former Lecturer in Latin at the Queen's University of Belfast and in Classics at the University of Birmingham. She has written on Latin poetry and on Late Antique Christian literature, and is joint editor (with Margaret Mullett) of *The Forty Martyrs of Sebesteia* (forthcoming, *Belfast Byzantine Texts and Translations*).

ACKNOWLEDGEMENTS

This book is our second collaboration on the historiography of Constantine and his immediate successors, part of an initiative that grew out of our mutual interest in Late Antique history when we were both working in the Classics and Ancient History Department of the University of Warwick. The Centre for Research in East Roman Studies there was an essential umbrella for our various projects and we would not have been able to bring these projects to fruition without it, nor without the financial help of the European Humanities Research Centre of the University of Warwick. The latter organisation provided the sponsorship which enabled us to host the symposium on Constantine and the Birth of Christian Europe in April 1993, and the papers presented at that meeting form the nucleus of the present volume.

We owe debts of gratitude to many individuals. The most immediate is to the symposium participants: to those who provided the papers published here; to those who read papers but were for various reasons unable to offer them for publication (Graham Gould, Stephen Hill, John Matthews and Averil Cameron who kindly contributed an introduction); and to all those who attended, and whose comments provoked such lively debate.

But perhaps we owe the most to our research associates, Mark Vermes at Warwick and Bill Leadbetter in Australia. They both did an enormous amount of work at various stages of the project – proofreading, checking references, re-formatting of disks, and the countless other editorial tasks whose invisibility is not a measure of their importance. They know the extent of our indebtedness.

We are also hugely grateful to the inexhaustibly patient, helpful and interested staff of the Library of the Institute of Classical Studies: Paul Jackson, Sue Willetts, Sophia Fisher and especially

ACKNOWLEDGEMENTS

Jenny Holden (on whom often devolved the dreary, and sometimes difficult, task of retrieving obscure volumes from the basement). Even when a move of premises was imminent, with all its attendant chaos, their professionalism and bibliographical expertise overcame any other preoccupations they may have had at a trying time. We would also like to thank Dr Ligotta and the other librarians of the Warburg Institute, London, for maintaining such an outstanding collection of texts, monographs and bound off-prints on the *Nachlaß* of Constantine and arranging the material in a manner which makes it readily accessible to the researcher.

Finally, special thanks go to Richard Stoneman, our commissioning editor at Routledge, and to his assistant Coco Stevenson. Richard attended the initial symposium and always had faith in and patience with this project, even when it only slowly came to fruition after the departure of one of us to the other side of the world. *Aut non tentaris, aut perfice.*

ABBREVIATIONS

Since there is no generally agreed set of abbreviations for the patristic and other sources used in this book, many of which are non-canonical and only available in obscure publications, full bibliographical details are given below. English and French translations have been indicated where available. References to Greek papyrological publications follow the standard abbreviations of J. F. Oates *et al.* in *Checklist of Editions of Greek and Latin Papyri, Ostraca and Tablets*[4], Atlanta 1992.

All dates are CE unless explicitly stated.

AB	*Analecta Bollandiana*
Adomnán	Adomnán, *De locis sanctis*, ed. and trans. D. Meehan, Dublin 1958
AE	*Année Épigraphique*
AJP	*American Journal of Philology*
Ald., *Carm. de virg.*	Aldhelm, *Carmen de virginitate*, in *Aldhelmi opera*, ed. R. Ehwald (MGH Auct. Ant. 15), 1919: 350–471; trans. M. Lapidge and J. Rosier, *Aldhelm: The Poetic Works*, Woodbridge 1985: 102–67
Ald., *De virg.*	Aldhelm, *De virginitate*, in *Aldhelmi opera*, ed. R. Ehwald (MGH Auct. Ant. 15), 1919: 211–323; trans. M. Lapidge and M. Herren, *Aldhelm: The Prose Works*, Ipswich 1979: 59–132
Ambrose, *ep.*	Ambrose, Epistulas, ed. and trans. G. Banterle, *Lettere Sant' Ambrogio: introduzione, traduzione, note e indice*, Milan 1988.
Amm.	Ammianus Marcellinus, *Res gestae*, ed. W. Seyfarth, 2 vols, Leipzig 1978; trans. J. C. Rolfe, 3 vols, LCL, 1935–52

Anat. Studs	Anatolian Studies: Journal of the British School of Archaeology at Ankara
Anon. Vales.	Anonymus Valesianus in Origo Constantini, Anonymus Valesianus, Teil 1, Text und Kommentar, ed. I. König (Trierer historische Forschungen 11), Trier 1987; trans. J. B. Stevenson in FCJ: 43–8
ANRW	Aufstieg und Niedergang der Römischen Welt. Geschichte und Kultur Roms im Spiegel der neueren Forschung, ed. H. Temporini et al., Berlin 1972
Athan., Apol. c. Ar.	Athanasius, Apologia contra Arianos, ed. W. Bright, Athanasius' Historical Works, Oxford 1881: 11–104; trans. M. Atkinson and revised by A. Robertson in NPNF Athanasius: 97–148
Athan., V. Ant.	Athanasius, Vita Antonii, PG 26; trans. H. Ellershaws, NPNF Athanasius: 188–221
Augustine, De unico baptismo	Augustine, De unico baptismo, ed. M. Petschenig (CSEL 53: 3–34), 1912
Augustine, ep.	Augustine, Epistulae, ed. A. Goldbacher (CSCO), Vienna 1902
Basil, de adulesc.	See Basil, ep.
Basil, ep.	Basil of Caesarea, Epistulae, ed. trans. R. J. Deferrari, The Letters, 4 vols, LCL, 1926–34; de adulesc. is translated in vol. 4
BCH	Bulletin de Correspondance Hellénique
Bede, HE	Bede, Historia ecclesiastica gentis Anglorum, ed. and trans. B. Colgrave and R. A. B. Mynors, Oxford 1969
BHG	Bibliotheca Hagiographica Graeca, 3rd edn, ed. F. Halkin, 3 vols, Brussels 1957
BHL	Bibliotheca Hagiographica Latina, Brussels 1898–1901 [repr. 1947]

BJb	*Bonner Jahrbücher des Rheinischen Landesmuseums*
BNgJ	*Byzantinisch-Neugriechische Jahrbücher*
Byz.	*Byzantion*
Byz. Aus.	Byzantina Australiensia, Canberra and Melbourne
BZ	*Byzantinische Zeitschrift*
CCSL	Corpus Christianorum, Series Latina, Turnhout 1967–
Cedrenus	Cedrenus, *Compendium Historiarum*, ed. I. Becker, 2 vols, (CSHB), 1838–9
Chron. Pasch.	*Chronicon Paschale*, ed. L. Dindorf, 2 vols, (CSHB), 1832; trans. M. and M. Whitby, *Chronicon Paschale 284–628 A.D.* (TTH 7), Liverpool 1989
CIL	Corpus Inscriptionum Latinarum
CJ	*Codex Justinianus*, ed. P. Krüger, *Corpus Iuris Civilis*, vol. 2, Berlin 1929
Const. Sirm.	*Constitutiones Sirmondianae*, eds T. Mommsen and P. Meyer, Berlin 1904; trans. C. Pharr *et al.*, *The Theodosian Code*, Princeton 1952: 477–86
CP	*Classical Philology*
CSCO	Corpus Scriptorum Christianorum Orientalium, Vienna and Louvain 1903–
CSEL	Corpus Scriptorum Ecclesiasticorum Latinarum, Vienna 1867–
CSHB	Corpus Scriptorum Historiae Byzantinae, 49 vols, Bonn
CTh	*Codex Theodosianus*, eds T. Mommsen and P. Meyer, Berlin 1904; trans. C. Pharr *et al.*, *The Theodosian Code*, Princeton 1952
Eph. Graec., *Enc. Bas.*	Ephrem Graecus, *In Basilium Magnum*, eds (1) S. Assemani, *Ephraemi Syri Opera omnia quae exstant graece (latine et syriace)*, vol. II, Rome 1743: 289–96; (2) S. G. Mercati, *Monumenta Biblica et Ecclesiastica 1, S. Ephraimi Syri Opera I 1: Sermones in Abraham et Isaac, In Basilium Magnum, In Eliam*, Rome 1915
Eus., *HE*	Eusebius, *Historia Ecclesiastica*, ed. E. Schwartz (GCS IX/1–3), 1903–09; trans.

	H. J. Lawlor and J. R. L. Oulton, *Eusebius etc., The Ecclesiastical History etc.*, 2 vols, London 1927–8
Eus., *Tric. Or.*	*Tricennial Oration*, ed. I. A. Heikel, *Oratio de laudibus Constantini* (GCS 7), 1902: 195–223; trans. H. A. Drake, *In Praise of Constantine: A Historical Study of Eusebius' Tricennial Orations*, Berkeley 1976: 83–102
Eus., *VC*	*Vita Constantini*, ed. F. Winkelmann, *Über das Leben des Kaisers Konstantin* (GCS 40 = Eusebius Werke I/1), 1975; trans. E. C. Richardson, NPNF, 2nd ser., I: 481–559. New trans. by A. M. Cameron and S. G. Hall is in preparation
FCJ	*From Constantine to Julian: Pagan and Byzantine Views*, eds Samuel N. C. Lieu and Dominic Montserrat, London 1996
FGrH	*Fragmente der griechischen Historiker*, ed. F. Jacoby *et al.*, Leiden 1923
FHG	*Fragmenta Historicorum Graecorum*, ed. C. Müller, 5 vols, Paris 1841–70
GCS	Die griechischen christlichen Schrift-steller der ersten Jahrhunderte, Leipzig 1897–1941; Berlin and Leipzig 1953; Berlin 1954–
Gildas	*Gildae de excidio Britanniae*, ed. H. Williams (Cymmrodorion Record Series 3), London 1899
Giraldus Cambrensis	Giraldus Cambrensis, *Topographia Hiberniae*, ed. J. J. O'Meara, *Proceedings of the Royal Irish Academy* 52 C 4 (1948–50) 113–77
GRBS	*Greek, Roman and Byzantine Studies*
Greg. Naz. *Or.*	Gregory Naziarizus, *Orationes*, PG 35–6; complete edition and translation ongoing in SC
Greg. Nyss., *In xl mart.*	Gregory of Nyssa, *In quadraginta martyres*, PG 46

Greg. Nyss., *In Bas. fratr.*	Gregory of Nyssa, *In Basilium fratrem*, in *Sermones Pars II*, ed. V. Jaeger *et al.* (= Gregorii Nysseni Opera X.1), Leiden 1990: 109–42
Greg. Nyss., *Serm.*	Gregory of Nyssa, *Sermones Pars I and II*, ed. G. Heil *et al.* (= Gregorii Nysseni Opera, vols IX and X.1), Leiden 1967 and 1990
Greg. Nyss., *V. Macr.*	Gregory of Nyssa, *Vie de S. Macrine*, ed. and trans. P. Maraval (SC 178), 1971
Greg. Nyss., *V. Moys.*	Gregory of Nyssa, *Vie de Moïse*, ed. and trans. J. Daniélou (SC 1ter), 1968
ILCV	*Inscriptiones Latinae Christianae Veteres*, ed. E. Diehl, Berlin 1924–31; corrected edn by J. Moreau and H. Marrou, Berlin 1961
ILS	*Inscriptiones Latinae Selectae*, ed. H. Dessau, Berlin 1892–1916
Irenaeus, *Adv. Haer.*	Irenaeus of Lyons, *Contre les hérésies* 3.2, eds A. Rousseau and L. Doutreleau (SC 211), 1974
JEH	*Journal of Ecclesiastical History*
Jerome, *Chron.*	Hieronymus [Jerome], *Chronicon*, ed. R. Helm (GCS 47 = Eusebius Werke VII), 1984
Jerome, *ep.*	Jerome, *Sancti Hieronymi Epistulae*, ed. I. Hilberg (CSEL 54–6), 1912
JHS	*Journal of Hellenic Studies*
JRA	*Journal of Roman Archaeology*
JRS	*Journal of Roman Studies*
JTS, n.s.	*Journal of Theological Studies*, new series
Julian, *ep.*	*imp. Caesaris Flavii Claudii Iuliani Epistulae Leges Poematia Fragmenta Varia*, ed. J. Bidez and F. Cumont, Paris and Oxford, 1922; trans. (of the letters) W. C. Wright, LCL Julian iii

Lact., *De mort.*	Lactantius, *De mortibus persecutorum*, ed. and trans. J. L. Creed, Oxford 1984
LCL	Loeb Classical Library, Cambridge, MA
Libanius, *Or.*	Libanius, *Libanii opera* vols I–IV, ed. R. Förster, Leipzig 1906
Malalas, *Chronographia*	Malalas, *Chronographia*, ed. L. Dindorf (CSHB), 1831; trans. E. Jeffreys, *The Chronicle of John Malalas* (Byz. Aus. 4), 1986
MAMA	*Monumenta Asiae Minoris Antiqua*
MEFRA	*Mélanges d'Archéologie et du Histoire de l'École Française de Rome. Antiquité*
Men. Rhet.	Menander Rhetor, ed. and trans. D. Russell and N. G. Wilson, Oxford 1981
MGH Auct. Ant.	Monumenta Germaniae Historica, Auctores Antiquissimi, Berlin 1877–1919
NGWG	Nachrichten. Gesellschaft der Wissenschaften zu Göttingen, philologische-historische Klasse
Not. Dig.	*Notitia Dignitatum accedunt notitia urbis Constantinopolitanae*, ed. O. Seeck, Berlin 1876: *Not. Dig. Occ.* = pp. 103–226; *Not. Dig. Or.* = pp. 1–102
Not. Dig. Occ.	see *Not. Dig.*
Not. Dig. Or.	see *Not. Dig.*
NPNF	The Writings of the Nicene and Post-Nicene Fathers, New York 1887–92 and Oxford 1890–1900
ODB	*Oxford Dictionary of Byzantium*, 3 vols, Oxford 1991
Origen, *Hom. in Ex.*	Origen, *Homiliae in Exodum*, ed. and trans. M. Borret, *Homélies sur l'Exode* (SC 321), 1985
Orosius, *adv. pag.*	Orosius, *Historia adversus paganos*, ed. C. Zangemeister, Leipzig 1889; trans. R. J. Deferrari, *The Seven Books of History Against the Pagans* (Fathers of the Church 50), Washington, DC 1964
Palladius, *Dial.*	Palladius, *Dialogus*, ed. P. R. Coleman-Norton, *Palladii Dialogus de vita sancti Joannis Chrysostomi*, Cambridge, MA 1928

Palladius, *Proem. in HL*	Palladius, *Proemium in Historia Lausaica*, ed. C. Butler, *The Lausaic History of Palladius, Texts and Studies*, 2 vols, 1898–1904; trans. R. T. Meyer, *Palladius: The Lausaic History* (Ancient Christian Writers 34), London 1965
Pan. Lat.	*Panégyriques latins*, ed. E. Galletier, 3 vols, Paris 1949–55; trans. C. E. V. Nixon and B. S. Rodgers, *In Praise of Later Roman Emperors: The Panegyrici Latini, Introduction, Translation and Historical Commentary*, Berkeley and Los Angeles, CA, and London 1994
Pass. Eusign.	*Passio Eusignii*, ed. P. Devos, 'Une recension nouvelle de la passion grecque BHG 639 de Saint Eusignios', *AB* 100 (1982) 209–28
Paul., *ep.*	Paulinus, *epistulae*, ed. G. de Hartel (CSEL 29), 1894
Paul., *V. Amb.*	Paulinus of Milan, *Vita Sancti Ambrosii*, revised text by M. S. Kaniecka, Washington, DC 1928
PG	*Patrologiae cursus completus, series Graeco-Latina*, ed. J. P. Migne, 162 vols, Paris 1857–1928
Philost., *HE*	Philostorgius, *Historia Ecclesiastica*, ed. J. Bidez and revised by J. Winkelmann (GCS 21), 1972; trans. of the summary of Photius by E. Walford in *Sozomen and Philostorgius*, Bohn's Ecclesiastical Library, London 1855: 429–528. A new translation by A. Emmett Nobbs is in progress
Phot., *Bibl.*	Photius, *Bibliotheca*, ed. P. Henry, 8 vols, Paris 1959–77; trans. codd. 1–165 only by J. H. Freese, *The Library of Photius*, London 1920
PL	*Patrologiae cursus completus, series Latina*, ed. J. P. Migne *et al.*, 221 vols, Paris 1844–1974
PLRE	*The Prosopography of the Later Roman Empire* I, eds A. H. M. Jones, J. R.

LIST OF ABBREVIATIONS

	Martindale and J. Morris, Cambridge 1971
Procopius, *De aed.*	Procopius, *De aedificiis*, ed. J. Haury, Leipzig 1913; trans. H. B. Dewing, LCL Procopius vii
Proem. in HL	See Palladius
Prudentius, *Peristephanon*	*Aurelii Prudentii Clementis Carmina*, ed. M. P. Cunningham, (CSEL 126), 1966
RAC	*Reallexikon für Antike und Christentum*, Stuttgart 1950–
RE	A. Pauly (ed.), *Real-Enzyclopädie der klassischen Altertumswissenschaft*, ed. G. Wissowa, Stuttgart 1893–1955
REG	*Revue des Études Grecques*
Rh. Mus.	*Rheinisches Museum für Philologie*
RQA	*Römische Quartalschrift für die christliche Altertumskunde und für Kirchengeschichte*
RRMAM	D. H. French, *Roman Roads and Milestones of Asia Minor*, 2 vols, (British Archaeological Reports, International Series 105 and 392), Oxford 1981–88
Rubisca	Rubisca, *The Hisperica Famina II: Related Poems*, ed. M. W. Herren, Toronto 1987
Ruf., *HE*	Rufinus, *Historia Ecclesiastica*, ed. E. Schwartz (GCS = Eusebius Werke II/2), 1908: 960–1040
SC	Sources Chrétiennes, Paris
SEG	*Supplementum Epigraphicum Graecum*, Leiden 1923–
SHA	*Scriptores Historiae Augustae*, ed. E. Hohl, rev. W. Seyfarth and C. Samberger, Leipzig 1965; trans. D. Magie, LCL *Scriptores Historiae Augustae*, 3 vols
Socrates, *HE*	Socrates Scholasticus, *Historia Ecclesiastica*, ed. G. C. Hansen, *Sokrates Kirchengeschichte* (GCS new series, vol. 1), 1995
Sozomen, *HE*	Sozomenus, *Historia Ecclesiastica*, ed. J. Bidez and revised by G. C. Hansen (GCS 50), 1960; trans. C. D. Hartranft in NPNF, *Socrates and Sozomen*: 239–427
TAM	*Tituli Asiae Minoris*

TAPA	*Transactions of the American Philological Association*
Thdt., *HE*	Theodoretus, *Historia Ecclesiastica*, ed. L. Parmentier and revised by F. Scheidweiler (GCS 44), 1954; trans. (with different chapter divisions) by F. Jackson in NPNF, *Theodoret and Gennadius*: 33–159
Thdt., *Quaest. in Ex.*	Theodoretus, *Quaestiones in Exodum*, PG 80
Thphn., *Chron.*	Theophanes, *Chronographia*, ed. C. de Boor, 2 vols, Leipzig 1883–5 (reprinted Hildesheim 1963); trans. C. Mango and R. Scott, *The Chronicle of Theophanes Confessor*, Oxford 1997
Trioedd	*Trioedd Ynys Prydein*, ed. and trans. R. Bromwich, Cardiff 1978
TTH	Translated Texts for Historians, Liverpool 1985–
TU	Texte und Untersuchungen zur Geschichte der altchristlichen Literatur, Leipzig and Berlin 1929–
Vegetius, *epit.*	Fl. Vegetius Renatus, *Epitome rei militaris*, Teubner, ed. A. Önnerfors, Stuttgart 1995; trans. N. P. Milner, *Epitome of Military Science* (TTH 16), Liverpool 1993
V. Sylv.	Anonymous, *Vita sancti Sylvestri papae et confessoris* (BHL 7725), ed. B. Mombritius, *Sanctuarium seu Vitae Sanctorum*, 2nd edn, 2 vols, Paris 1910, vol. II: 508–31 (reprinted with modern section and line numbering by P. De Leo, *Il Constitutum Constanti: copilazione agiografica del sec. VIII: Note e documenti per una nuova lettura* (Ricerche sui falsi medioevali I), Reggio di Calabria 1974: 153–221)
Zon.	Zonaras, *Annales*, eds M. Pinder *et al.*, 3 vols (CSHB), 1841–97
Zos.	Zosimus, *Historia nova*, ed. L. Mendelssohn, Leipzig 1887; trans. R. T. Ridley, *Zosimus: New History* (Byz. Aus. 2), 1982
ZPE	*Zeitschrift für Papyrologie und Epigraphik*

1

INTRODUCTION

Averil Cameron

Constantine the Great (sole emperor 324–337) has been for centuries a figure of major importance and major disagreement among historians. Nothing has happened in recent years to lessen either the interest or the controversy which his reign has aroused. Perhaps the extreme hostility and scepticism felt towards him in the nineteenth and early twentieth centuries as a Christian emperor have abated somewhat, as religious partisanship itself has ceased to occupy the central ground in historical consciousness. Historians of the Roman empire today are indeed interested in religious history, but their interest takes a very different form, and few will venture to produce a kind of history overtly dictated by their own personal religious agenda. This ought to be a good moment, therefore, at which to attempt a new assessment of the historical Constantine.

Most, though not all, of the chapters in this volume originated as papers at a conference organised by Sam Lieu and Dominic Montserrat at the University of Warwick in 1993; the chapters by Bill Leadbetter and Jane Stevenson are additions. The contributions are, tellingly, divided into two sections, 'History and historiography', and 'Legend', and with some qualification, this can fairly be said to represent the major directions of recent research. In the 'History' section, while Barnes, Tomlin and Mitchell address general historical questions, Hall returns to the analysis of the *Vita Constantini* as an historical source; the rest of the contributions in the volume address in different ways the history and legend of Constantine, and in particular, the ways in which he was transformed into a Christian saint and hero, whether in the history of Constantinople, or in relation to the wider Christian world. Literary, rather than historical, analysis (here represented in

1

Anna Wilson's chapter on the *Vita Constantini*) is another direction observable in recent scholarship.

The appearance of this volume is timely. Books and articles on Constantine continue to appear in uninterrupted sequence. But the appearance of Paul Magdalino's edited collection[1] indicates a new and lively interest in the history of the Constantine myth and in the imperial image which Constantine was thought to represent. F. Winkelmann's critical edition of the *Vita Constantini* (1975, revised edition 1993), and the collection of his numerous supporting articles,[2] had already drawn attention to the later and legendary lives of Constantine, as had publications on their evolution in the Early Byzantine period.[3] Sam Lieu and Dominic Montserrat have themselves recently published a volume of annotated translations of some of these texts.[4] Also relevant is the current interest in the history of the empire as a city and as capital of an empire, for which the reality of Constantine's achievements and the way in which they were later perceived are equally relevant. To Gilbert Dagron's fundamental *Naissance d'une capitale*,[5] we must add Cyril Mango, *Le développement urbain de Constantinople (IVe–VIIe siècles)* (Paris 1985), and the essays in C. Mango and G. Dagron, *Constantinople and its Hinterland* (Aldershot 1995).

The sources for the reign of Constantine itself have also received attention. Commentaries such as those of H. A. Drake on Eusebius' *Tricennalian Oration*, J. L. Creed on Lactantius' *De mortibus persecutorum*, I. König on the *Origo Constantini* and C. E. V. Nixon and B. S. Rodgers on the *Panegyrici Latini* are making the period more accessible, and opening new solutions to traditional problems. The nature of the *Vita Constantini*, now recognised as not only Eusebian, but characteristically Eusebian, has attracted detailed attention from T. D. Barnes.[6] Anna Wilson's chapter in this volume recognises the artfulness of the writing of the *Vita Constantini*, a text strangely neglected by students of biography or hagiography, and enables us to link it to the classic fourth-century Greek works that were to follow, including Gregory of Nyssa's *Life of Moses* and *Life of Macrina*. Stuart Hall in this volume addresses the old problem of the Constantinian documents quoted at length in the *Vita Constantini*; elsewhere he has shown with what scrupulous attention to detail Eusebius has crafted a subtly changed narrative in the *Vita Constantini* from the account he himself wrote of Constantine's rise more than twenty years earlier. Wilson's study here marks a contribution to the necessary rescue of Eusebius' life from the realm of source-criticism to that of

INTRODUCTION

literature; the next step is to set it side by side with another highly political, and artful, life, the *Life of Antony*.[7]

Despite T. D. Barnes' *Constantine and Eusebius*, which sets out a strongly argued case for seeing Constantine as a committed and proselytising Christian, the argument as to the date and degree of his commitment continues. Understanding Eusebius is critical to providing the answer, but his claims must be set against what is stated or can be deduced from other sources. In this volume, Barnes extends the argument of his *Athanasius and Constantius*, arguing against the traditional view of the church at this period as being dominated by the state, and of Constantine himself as 'Caesaropapist'. Stephen Mitchell's conclusion that there is little evidence for extensive church building in this period, despite the space devoted to this topic in the *Vita Constantini*, fits well with the argument of Cyril Mango, that contrary to Eusebius' claims for its fully Christian character, Constantinople grew to be a Christian city only slowly.[8] By the fifth and sixth centuries, however, Constantine himself was firmly established in the popular Byzantine mind as the saintly Christian founder of the capital, and, with his mother Helena, as the one responsible for finding the True Cross in Jerusalem. The True Cross figures more and more prominently in the later legendary accounts, until it all but obliterates the historical Constantine. All the more remarkable, then, that Eusebius never mentions the discovery in the *Vita Constantini*. Some scholars, indeed, have found this so hard to understand that they are willing to argue that Eusebius deliberately suppressed it.[9] This seems unlikely. But the loss of the historical Constantine was real enough. The *Vita Constantini* was not much read in Byzantium, it seems; it passed into the limbo shared by early pagan versions of Constantine's reign and was rescued only at the end of the Iconoclast period, though even then it met with little favour. Eusebius himself had been temporarily paraded as a newly discovered iconoclast writer, but the legendary *Lives* of Constantine show little or no knowledge of the original *Vita Constantini* from which, in a sense, they derive. Meanwhile, amid the tangle of translations and versions of apocryphal texts in the early medieval period, the legendary Constantine had passed to literature in Coptic, Syriac and other languages, and to the West, through the stories studied here by Sam Lieu, where the Constantine legend was used to justify the claims of the Roman Church; yet other details are traceable in the Irish and Anglo-Saxon traditions discussed by Jane Stevenson.

3

The influence of Constantine himself continued to the end. It was believed that the eighth-century Iconoclast emperor Constantine V would return on his horse and lead Byzantium to victory. The last emperor of Byzantium was another Constantine, and fell in the last day's fighting when Mehmet II's army entered the city in 1453; to some, however, he lived on, and his descent was claimed until the present century.[10]

This volume is not just about Constantine I, the first Christian emperor and founder of Constantinople. It takes the reader from the historical circumstances of Constantine's reign, and the historical problems surrounding them, through the developing thickets of story and legend, and on to the Constantine whom the Byzantines knew as a saint or an imperial prototype, and whom the Western Church claimed as its own patron. Like the fabled phoenix, as Eusebius claims, or his eponymous successors, Constantine possessed the gift of immortality, the immortality that is conveyed by history and legend and which, rather than Constantine himself, is the real subject of this volume.

NOTES

1 Magdalino 1994.
2 Winkelmann 1993.
3 In particular Dagron 1984, Cameron and Herrin 1984, Kazhdan 1987.
4 Lieu and Montserrat 1996.
5 Dagron 1974.
6 Barnes 1989a; Barnes 1994 – but see Cameron 1997.
7 For which see Cameron 1997.
8 Mango 1985.
9 So, out of several examples, Borgehammar 1991.
10 See Nicol 1992.

Part I

CONSTANTINE
History and historiography

2

CONSTANTINE, ATHANASIUS AND THE CHRISTIAN CHURCH

Timothy Barnes

It is undeniably true, as Fergus Millar has recently reminded us, that the conversion of Constantine in 312 was not 'the moment when Christianity became "the official religion of the Roman Empire"'.[1] But it is misleading to assume, as many including Norman Baynes have done, that 'for the student of the religious policy pursued by Constantine the crucial period is that which lies between the Battle of the Milvian Bridge and the Battle of Chrysopolis' in 324.[2] Such an exclusive concentration on the conversion of Constantine in 312 and its immediate consequences leads directly to the erroneous inference that at no point in his reign did Constantine do more than make Christianity 'the religion of successive emperors other than Julian'.[3]

That is simply to leave out of account what Constantine did after he conquered the East in 324. For when Constantine defeated Licinius in a war which he advertised as a religious crusade to rescue the Christians of the East from persecution, he was able to go much further than he had gone after he defeated Maxentius. In the winter of 312–13 Constantine began a systematic policy of giving honours, privileges and donations to the Christian Church and Christian clergy. In 324–5, as the new master of the East, he prohibited the cultic activities which until then had characterised the traditional religions of the Roman empire, and he thus affirmed the status of Christianity as the official religion of the state and its rulers. Constantine outlawed the performance of animal sacrifice, ordered that no new cult statues of the traditional gods be dedicated, and forbade magistrates and governors to begin

7

official business with the traditional act of casting incense or some other similar offering on an altar standing in their court for this ceremony.[4] Since the persecutions between 303 and 324 had been predicated on the assumption that all inhabitants of the Roman Empire except Jews had an obligation as citizens and faithful subjects to perform such an act of symbolic sacrifice on every official occasion, this prohibition indicated that the traditional religions had now lost their established status.

Whether Constantine also in the years after 324 bestowed on Christianity the privileged standing of which he deprived paganism is a question on which my views are well known and controversial.[5] In this chapter, however, I do not wish to traverse this boggy terrain yet again. My purpose is, rather, to set out some of the more important general conclusions which seem to me to follow from my detailed reconstruction of the episcopal career of Athanasius.[6]

In recent scholarship, the dominant model of the relationship between the Christian Church and the Roman state under and after Constantine has been one which was developed by scholars, especially Eduard Schwartz, who wrote in German between 1870 and 1914. It operates with terms such as 'Reichskirche' and 'kaiserliche Synodalgewalt':[7] it holds that the emperor not only convened important councils of bishops but also either presided himself (as he is often imagined to have done at Nicaea in 325)[8] or appointed an imperial official to preside in his place (the prime example being the *comes* Dionysius at the Council of Tyre in 335).[9] And it reduces the role of bishops at councils such as Nicaea and Tyre to utter insignificance by assimilating them to members of the imperial *consilium*, whose advice was not binding on the emperor. Hence, according to this model, all the decisions taken at Nicaea were, strictly speaking, decisions of Constantine alone, since he could have disregarded the merely advisory opinions of the bishops whom he had summoned to the council. As Eduard Schwartz put it in his classic study of Constantine and the Christian Church, at the Council of Nicaea in 325, 'die Form der Verhandlung war keine andere als die eines vom Kaiser abgehaltenen Schiedsgerichts'.[10] Similarly, Klaus Girardet asserted in 1975 that at the Council of Tyre in 335 'der iudex in diesem Prozeß ist Konstantin, die Bischöfe sind seine *consiliarii*'.[11] More paradoxically still, Girardet has subsequently applied the same analysis to the Council of Rome in October 313 at which Miltiades and a dozen or so other Italian bishops pronounced on the

Donatist controversy, so that this council at Rome, in Girardet's view, was the first 'Reichskonzil': for Constantine, though hundreds of miles away and not, so far as we know, represented by a *comes*, was acting as a *iudex* in a traditional manner, the only historically significant innovation being that the imperial *consilium* was not constituted of the usual officials and courtiers, but of bishops performing the same function.[12]

It is my contention that this model is not based on impartial evaluation of our evidence for the fourth century, but took its inspiration from the situation of the Church in the Germany of Bismarck and Kaiser Wilhelm II. It is significant and telling that Jacob Burckhardt's observation that 'Constantin wollte eine Reichskirche, und zwar aus politischen Gründen' occurs only in the *second* edition of his classic book about Constantine and his age, published in Germany in 1880, but is absent from the corresponding passage of the first edition, published in Switzerland shortly after the failed revolutions of 1848.[13] Even in the second edition, however, it should be noted, Burckhardt immediately went on to observe that the Church of the fourth century was able to challenge the political power of the emperors. Edward Gibbon's view had been similar: 'the distinction of the spiritual and temporal powers, which had never been imposed on the free spirit of Greece and Rome, was introduced and confirmed by the legal establishment of Christianity' and, as a result, 'a secret conflict between the civil and ecclesiastical jurisdictions embarrassed the operations of the Roman government'.[14]

This model of the relationship between Constantine and the Christian Church, though long dominant in German writing about the fourth century, has been vigorously challenged by scholars belonging to other scholarly traditions. The English theologian and patristic scholar, J. N. D. Kelly, who had studied with Hans Lietzmann in Berlin in the 1930s, dismissed Schwartz's view that Constantine imposed on the bishops at Nicaea 'the obligation of finding a formula for the admission of clergy to, or their exclusion from, the new state Church' as exaggerated, and he charged Schwartz with consistent exaggeration of 'the degree of the Church's absorption in Constantine's "Reich"'.[15] And the French legal historian Jean Gaudemet elegantly rejected the notion of Caesaropapism as if it were as implausible as the claim (which no-one has ever seriously entertained) that the Roman empire of the fourth century was a theocracy: the relationship between Church and state was one of collaboration in which each party had rights and duties of its own to uphold and perform.[16] But the protests of Kelly, Gaudemet and others have until now failed to impair the continuing wide acceptance of the paradigm laid down by Schwartz, which is still dominant in German scholarly writing about the Church in the Constantinian empire and often tacitly, or even explicitly, accepted by scholars of other nationalities.[17] Let me, therefore, set out in some detail the model of the relationship between the emperor and the bishops which my work on Athanasius partly assumes and partly attempts to establish as valid.[18]

In the period between Constantine's conquest of the East in 324 and the accession of Theodosius in 379, neither the emperor nor any of his officials ever presided over or even sat as a member of a council, except in the extraordinary circumstances of 359, when Constantius took an abnormally prominent role in theological debate, a role which had no precedent. In 359 the emperor ordered the bishops of the West and the East to meet at separate councils in Ariminum and Seleucia in order to ratify a creed which had been presented and subscribed in his presence at Sirmium on 22 May, and which thus had his prestige and authority behind it. Hence both the praetorian prefect Taurus at Ariminum and the *comes* Leonas at Seleucia, acting with Bassidius Lauricius, the governor of Isauria, played an active part in securing the compliance of the assembled bishops with the emperor's wishes. However, the historically significant fact is not that the emperor's will eventually prevailed in 359–60, but that it took the prolonged use of strong-arm tactics and deceit to extort from the bishops an acceptance of the official homoean creed which was both grudging and temporary.

The test cases for determining normal practice must be the Council of Nicaea in 325 and the Council of Tyre in 335. In the former case, despite the familiar image of Constantine seated among the bishops and presiding over their discussions, the evidence makes it clear that the emperor was not technically a member of the council at all: he took part in its discussions as an interested layman who was present, but was not a voting member of the assembly. The council proper comprised bishops, priests and deacons, and it was presided over by Ossius, the Bishop of Corduba. In the latter case, there is *prima facie* evidence that Dionysius presided: Athanasius says so and modern scholars have been very reluctant to disbelieve his testimony. But everything that Athanasius says about the Council of Tyre must be

10

evaluated carefully, not taken on trust as if his testimony were impartial. Athanasius consistently tried to discredit the Council of Tyre and its verdict against him in every way possible. Yet in his eagerness to document the bias, partiality, and improper procedures of his enemies, he quotes letters exchanged between Dionysius and the bishops at Tyre which show that the *comes* was not even present at some of the crucial sessions of the council.[19]

In both cases, a distinction must be drawn between the formal opening ceremony and the substantive deliberations of the council. Eusebius of Caesarea attended the Council of Nicaea and has left a brief and tantalising account of the opening ceremony which, though deficient in precise detail, shows that Constantine played a central role, indeed, that the ceremony was to a large degree an act of homage to the emperor by the council.[20] At Tyre in 335, the council opened with a ceremony in which the imperial *notarius* Marianus read aloud a letter from Constantine welcoming the bishops and defining the agenda of the council:[21] there is no difficulty or implausibility in holding that Dionysius presided at the opening ceremony, but then put the substantive matters and the conduct of the council wholly in the hands of the bishops.

Councils met both with imperial permission or at imperial command and without any consultation of the emperor and his officials. There had been councils of bishops even in the days when Christianity was a capital crime,[22] and there is no hint that pagan emperors were ever asked to grant permission for councils to be held in the late third and early fourth centuries. Alexander convened a council which excommunicated Arius, and Arius' supporters held counter-councils which vindicated him without any reference to Licinius until the emperor prohibited councils of bishops from meeting altogether – which may have been a partisan intervention inspired by Eusebius of Nicomedia. It was entirely predictable, therefore, that this long-standing practice should continue under Christian emperors, and there were numerous councils between 324 and 361 which met without seeking imperial permission to do so. The novelty was that after 324 the emperor sometimes summoned councils and set their agenda.

It is not certain that it was Constantine rather than the bishops, who met in Alexandria in the late autumn of 324, who summoned the council which was expected to meet at Ancyra in 325, but it was certainly the emperor who transferred the planned council from Ancyra to Nicaea.[23] Moreover, Constantine set at least part of the agenda and subsequently claimed credit for some of the decisions in which he had participated just as if he were a bishop. For some later councils in his reign, it seems certain that Constantine both summoned the bishops to meet and defined their agenda (which did not prevent them from discussing other matters too), and on occasion compelled the attendance of both bishops and other interested parties. A papyrus shows the compulsion used to secure attendance at the Council of Tyre in 335, and it was Constantine who both ordered a council to meet at Caesarea in Palestine in 334 to try Athanasius for murder and cancelled the council when Athanasius convinced him that the charge was false. Constantine also took the initiative in summoning councils of bishops to meet in Nicomedia in 327–8, in Jerusalem in 335, and in Constantinople in 336: he attended the Council of Nicomedia in December 327 or January 328; he ordered the bishops assembled at Tyre to adjourn to Jerusalem to dedicate the Church of the Holy Sepulchre in September 335, requesting them again to readmit Arius to communion; and he attended the Council of Constantinople in 336, which condemned Marcellus of Ancyra.

On the other hand, it is not necessary to suppose that the bishops who met at Antioch in 327 and deposed Eustathius and other bishops of Syria, Phoenice, and Palestine sought imperial permission before they met. And the Councils of Alexandria in 338 and 352, which pronounced Athanasius innocent of the charges on which he had been condemned and deposed, clearly assembled in defiance of the wishes of Constantius, since the councils whose verdicts they disputed had just met with the obvious approval of the emperor, who certainly attended the Council of Sirmium in 351 and probably also the Council of Antioch in early 338. Moreover, Julius did not consult Constans before holding the Council of Rome which exculpated Athanasius and Marcellus in 341: indeed, no bishop of Rome would have seen any need to seek imperial permission to hold a council in Rome under any circumstances. Nor again did Eusebius of Vercellae and Athanasius even consider consulting Julian before they convened the Council of Alexandria in 362.

The agenda of a council might include any or all of three types of business: the adjudication of disputes concerning the status of individuals; the definition of what constituted true doctrine; and disciplinary matters concerning both clergy and laity. And its membership might comprise the bishops of a single province, of several provinces or a region or, in theory, of the whole empire or whole world. But what if two councils came not merely to different decisions but to opposing ones? The ecclesiastical history of the reign of Constantius provides examples enough of this phenomenon, the clearest cases being the two councils of 338 (Antioch and Alexandria), the two councils of 341 (Antioch again and Rome) and the divided Council of Serdica in 343. There was as yet no agreed procedure for resolving such disputes. Admittedly, the synodical letters and the polemical literature of the middle of the fourth century contain appeals to the ecumenical nature of the Council of Nicaea as endowing its decisions and above all its creed with a supreme and inviolate status,[24] and Athanasius frequently argues that the decisions of a council attended by a large number of bishops ought to prevail over those of a council attended by few bishops, but the earliest clear statement of a formal hierarchy subordinating provincial to regional councils and the latter to ecumenical councils occurs at the very end of the century.[25]

Constantine declared that the decisions of councils of bishops were divinely inspired,[26] and he gave them legal force. In recording this enactment, Eusebius states that:

> He put a seal of approval on the rulings of bishops declared at councils, so that the governors of provinces were not allowed to rescind what they had decided, for he said that the priests of God were more trustworthy than any magistrate.
>
> (Eus., VC 4.27,2)

Although Eusebius mentions only the duty of provincial governors to respect and enforce the rulings of church councils, both consistency and Constantine's public pronouncements about the status of the decisions of councils required that even the emperor lacked the right to countermand them. That was a startling innovation, since the Roman emperor had traditionally been regarded as the ultimate arbiter of all disputes among his subjects.[27] Constantine denied himself the right to try bishops, who could only be condemned and deposed by a council of their peers. He did on occasion conduct a preliminary examination, which could (and sometimes did) result in the dismissal of the accusation and the acquittal of the bishop. But if he found that there was a *prima facie* case, he thereupon convened a council of bishops and submitted the whole matter to them.

Constantine's attested dealings with Athanasius fall into this pattern. When he heard Athanasius at Psammathia in 331–2, it is wrong to describe the proceedings as an imperial trial or *cognitio*, as Girardet does:[28] had Constantine not dismissed the charges as unfounded, he would not have condemned or deposed Athanasius himself, but would have submitted the case to a council of bishops. Similarly, when Athanasius was accused of murdering Arsenius, Constantine ordered the *censor* Dalmatius to investigate the charge. But he planned no 'trial for murder in Antioch', as asserted by Girardet:[29] the 'court of the *censor*' derided by Athanasius was the abortive Council of Caesarea which was instructed to meet in order to render a verdict on the charge of murder. The emperor (or his deputy) merely conducted a preliminary hearing: if he decided that there was a *prima facie* case against the accused bishop, the matter was then referred to a council of bishops who functioned as the court of both primary and ultimate jurisdiction.

After a bishop had been tried and condemned by his peers, it was both proper and necessary for the emperor to enforce his deposition by means of exile, using force if necessary. That was not in itself an innovation by or under Constantine. There was a precedent in the third century when Paul of Samosata refused to accept his deposition by a Council of Antioch: Christians of Italy, acting on behalf of their colleagues in Syria, submitted a petition to the Emperor Aurelian requesting him to compel Paul to surrender the church in Antioch.[30] What was new in the Christian empire of Constantine was the automatic enforcement of the decisions of church councils. Aurelian could have reviewed and reversed the decision of a third-century council: Constantine had bound himself in advance to accept and enforce the condemnation of a bishop by his peers meeting as a council. In practice, that did not prevent a deposed bishop like Athanasius (and perhaps Eustathius of Antioch before him) from attempting to persuade the emperor to reconsider his case, but there is only one example between 324 and 361 when a synodical condemnation was overruled by imperial fiat – in 337 when Constantinus issued an edict restoring all the bishops exiled under his father. Significantly, the Council of Antioch in 339 regarded this restoration as canonically invalid – precisely because Athanasius had returned to Alexandria without the vote of a council of bishops.

The first exile of Athanasius does not neatly fit into this pattern, since it cannot legitimately be regarded as the automatic enforcement of his condemnation by the Council of Tyre.[31] On this occasion, Constantine did not accept the decision of a council.

He was persuaded by Athanasius that it had proceeded improperly and unfairly – but before he knew of its verdict. The letter which he wrote to the bishops at Tyre did not overrule their synodical decision. He commanded them to come to him so that he could ensure fair play: in other words, he felt that he had a duty to guarantee due process – which would enable the council as a whole to reach a just verdict. But that letter, despite its prominence in Athanasius' account of his exile in 335, was immediately overtaken by events. Constantine rendered it null and void when, after the arrival of two delegations from Tyre, one bringing the council's condemnation of Athanasius, the other protesting that it was unjust, he interviewed Athanasius and sent him to Gaul. That action, however, did not reinstate the condemnation of Athanasius by the Council of Tyre as a valid deposition. The emperor refused to allow the successor whom the council had appointed in his place to become bishop of Alexandria: although he was in exile and debarred from the normal exercise of his episcopal functions, Athanasius was technically still the lawful bishop of Alexandria.

The situation of Athanasius in 335–7 was highly anomalous. In contrast, both his exile in 339 and his flight in 356 fit perfectly into the pattern of deposition by a council followed by imperial enforcement of its verdict. In 339 the decision of the Council of Antioch was put into effect at once. In the 350s, more than four years passed before Constantius could enforce the deposition of Athanasius by the Council of Sirmium. But the delay did not alter the legal basis of his supersession. Athanasius' eloquence in his *Defence before Constantius* should not be allowed to obscure the fact that the Council of Sirmium had deposed him in 351 – nor should his eloquence elsewhere be allowed to obscure the fact that he was often condemned by councils of bishops, whose verdicts he steadfastly refused to accept.

The normal pattern was that a bishop deposed by a council of bishops was automatically exiled by the emperor or a subordinate official. In 355, for example, Lucifer of Caralis was deposed by the Council of Milan for refusing to set his name to the synodical letter of the Council of Sirmium four years earlier. Two passages of his tract *Moriundum esse pro dei filio* disclose that Liberius was interviewed by Constantius at a meeting of the imperial *consistorium* in the palace before he departed into exile in Egypt (1.53–57; 4.7–12). Similarly, in 356, when Hilary of Poitiers was deposed by the Council of Baeterrae, it was the Caesar Julian who sent him into exile in Phrygia after receiving his formal condemnation from the council. Moreover, there is what I believe to be an example of a council ordering imperial officials to enforce their verdict in a passage of Sozomen that seems never to have received from historians the attention that it obviously deserves. The Council of Constantinople in early 360 deposed a number of bishops, among them Basil of Ancyra. Sozomen had read the *acta* of the council, presumably in the collection of such documents made by Sabinus of Heraclea *c.* 370, and he provides a detailed summary of the charges on which Basil was condemned. One of the crimes alleged against Basil was that

> he gave orders to the civil authorities to sentence clergy from Antioch, from the area by the River Euphrates, from Cilicia, Galatia and Asia, to exile and other penalties without a hearing, with the result that they endured iron chains and also spent their substance on the soldiers who escorted them in order to avoid maltreatment.
>
> (Sozomen, *HE* 4.25.5)

His enemies' description of Basil's action is clearly tendentious. The bishop can hardly be imagined to have given 'orders to the civil authorities' in a private letter. What he did was to write to them in the name of a council of bishops over which he presided to inform them that the council had condemned the clergy in question – and to request that they remove or exile them in accordance with the rule laid down by Constantine. The authorities then took action without further ado: since there was no need for any sort of judicial hearing in their court, they simply enforced the ecclesiastical condemnation by bundling the condemned men into exile.

Constantine gave bishops important privileges in the new Christian empire. They could act as judges in disputes between Christians by virtue of the newly introduced *episcopalis audientia*,[32] they could preside over the manumission of slaves in church,[33] and they soon began to act regularly as ambassadors in matters of high political import.[34] In significant ways the Christian bishop was now outside the normal legal system. Theodosius ruled that bishops could not be compelled to appear as witnesses in court.[35] It should not be assumed that this ruling represented an innovation. For the bishop's privilege of trial by his peers, though not explicitly attested until 355, surely goes back to Constantine. On 23 September 355

Constantius wrote to one Severus, whose office is unknown, in the following terms:

> By <this> law of our clemency we forbid bishops to be accused in <secular> courts, lest there be an unrestrained freedom for deranged minds to denounce them, in the belief that <false accusations> will not be punished because of the benevolence of the bishops. Accordingly, if anyone at all lodges any complaint <against a bishop>, it is appropriate for it to be examined only before other bishops, so that a suitable and convenient hearing be provided for the investigation of all <relevant matters>.
>
> (*CTh* 16.2.12)[36]

The principle that only a council of his peers could try, condemn and depose a bishop can be observed in operation in the reign of Constantine, particularly and with the greatest clarity in the case of Athanasius. It also encouraged the formation within the church of coalitions of bishops which functioned in a very similar way to modern political parties – a broad ideological (or theological) cohesiveness furthered and sometimes hindered by personal ambitions.

Not the least among the privileges which bishops enjoyed was a relative immunity from coercion by secular authorities. No matter what his crime, a bishop could only be deposed and exiled, not legally tortured and executed.[37] This encouraged the development of an attitude of independence and even defiance, which was fully fledged by the end of the reign of Constantius and which had clear political implications. Athanasius, Hilary of Poitiers, and Lucifer of Caralis all argue that because Constantius maltreats the church, he is a persecutor and a tyrant who no longer deserves to be emperor. During the fourth century Christian orthodoxy was added to the traditional list of virtues required in a legitimate emperor. Athanasius himself thought through the implications of regarding church and state as opposing entities,[38] and it was in the reign of Constantius that the classic antithesis was first voiced in its most familiar form.[39]

Ossius of Corduba, as quoted by Athanasius in the *History of the Arians*, begged Constantius to emulate his brother Constans in granting the church real independence:

> Stop using force, and do not write or send *comites*. Release those who have been exiled, so that they do not perform

greater deeds of violence because you are accusing them of using violence. What <action> of this sort was ever taken by Constans? What bishop was exiled <by him>? When did he ever participate in an ecclesiastical decision? What palatine official of his compelled people to subscribe to the condemnation of anyone?

Stop, I beg you, and remember that you are a mortal man: fear the day of judgement and keep yourself pure for it. Do not intrude yourself into the affairs of the church, and do not give us advice about these matters, but rather receive instruction on them from us. God has given you kingship, but has entrusted us with what belongs to the church. Just as the man who tries to steal your position as emperor contradicts God who has placed you there, so too you should be afraid of becoming guilty of a great offence by putting the affairs of the church under your control. It is written: 'Render unto Caesar the things that are Caesar's, and unto God those that are God's' (Matthew 22.2). Hence neither do we <bishops> have the right to rule over world nor do you, emperor, have the right to officiate in church.[40]

ACKNOWLEDGEMENTS

It was a great honour and a great pleasure to address the symposium organised by Sam Lieu and Dominic Montserrat at the University of Warwick in April 1993 to celebrate the establishment of the Centre for Research in East Roman Studies. I must thank Sam Lieu for choosing Constantine as the theme of the symposium and for inviting me to speak on a controversial subject upon which I have unorthodox views. [Editors' note: We are grateful to Harvard University Press for kind permission to publish this chapter which includes material published in the author's book, *Athanasius and Constantius: Theology and Politics in the Constantinian Empire*, Cambridge, MA 1993].

NOTES

1 Millar 1992: 103.
2 Baynes 1931: 95.

3 Millar 1992: 103.
4 Eus., *VC* 2.45.1. In defence of Eusebius' veracity, and on the importance of his testimony in interpreting the religious policies of Constantine, see Barnes 1984: 69–72. It is expressly discounted by Lane
  Fox 1986: 609–62, 775–84, especially 635–7 with 779 n. 1 (using
  the repeated qualification 'in Eusebius' view').
5 See Barnes 1981: 210–12, 245–50; Barnes 1986: 39–57; Barnes
  1985; Barnes 1989c: 310–37; Barnes 1989a: 94–123; Barnes
  1992b: 635–57 (these articles are reprinted in Barnes 1994 as nos
  V, VI, VIII, XI and IX respectively).
6 In Barnes 1993. What follows is very closely based on Chapter XVIII
  of that book, 'The Emperor and the Church' (pp. 165–75), and I am
  most grateful to Harvard University Press for granting permission for
  me to use it here.
7 For example, Aland 1960: 257–79; Schneemelcher 1970: 11, 13, 17,
  19; Girardet 1975: 1: 'Eine der Folgen der "Konstantinischen
  Wende" ist die "kaiserliche Synodalgewalt"'.
8 For example, by Seeck 1921: 415. It has recently been argued by
  Leeb (1992) that Constantine claimed complete control over the
  Church by the comparison of himself to Christ manifest in the
  constant use of 'Christ-typology and Christ-symbolism' in official
  representations of himself, especially after 326.
9 So, recently, Frend 1984: 527.
10 E. Schwartz 1936: 127.
11 Girardet 1975: 67–8.
12 See Girardet 1989.
13 Burckhardt 1880: 264 (= ed. B. Wyss, Bern 1950: 449); Burckhardt
   1853: 412.
14 Gibbon [1776] 1909 II: 314–15 (= Chapter XX).
15 Kelly 1972: 212.
16 Gaudemet 1957: 179–81. However, for a subtle argument which
   finds signs of incipient 'Caesaropapism' towards the end of Constantius' reign, see Piétri 1989: 113–72.
17 For German doubts about the aptness of the term, see Baus 1973:
   91–3 (= 89–90 in the English translation by A. Biggs, New York
   1980). Significantly, the volume itself has the title *Die Reichskirche
   nach Konstantin dem Grossen*.
18 The following discussion assumes the historical reconstruction
   argued in detail in Barnes 1993: 19–164.
19 On Athan., *Apol. c. Ar.* 71–85, see Barnes 1993: 29–30.
20 Eus., *VC* 3.10–12.
21 Eus., *VC* 4.42, cf. Warmington 1985.
22 Hefele and Leclercq 1907; Marot 1960: 19–43. For an assessment of
   the impact of Constantine on conciliar practice, see de Vries 1971:
   55–81, who concludes that 'die bisher verfolgte, aber freie Kirche,
   wird langsam zur "Reichskirche"'.
23 Barnes 1981: 212–14, 378, n. 35.
24 The term 'ecumenical council' is first attested in 338: Eus., *VC*
   3.6,1; Athan., *Apol. c. Ar.* 7.2. Chadwick 1972 argues that the
   term was used in 325 itself and 'had some association in the first

instance with the church's plea for exemption from tax' – and he draws the inference that the decisions of the council were so widely accepted because it succeeded in 'obtaining important fiscal relief'.

25 Gaudemet 1957: 144, citing Augustine, *De baptismo* 2.3.4 (CSEL 51.178).

26 See the *Epistula Constantini ad episcopos catholicos* in Optatus (see Appendix 5 in *S. Optati Milevitani Libri VII*, ed. C. Ziwsa, 1893 (CSEL 26: 203.23–5): the date is 314); Ruf., *HE* 10.5 = Gelasius of Cyzicus, *HE* 2.27.10 (325) – from Gelasius of Caesarea.

27 Millar 1977, especially 363–590.

28 Girardet 1975: 60–2.

29 Ibid.: 63, 67.

30 Eus., *HE* 7.30.19–20, cf. Millar 1971.

31 Despite Girardet 1975: 66–75.

32 *CTh* 1.27.1 (?318); *Const. Sirm.* 1 (333), cf. Barnes 1981: 51, 312, nn. 78–82. For the modern bibliography on this contentious topic, see now Elm 1989: 209–17. The papyrus she discusses provides an example of episcopal jurisdiction in a case concerning the theft of some books. The name of the bishop is Plusianus: since the first editor of the papyrus (Ulrich Wilcken) dates the papyrus to the fourth century and gives its provenance as 'Hermupolis (?),' there is a chance that he may be none other than Plusianus, the Bishop of Lycopolis, who was alleged to have burnt the house of Arsenius on Athanasius' orders (Sozomen, *HE* 2.25.12).

33 Sozomen, *HE* 1.9.6; *CJ* 1.13.1 (316); *CTh* 4.7.1 = *CJ* 1.13.2 (321).

34 J. F. Matthews *RAC* 10: 653–85, s.v. 'Gesandtschaft', especially 679.

35 *CTh* 11.39.8 (381).

36 My own, deliberately free translation. The subscription reads: *data epistula viiii kal(endas) Octob(res), acc(epta) non(is) Octob(ribus) Arbitione et Lolliano cons(ulibu)s*. Seeck 1919: 11 construed the phrase *data epistula* as a reference to a letter of the praetorian prefect forwarding the emperor's instructions.

37 The execution of Priscillian is not an exception, since he was not a validly ordained bishop: see Girardet 1974 and (briefly) Barnes 1990: 163.

38 Hagel 1933: 15–77, especially 47–58. See also Barnard 1977.

39 Gaudemet 1957: 181–2.

40 *History of the Arians* 44.6–8. Klein 1982: 1002–10 argues that this is yet another invented quotation and that the sentiments are those of Athanasius rather than Ossius. It would not much affect the point at issue here if he were correct, but Athanasius claims to have read the letter (*History of the Arians* 43.4).

3

CHRISTIANITY AND THE LATE ROMAN ARMY

Roger Tomlin

My text is taken from the second book of St Ambrose, *Concerning the Faith*: 'The army is led, not by military eagles and the flight of birds, but by Your name, Lord Jesus, and Your worship'.[1] For St Jerome, symbols of the Empire's Christianization are spiders and owls in the deserted temples of Rome, and 'the insignia of the Cross on the soldiers' flags'.[2] What then was the impact of Constantine's new religion upon the army in the century that elapsed between his Christian victory at the Milvian Bridge (28 October 312) and the Gothic sack of Rome (24 August 410), those milestones in what Gibbon calls the triumph of barbarism and religion? If one takes Eusebius literally, 'the historic world conversion from heathendom to Christianity was first of all effected in the army'.[3] But was the army really Christianized? How far did Christianity affect the behaviour of fourth-century soldiers, their loyalties and morale? These questions must be pursued through a maze of anecdotal evidence, and the answer will be a series of impressions reflecting only too faithfully the fragmented, tendentious quality of the sources.

The Church was now the conscience of the Roman State. First, some animal stories. Honorius' third consulship (396), was celebrated in Milan with a wild beast show and a panegyric from Claudian which likens the timid emperor to a lion cub.[4] One of the exhibits in the show, a convicted criminal called Cresconius, unfortunately escaped and sought sanctuary in the Cathedral. In spite of the clergy's protests, he was dragged out by soldiers of the commander-in-chief; but when they made their report, they were set upon by another of the escaped exhibits, some leopards, which mauled them badly. In consequence it was necessary to pardon Cresconius, although he was admittedly very guilty.[5] It is a far cry from the martyr Ignatius' famous description of himself as God's wheat: 'I am ground fine by the lions' teeth to be made purest bread for Christ.' On his way to Rome under military guard, he wrote that he was already battling with the beasts, 'chained as I am to half-a-score of savage leopards, who only grow more insolent the more gratuities they are given'.[6] What would he have thought of the sixth-century abbot who converted a lion to vegetarianism on a diet of bread and mushy peas?[7] But he might have been heartened by the story of the hermit Arsacius, who lived in one of the towers of Nicomedia for almost forty years, until his death in the great earthquake of 24 August 358 which he had predicted. Arsacius, a Persian, had been a Christian soldier in the army of Licinius and a conscientious objector: he resigned his post as keeper of the imperial lions.[8]

Ignatius under arrest fared differently than John Chrysostom three centuries later, when in 404 he was hustled into exile on the eastern frontier. His soldier guards treated him so well, he wrote, that he had no need of servants. But when they reached Caesarea in Cappadocia, an Isaurian raid was imminent and, worse than this, the house was mobbed by Christian monks. His guards fled to him, and said: 'Save us from these animals, even if we run into the Isaurians instead.' The provincial governor was unable to control the monks, and the local bishop was afraid to let Chrysostom stay. The monks grew still more violent, and he had to leave carried on a stretcher, by night, with the torches put out for fear of attracting Isaurians.[9]

The State might use soldiers to impose its will on bishops, but it did not follow that Christian clerics and Roman soldiers were at daggers drawn. Here is some more natural history. A clergyman in the 340s wrote to Abinnaeus, the commandant of the fort of Dionysias in the Egyptian Fayyûm: 'We know your excellence and your love for us; it is for God's sake that you so act, and I pray to Him that He will requite you the love which you show; for you act for Him.'[10] The action required is this: the loan of nets stored in the headquarters building, to catch gazelles which have been eating the crops. The same clergyman also writes on behalf of his brother-in-law, who has been drafted into the army:

> If you can release him again, it is a fine thing you do, first
> of all on God's account, secondly on mine, since his

mother is a widow and has none but him. But if he must serve, please safeguard him from going abroad with the draft for the *comitatus*, and may God make return to you for your charity and elevate you to greater things.[11]

Conscription into Licinius' army had already converted one Egyptian to Christianity. St Pachomius, aged about 20, was locked up with other recruits at Luxor, and people called 'Christians' brought him food and drink, which made him ask what they were. When he found out, he swore to serve the Christian God for the rest of his life after he was released; the monasteries he organized, with their perimeter walls, specialized buildings, and barrack-like houses, recall the forts he had known; after all, the army was also organizing tight-knit communities against a hostile world.[12] But the old imperial army, for all its religiosity expressed in thousands of altars, hundreds of temples, and even an official religious calendar, played something of a passive role in the conversion of the Empire to Christianity.[13] It was certainly a prime medium for the spread of other eastern cults, like those of Jupiter Dolichenus and Mithras; indeed, Manichaeism, a synthesis of dualism with Christianity, is said to have been introduced to Palestine by a veteran soldier of Mesopotamian origin.[14] But the sheer variety of beliefs in the army was an obstacle to the progress of a single, exclusive cult; nor did the subversive 'atheism' of Christianity and its pacific message appeal to soldiers in particular.[15] The teaching of the Bible itself was ambivalent. In simplistic terms, the prohibition on the shedding of blood, the Gospel exhortations to turn the other cheek, to put down the sword, conflicted with Old Testament examples of righteous warfare and, even in the New Testament, examples of virtuous centurions and the teaching of John the Baptist to baptized soldiers: 'Do violence to no man, neither accuse any falsely; and be content with your wages'.[16] Arguably, a Christian could serve in the Roman army. Tertullian, for example, at first proudly claimed that his fellow-Christians 'filled' the army bases, but later he believed that military service was wrong because it entailed idolatry.[17] He writes about the martyrdom of a soldier who refused to wear a wreath at a donative parade, but lets slip a significant detail: other soldiers, who included Christians 'talking like pagans', complained: 'Why should he make trouble for the rest of us over dress? Why be so rash and eager to die? Is *he* the only

Christian?' Tertullian comments they wanted to abolish martyr-dom, because the martyr was putting their quiet lives at risk.[18]

There are indeed some authentic military martyrs in the third century, the first attested being an *optio ad spem* called Marinus in *c.* 260, who seems to have served many years without being aware of any conflict of duties; it was only when he was denounced by a rival for promotion to centurion, on the grounds that he would be unable to sacrifice in the imperial cult, that his bishop confronted him with a formal choice between the Bible and the sword.[19] The centurion Marcellus, who was executed in 298 for throwing down his belt and vine stock because he could not serve Christ in the army, is not said to have been a recent convert.[20] As the proconsul of Africa said to a conscientious objector in 295: 'There are Christian soldiers in the sacred *comitatus* of Our Lords Diocletian, Maximian, Constantius and Galerius, and *they* serve.'[21] This remark is supported by a small number of third-century Christian soldiers' tombstones.[22] The most remarkable is that erected by an eastern veteran to his wife, which in fact details his own career: 'Aurelius Gaius, so far from turning the other cheek, had risen through the legionary cavalry to be *optio* in the élite cavalry regiment of *Comites*, and in the course of twenty years served in twenty-three provinces and crossed five different imperial frontiers. He served Maximian in Mauretania, Diocletian in Egypt, and Galerius in Mesopotamia.'[23]

The formidable Gaius may have left the army in the purge which preceded the Great Persecution forced on Diocletian by his *Caesar* Galerius, when Eusebius says that many soldiers pre-ferred to be dismissed rather than apostatize.[24] By implication, it was the first time they had been forced to choose. In consequence the greatest of the persecutors, Galerius, was able to rely on his army in the gruesome struggle which ultimately ensued.[25] In the western empire, his colleague Constantius may have purged his own army, if there is anything in Libanius' claim that his succes-sor Constantine won the Battle of the Milvian Bridge with 'an army of Gauls which attacked the gods after previously praying to them'.[26] Eusebius ingeniously combines two traditions with his implausible story that Constantius actually threatened to purge Christians if they did not apostatize – and then retained only those who refused.[27] How far he actually sympathized with the Chris-tians is difficult to say; it would seem that he was himself a worshipper of the Sun, who was unwilling to do more to them than demolish their churches.[28] In fact, a purge may not have been necessary: there would not have been many Christian soldiers in an army recruited from the sons of soldiers and veterans, and from peasants, who in Gaul almost a century later, during the ministry of St Martin in the 380s, were still largely pagan.[29] Christians in third-century Britain and Gaul, so far as we know, were a small, urban-based minority. The army inherited by Constantine from his father was enlarged, not from the towns, but from Germans: refugees, prisoners-of-war and volunteers, who were drafted into the new *auxilia*, the late Roman army's battalions of shock troops.[30] Many years after the Battle of the Milvian Bridge, Constantine swore to Eusebius that his famous vision of the Cross had been shared by his whole army — which would seem to make his subsequent efforts to indoctrinate it unnecessary — but Lactantius in his contemporary account says only that he received a dream which made him mark Christ's initials, the *Chi-Rho*, on his soldiers' shields.[31] According to Eusebius in *Vita Constantini* 4.21, this became standard practice.

Eusebius, who is writing just after Constantine's death (22 May 337), is here describing his hero's deliberate Christianization of the army, and this detail happens to be one which we can check. It turns out to be only partly true. No fourth-century shield survives, unfortunately, but more or less authentic representations are available.[32] One of the most explicit is a silver dish found in the Crimea, which depicts Constantius II on horseback attended by a long-haired guardsman and Victory; the Germanic guardsman carries a circular shield with decorated rim and a large central *Chi-Rho*, much like the guards of Justinian on the famous mosaic in the chancel of San Vitale at Ravenna.[33] That the motif was familiar is suggested by a glass beaker from Cologne, which is engraved with soldiers bearing various shield-devices including a diminutive *Chi-Rho*.[34] *Chi-Rho* shields were carved in stone at the new Christian capital, on the Columns of Theodosius and Arcadius at Constantinople.[35] The thirtieth anniversary of Honorius' accession was celebrated at Ravenna in 422 with a gold *solidus* on which he appears full-face, wearing a helmet, armed with a spear and small *Chi-Rho* shield.[36] But no such shield appears on the Arch of Constantine at Rome. This omission may be deliberate, since the Senate and People of Rome recognized only an unspecific 'divine inspiration' in Constantine's victory.[37] But the Arch is explicit in illustrating Maxentius and his armoured cavalry drowning in the Tiber, a débâcle seen in biblical terms by Eusebius, and it also depicts a soldier with a new, non-Roman shield which carries the motif interpreted as 'horns' or 'opposed animal heads'.[38] This is found on other fourth-century shields, notably that of a guardsman on the Geneva silver dish of Valentinian, and among the shield devices of the *Notitia Dignitatum*.[39] How far these *Notitia* devices are authentic is open to question, but some at least can be paralleled, for example by shields on the Arch of Galerius at Salonika or in the Herod scene on the ivory reliquary casket of Brescia.[40] Often the *Notitia* shield devices are geometric, sometimes they include faces or figures of divine beings, emperors and other animals, but there is not one instance of a *Chi-Rho*. So we do not know who actually carried a *Chi-Rho* shield in the fourth century, but it was patently not the army as a whole; indeed, had it been, then how could the Alamanni have distinguished specific Roman units by their shield devices?[41] Was it only poetic licence that gave the battalion of *Leones* their lion shields?[42] The *Chi-Rho* was not even restricted to the élite Guards units, the *scholae*, since their shields are carefully illustrated by the *Notitia*, with not a *Chi-Rho* among them.[43] Judging by the silver dish of Constantius II, the *Chi-Rho* shield may have been carried only by the Christian emperor's personal bodyguards, the forty *candidati* seconded from the *scholae*. We know little about them. A *candidatus* of Constantius II has gained a niche in Christian literature. He was a Frank who consulted the Palestinian hermit Hilarion and, according to Jerome, by a miracle he spoke spontaneously in Syriac; after the consultation was over, he naïvely offered a fee of ten pounds of gold, but it was declined.[44] But even these *candidati* are uncertain candidates for the *Chi-Rho* shield: the carefully observed guardsmen on the Madrid *missorium*, the great silver dish of Theodosius I, duly carry shields, but these only have geometric patterns.[45]

The real place of the *Chi-Rho* in late Roman military art is on the new battle flag, the *labarum* as it came to be called, which Constantine developed from the old *vexillum*. Soon after his conquest of Rome it entered the Forum itself, brandished by the colossus of the new emperor which was inserted like a monstrous cuckoo into the Basilica of Maxentius.[46] Legends accumulated around the *labarum*. It protected the standard-bearer, and (so Constantine told Eusebius) someone who passed it to another was himself promptly killed; and Licinius warned his men not to attack it or even look upon it, for 'it possesses a terrible power, and is especially hostile to me'.[47] Strangely enough, the *labarum* is never mentioned by the military theorist Vegetius, a Christian bureaucrat writing in the reign of Theodosius, but then he did not understand the *vexillum* either, and he would have had no place for Constantine's new flag in his archaizing picture of the old legions.[48] But we do not need Jerome to tell us that it was a major Christian symbol of victory: it appears on the coins of Constantine, first triumphant over 'that snake' Licinius, and then on those of his Christian successors; and when Julian was trying to undo the Constantinian revolution, he abolished the *labarum*.[49]

Constantine, Eusebius tells us, indoctrinated the army: 'instructing it in the mild and sober precepts of godliness, he carried his arms as far as the Britons, and all the nations that dwell in the very bosom of the western ocean'. The Goths submitted in consequence, and Roman power reached as far as Ethiopia and India.[50] Sozomen even conjectures that Constantine invented the miraculous *labarum* to convert his soldiers from paganism.[51] Sunday was made a day of rest. Christian soldiers were free to attend church:

> His trusty bodyguard, strong in affection and fidelity to his person, found in their emperor an instructor in the practice of piety, and like him held the Lord's salutary day in honour, and performed on that day the devotions which he loved.

Non-Christians attended a special parade to recite a safe, monotheistic prayer like the one dictated by the angel to Licinius, acknowledging God as the giver of Victory, and commending Constantine and his sons to His protection.[52] Constantine advertised his own trust in the Lord of Hosts by constructing a tent-chapel which accompanied him on campaign: like Moses, he would 'rush from the tabernacle, and give orders to his army to move at once, and draw their swords'; victory always followed.[53] Sozomen adds to Eusebius' account that each military unit was issued with a mobile chapel of its own, and spiritual advisers, but these army chaplains are not actually attested until the early fifth century.[54] Jerome, by contrast – but here he is making a rhetorical point, not really contributing to ethnology – takes the climax of the spread of Christianity to be not the *labarum*, not the crowds of monks from India, Persia and Ethiopia, not even the newly pacific Armenians and psalm-singing Huns, but the tented churches that travel with the Goths and enable them to fight the Romans on equal terms.[55]

To seek the truth that lies behind such rhetoric can be like using Gildas as a source for sub-Roman Britain: a subjective search after coincidences. Jerome's remarks find confirmation of a sort in a mid-fifth-century sermon, probably by Prosper of Aquitaine, which claims that barbarians who served in the Roman army were converted to Christianity and took their new faith home with them.[56] This is fascinating testimony to the late Roman army as a medium of Christian conversion, but it is hard to parallel. Archaeology is not likely ever to confirm Jerome's Gothic tented chapels. We may suspect him of being intoxicated by his own rhetoric, but perhaps the inspiration was, so to speak, the Constantinian Portachapel. Jerome's would then be the only evidence that it persisted, but there is a scatter of evidence for 'garrison chapels', churches associated with late Roman military sites. The masonry font of a fourth-century church survives just outside Cologne cathedral; perhaps this is where the usurper Silvanus was going in 355, on his way to church, when he was murdered by his own troops at the instigation of imperial agents including our informant, the pagan Ammianus Marcellinus.[57] At Mainz in 368, the population was at church when the Alamanni caught them by surprise.[58] Small churches have been found inside the walls of three forts on the Rhine, at Boppard, Kaiseraugust and Zurzach, and this may be the explanation of two strange towers found in the circuits of a pair of Danubian forts: each tower is rectangular with an apse, and is perhaps a chapel. A small church and font also seem to have been built inside the last base of the Second *Augusta* Legion, the Saxon Shore fort at Richborough.[59] A systematic search in the archaeological record might swell this evidence, but overall it does seem rather slight, compared with the hundreds of pagan temples that clustered round the forts of the Principate, each fort with its own *aedes*, its chapel of the Standards.[60]

When Julian the Apostate was mobilizing the Gallic army for civil war against Constantius II, he thought it expedient to go to church 'to win the favour of all men and have opposition from none'.[61] Christian emperors, like pagan *imperatores* taking the auspices, consulted a holy man before a decisive battle. During the Battle of Mursa, Constantius II had been in church, and it was the local Arian bishop Valens who first told him that Magnentius was in flight; Valens claimed to have heard this from an angel, and in consequence was credited by Constantius with the victory.[62] By contrast, the other Arian emperor Valens left Constantinople for his last campaign to the yells of the monk Isaac that God had roused the Goths against him because of his persecution of the orthodox.[63] The Catholic Theodosius consulted the Egyptian hermit John of Lycopolis before both his successful civil wars.[64] The Battle of the Frigidus he fought allegedly against his generals' professional judgement: he was strong in the Cross, Theodoret tells us, 'although the men left him were few in number and much discouraged'. (This is not surprising, since in the first day's fighting, their emperor had lost 10,000 of his Gothic federates.) But Theodosius prayed all night, and was rewarded with a vision of St John the Evangelist and St Philip.[65] Next day the wind blew into his enemies' faces, and they were scattered. Such visions were not exclusive to emperors. The Berber prince Mascezel, commanding a small north Italian expeditionary force of 5,000 men against his own brother and 70,000 rebels in Africa, after reinforcing his army with monks from the island of Capraria saw in Africa St Ambrose (who had just died) strike the ground three times with his walking stick. This predicted victory against the odds three days later.[66]

These are stories told us by interested parties, of course, and they all belong after the event. One side or the other was bound to win.[67] The reasoning is transparent in Philostorgius' gloss on the authentic apparition of the Cross at Jerusalem on the morning of 7 May 351. It was also seen by the two armies about to fight a civil war, he notes, but it made Magnentius and his men, who were pagans, helpless with fear, whereas Constantius and his men were inspired with irresistible confidence.[68] From the pagan side we hear of Constantine's vision of Apollo, and that he even ascended the Roman Capitol 'for fear of the soldiers', and took part in pagan ceremonial.[69] This too is tendentious, part of the pagan thesis which dates the Conversion after the murders of Fausta and Crispus, but it may be supported by the famous acclamation of the veterans: 'Constantine Augustus, may the gods [plural] preserve you for us.' The inference that the army remained pagan, however, depends on the transmitted date of this acclamation, 1 March 320, which is a problem, and so the argument cannot be pressed.[70] In general, it should be said that the army was motivated by military success and charisma, both of which Constantine had by the bucketful, and that there is no sign of religious considerations affecting its loyalty. The same is true of Julian's army or Arbogast's.

This flexibility, shall we call it, of the evidence can also be seen in Eusebius' remark that when Constantine decided to confiscate pagan cult statues and treasures,

> he considered no soldiers or military force of any sort needful for the suppression of the evil; a few of his friends sufficed for this service, and these he sent by a simple expression of his will to visit each several province.[71]

Next, Eusebius describes the demolition of temples – by squads of soldiers. The pagans were demoralized by soldiers' feet trampling their most intimate shrines.[72] During the fourth century we hear from time to time of soldiers seconding bishops in the demolition of temples: at Alexandria in 360, for instance, when the *Dux* Artemius stripped the Serapeum and dispersed a protesting mob.[73] At Apamea in *c.* 386 the new bishop, Marcellus, 'trusting rather in God than in the hands of the multitude', was able to destroy the Temple of Jupiter with the aid of two regular army battalions provided by the Praetorian Prefect in person. This would have been Cynegius, the nameless villain of Libanius' ineffectual protest at the demolition of temples by Christian mobs under official protection.[74] The final demolition of the Serapeum in 391 by Theophilus, Bishop of Alexandria, is satirically described by the pagan Eunapius as a 'war' fought by Romanus the *Comes Aegypti* against no opposition. But Sozomen's circumstantial account shows that Theophilus took the initiative supported by Romanus, and that troops must have been available, even if they are not explicitly mentioned.[75] There is an irresistibly vivid picture of armed intervention at Gaza in 401, where the local pagans were dispersed by soldiers after the imperial order had been read to them. The soldiers took ten days to demolish the other temples – this is more than sixty years after the death of Constantine – before setting light to the greatest of them all, the Temple of Marnas. As it burnt, the soldiers began to loot. When the officer in charge had a looter flogged, a burning beam fell on him and dashed out his brains.

> And straightway the soldiers which believed and the Christ-loving folk, knowing that the tribune's heart had been inclined towards idols, glorified God and sang the

Fifty-second Psalm, 'Why boastest thou thyself in mis-
chief, O mighty man? The goodness of God endureth
continually.'

If the officer was indeed a secret pagan, as is alleged (admittedly
the reasoning is contemptible), then his maintenance of military
discipline would be the army's only protest at being used to
suppress paganism. But this unique detail, like the whole splendid
story, cannot be regarded as authentic.[76]

If the army did not object to destroying paganism, or to
suppressing heretics, does this mean that it was a willing instru-
ment in the hands of Constantine and his Christian successors?
Julian thought so, at least according to Theodoret: even after
Constantius' death he concealed his paganism for a while for
fear of the troops

who had been instructed in the principles of true religion,
first by Constantine, who freed them from their former
error and trained them in the ways of truth, and afterwards by his sons, who confirmed the instruction given by
their father.[77]

But Theodoret is muddled here, if not being disingenuous. His
prime interest is Julian's reinstatement of the bishops exiled by
Constantius; only after this (he implies), did Julian make his
paganism known. Like Ammianus Marcellinus and Libanius,
Theodoret seems to have merged Julian's first overt paganism
with his formal legalization of pagan cult.[78]

In praising Constantius for his piety, Theodoret slides past the
embarrassing fact that he was an Arian heretic; at least he could be
credited with requiring that his troops attended church before
they campaigned against Magnentius.[79] Julian himself is said to
have remarked of the small military escort given him by Constantius in 355, two years after Magnentius' death, that 'they
knew nothing except how to pray'. This quip was a pagan commonplace.[80] When Julian inherited the eastern army, its soldiers
were demoralized, Libanius alleges, 'not just by bad leadership,
but because they went into battle without the gods supporting
them'; in other words, because they were doctrinaire Christians.[81]
After all this, therefore, it is disconcerting to find the Christian
poet Ephrem of Nisibis attributing their failures against the
Persians to their covert paganism.[82]

One of the saving pleasures of studying the religious beliefs of the late Roman army is that the sources are brightly coloured by their prejudice; the true facts – which could hardly have been determined even at the time – remain obscure. What Theodoret says about Constantius' and Julian's armies follows from Eusebius' statement that Constantine indoctrinated his army and, indeed, it is supported by Julian's hypocritical visit to that church in Vienne before Constantius died. But is Theodoret right? Did Julian have to convert his army to paganism? The Gallic Army hardly needed re-indoctrination. Julian was uncertain of its loyalty before leaving Gaul, and made a secret sacrifice to Bellona before he addressed his troops; but in reply they swore allegiance to him, 'putting swords to their throats', just like the chieftains of the Quadi to Constantius.[83] The oath itself – 'they swore grimly to do anything for him, even if it meant losing their lives' – sounds like the regular military *sacramentum*: Vegetius quotes it, 'they would do all that the emperor commanded, they would never desert or refuse to die for the common good'.[84] The un-Roman character of Julian's proclamation at Paris is well known: he was the first *Augustus* to be lifted on a shield like a German chieftain, something which now entered the accession ceremonial, which in the fourth century had not yet acquired a Christian veneer. But although Julian himself saw the gods' hand in his elevation, there is no evidence that the troops proclaimed him at Paris for religious motives. Quite the reverse: they did not even know he was a pagan. When they invaded Illyricum in the civil war, they were aspersed by rain in the sign of the Cross,[85] but Julian had no reason to fear a Christianity which proved to be as superficial as raindrops. At Naissus, when the unexpected news arrived of Constantius' death, he seems in fact to have been pleasantly surprised about his army: 'I worship the gods openly', he wrote to his theurgic guru, Maximus the philosopher; 'and the whole mass of the troops who are returning with me worship the gods.'[86]

The Gallic Army, after five years of defeating the Franks and Alamanni, had just embarked on a civil war against the odds – and won it by a walkover. It was recruited in any case, not from theologians, but from soldiers' sons, Gallic peasants, and German tribesmen. So its loyalty to the young, dynamic and engagingly eccentric Caesar is not surprising. But Julian seems to have had no difficulty in winning the loyalty of Constantius' army either. Like his revolutionary uncle Constantine, who 'sought Divine assistance, deeming the possession of arms and a numerous soldiery of secondary importance', Julian 'considered superiority in numbers, force of steel, strength of shield, and every single thing to be quite pointless if the gods were not on his side'.[87] He therefore re-indoctrinated Constantius' army: 'he induced the hand that grasped the spear to grasp offerings of incense and libation . . . if persuasion proved insufficient, gold and silver co-operated to ensure adherence'.[88] How this was actually done is described in rhetorical but revealing terms by Julian's sometime fellow-student, St Gregory of Nazianzus: he seduced the army, which knew only one law, the emperor's will; much of it, then and previously, consisted of corrupt time-servers.[89] There was a shameful donative parade, at which each man was required to offer a pinch of incense before receiving his pay. Julian was exploiting soldiers' innate stupidity and greed, Gregory comments: the whole conquering army was conquered by a flame, by gold, by a puff of smoke; most of them were even unaware that they had been murdered spiritually, and that was the worst thing of all. They kissed the emperor's hand, without realizing it was their executioner's.[90] At dinner afterwards some soldiers are said to have crossed themselves, which prompted the comment by a messmate: 'Don't you even realize you are apostates?'[91] It takes an effort to share Gregory's sense of outrage. True, he may be an over-educated outsider ignorant of how armies work, ignorant of their discipline and the strength of habit, a propagandist pining for someone to be martyred, but to be fair to him, perhaps he is also articulating the sort of dread the East India Company's sepoys felt in 1857, that their cartridges had been greased with the fat of unclean beasts to seduce them into Christianity.

This dread would have affected morale, but can we really detect it in Constantius' 'time-serving' army? Even in Gregory's own account, it is evident that the army was disciplined, it was used to being paid regularly, it took Julian's paganism in its stride. Church historians claim that Julian excluded Christians from the army and the administration,[92] but authentic military martyrs are hard to find. A brace of them is offered by John Chrysostom, soldiers who complained at a drinking party that life was no longer worth living: 'Everything groans with the smoke of sacrifice, we cannot even breathe pure air.'[93] They were arrested for treason and executed; Chrysostom implies this was because they refused to apostatize, but the Antiochene tradition only saw them as guardsmen who joined the Christian mob shouting insults at Julian.[94] They were executed – for their breach of military discipline

– though naturally enough they were treated as martyrs. The Church's need for martyrs and confessors stimulated the supply after Julian was dead. Thus the future emperor Valentinian is said to have resigned his commission in protest: the various versions of the story make him commander of four different regiments, and assign him three different places of exile. The truth seems to be that he was cashiered in 357, when Julian believed he had disobeyed orders, and was not reinstated.[95]

Ephrem calls Constantius' army 'crypto-pagans'; but Gregory calls them 'time-servers', and this is closer to the truth. A Christian soldier in Julian's army might have reflected upon the ideas put into words by St Augustine. The powers of this world, just and unjust, are established by God for our 'discipline' and thus St Paul ordered slaves to obey their masters. Julian was an idolater and an apostate, but it was right for Christian soldiers to obey him. If he ordered them to sacrifice, they would of course prefer their Christian duty; but if he gave them a military order, then they would obey at once.[96] We may add that, in practice, the issue was not so clear-cut. Gregory's narrative shows how easily a military ceremony could be given pagan overtones. It was a brave, not to say a wayward soldier who thought of resisting an emperor who had defeated the Germans against the odds, and had just won a civil war by his Christian opponent's sudden death at the age of 44. The usurper Magnus Maximus, not a pagan but an aggressive Catholic, was able to defend his own usurpation by the argument that power had been thrust upon him by God's will: the proof was his unexpected victory over the irreproachably Catholic emperor Gratian. The logic of this – that God is for the big battalions, so to speak – was accepted by St Martin himself.[97]

Julian rewarded the army for its outward paganism by glutting it with the meat of sacrificial victims at Antioch, while corn ran short.[98] That summer (363) it was accompanied by professional soothsayers with whom Julian's court philosophers 'argued obstinately over things of which they were ignorant'.[99] When Julian fell in battle – killed by a demon, according to the epic written by one of his staff, killed by saints in Christian legend, but in fact speared by an Arab horseman[100] – one last animal was sacrificed next morning for Jovian, his Christian successor, and its entrails were inspected by the soothsayers.[101] Less than twenty-four hours: that is how long Julian's indoctrination of the army really lasted. There is no need to believe Theodoret that Jovian refused to command an army of pagans unprotected by Providence: 'Your

Majesty need have no fear', they allegedly replied; 'you will be commanding Christians brought up in the truth, for our veterans were schooled by Constantine himself, and their juniors were taught by Constantius.'[102] This is a doublette of Theodoret's own comment on Julian's accession in 361.[103] But an odd episode occurred when Jovian was leaving Antioch: some Arians from Alexandria petitioned him to appoint a new bishop, and when he told them he had recalled Athanasius, they protested. At this moment an unspecified soldier suddenly intervened: 'Your Majesty, these are the scum of Cappadocia, the residue of the unholy George who desolated Alexandria and the world.'[104] In other words, they were Arians. Jovian's army evidently contained one Catholic theologian, a survivor who had kept his head down during the reigns of Constantius and Julian. However, it was not pagans or heretics whom Jovian had to fear, but potential usurpers: notably Jovinus, one of Julian's most trusted generals, who had been left in command of the Gallic army. Like Jovian himself, he was a Catholic Christian, and he founded a church at Rheims to be the living home of his mortal remains.[105] Jovian's election in 363, like the more considered imperial election of 364, was marked by tension between Julian's men and Constantius'; both Jovian and Valentinian were compromise-candidates. The division was never on religious lines.[106]

Some reasons may be briefly stated. The army was conservative, a creature of habit; it was slow to Christianize even its externals; it was used to obeying orders. It was recruited from diverse sources, some of them not even Roman, and internal tolerance of different beliefs had always been necessary for it to function efficiently. As late as 408, when a pagan general threatened to resign, Honorius was forced to withdraw his new directive that court officials, civil and military, should be Catholic Christians.[107] That fine historian Socrates, a Catholic, was shocked by the new Bishop of Constantinople telling Theodosius II in 424: 'Your Majesty, give me the earth purged of heretics, and I will give you heaven in return. Help me destroy heretics, and I will help you conquer the Persians.'[108] Even the government's response was lukewarm. It now excluded heretics from the public service, but with two significant exceptions: the staffs of provincial governors which, as Sozomen remarks, are 'the most arduous and least honourable Roman service'; and the armed services themselves.[109] The army had more pressing concerns: to paraphrase Piganiol's criticism of Theodosius the Great, it was not going to build the City of God with the walls of the empire tumbling about its ears.

The army's conservatism has already been noticed in the *Notitia*, which reached its present form after the Battle of the Frigidus (5 and 6 September 394), the last time a Roman army went into action under pagan auspices.[110] There is no *Chi-Rho* shield in the *Notitia*, but if one looks very carefully, not at the line-drawings in Seeck's edition, but at the manuscript itself, one can see a few tiny Crosses and ambiguous figures which might be angels or Victories. But the senior legion of them all, the *Ioviani*, still bears the same shield device as on the Arch of Galerius: Jupiter's eagle, for all that Ambrose might have said to the contrary in 378.[111] The legion retained its pagan title too, like its twin the *Herculiani*, and they are both glossed by a Church historian without a tremor as 'the legions which have received this title in honour of Jupiter and Hercules'.[112] Other 'theophoric' units of Diocletian and his colleagues likewise retain their original names.[113] Abinnaeus' old regiment remains at *Dionysias*, the Fort of Bacchus.[114] This was only a matter of habit; after all, we still name the days of our week after pagan gods without worshipping Woden. Nomenclature did not really change: new army units in the fourth century were still named in the old way, from their ethnic origins or previous station, or from the emperor who raised them, not after the Saints or the Trinity.[115] Religious censorship is hard to find.[116] None of this is evidence of residual paganism, only that the army was not being aggressively Christianized; that it preferred the traditional names, just as Vegetius (a Christian) uses the adjective 'old' eight times as often as the noun 'God'.[117]

The army's conservatism, which Nock in a brief, luminous survey has rightly called its 'relative indifference to religious changes', is apparent in the role it played – or rather, did not play – in Church politics.[118] Constantius used it to impose an Arian settlement. At Constantinople in 342 the Master of Cavalry was lynched when he tried to depose the new Catholic bishop; the Praetorian Prefect was then sent with an armed escort, with which he installed an Arian bishop; but when the crowd failed to disperse, the soldiers drew their swords, and 3,150 people are said to have been killed.[119] At the request of this new bishop, four army battalions were directed against a Novatianist village in Paphlagonia – and were almost wiped out in the battle which ensued.[120] The turbulent priesthood of Athanasius was marked by military intervention. He slipped into hiding in 356 when the *Dux* of

Egypt stormed his cathedral to arrest him. Two years later, the *Dux* Sebastianus violently dispersed a Catholic congregation, and his soldiers beat up the clergy and stripped and insulted nuns.[121] In 359 the Council of Rimini tried to depose Basil of Ancyra because he had had clergymen arrested, 'so that many had been loaded with chains, and had been compelled to bribe the soldiers who were taking them away, not to maltreat them'.[122] Naturally, we hear of all this when the orthodox suffered, but there is no reason to suppose that Constantius had turned his troops into Arians. The Roman army could always treat civilians brutally without needing the excuse of religion. The massacre at Constantinople, which was really due to the crowd pressing upon the soldiers in a confined space where neither of them could move, is only a horrible accident compared with the bloodbath at Thessalonica, when a peaceable circus audience was massacred as an act of policy, a deliberate retribution for the lynching of another commander-in-chief, by order of that most Catholic emperor Theodosius the Great. Ambrose, to his credit, protested. His prestige had been unassailable since the Siege of the Basilicas, where we find soldiers obeying the letter of their orders but, at least according to Ambrose, openly sympathizing with their victims: they picketed his church and, when they entered it amid incipient panic, they said they had come 'to pray, not to fight'; and finally, when the imperial court backed down, 'the soldiers eagerly brought the news themselves, running to the altars and kissing them'.[123] Ambrose was a special case: a man of iron self-confidence, entrenched in his Catholic see against an isolated Arianizing court aware of the self-appointed Catholic liberator biding his time across the Alps. John Chrysostom's popularity made him formidable too: when his enemies dispersed his congregation and arrested him, they used a pagan Guards officer and 400 Thracian recruits, who might be expected to have no personal loyalty towards the bishop.[124]

Athanasius' adversary, the *Dux* Sebastianus, was a Manichaean. After serving the Arian Constantius, he became joint-commander of the pagan Julian's second army in Mesopotamia; then he was purposely chosen by Valentinian, a Catholic, for service in the West, from which he returned in 378, not for religious reasons but because he disliked the eunuchs at the court of Gratian.[125] Sebastianus, who died with the Arian Valens at Adrianople, is the most striking instance of fourth-century emperors' indifference to the religious orientation of their high command and, indeed, vice versa; but this indifference is confirmed by his senior colleagues in the army of Valens: a coterie of pious Catholics, not an Arian among them.[126] Three of them, Victor, Arinthaeus and Traianus, are said to have criticized Valens to his face for his Arianism, but this allegation only betrays a Church historian's unease that Catholic generals should have served a heretic emperor. Victor and Arinthaeus, the most senior surviving generals of Constantius at the court of Julian, were Valens' joint commanders-in-chief for almost the whole of his reign.[127] Victor was a good Catholic who patronized Valens' critic, the monk Isaac at Constantinople; he was not even a Roman by birth, but a Sarmatian who had married a Christian Arab princess. Her fellow tribesmen, indirectly recruited for the empire by the evangelizing of a Catholic monk, fought for the Romans with a blood lust which made Goths recoil.[128] Arinthaeus was a correspondent of Valens' Catholic opponent Basil of Caesarea, who wrote a letter of consolation to his widow after the general's death-bed baptism. The third of Valens' alleged critics, Traianus, was, like Sebastianus, *Dux* of Egypt (in 367), when he arrested and expelled the Arian claimant to Athanasius' see; in Armenia as *comes* he directed Valens' economical intervention, and eliminated an embarrassing but more or less Christian king by assassinating him over dinner. Traianus' daughter became a nun and a vegetarian.[129] Like his colleague in Armenia, the *comes* Terentius, Traianus received letters from St Basil. Terentius, like Sabinianus who resorted in emergency to the martyrs' shrines at Edessa, was a Christian general covertly disliked by Ammianus Marcellinus: 'he walked with eyes downcast, almost mournfully, but he was a lifelong promoter of quarrels'.[130]

The paradox of these Catholic and capable generals serving an Arian emperor is echoed a few years later in the West, where the court of Gratian was dominated by Frankish-born generals, four of whom were pagans. Bauto and Rumoridus opposed Ambrose in favouring the restoration of that over-studied heirloom, the Altar of Victory.[131] Richomeres, like Victor and Saturninus a survivor of the disaster at Adrianople, was later chosen by the Catholic Theodosius to command in both his civil wars.[132] Finally, Arbogast, the nephew of Richomeres, succeeded Bauto because the army liked him; according to a pagan, it was 'because of his bravery, military knowledge and contempt for wealth'.[133] His wine waiter, a Christian, reported a conversation he had overheard between Arbogast and some Frankish chieftains. Did he know

Bishop Ambrose, they asked him. Yes, he did (Arbogast replied); he was a friend of his and often dined with him.[134]

The careers of these generals are not really a paradox, unless we expect emperors and their advisers to choose officers and promote commanders-in-chief, not for their military skill (a vital commodity in quite short supply), but for their religious faith. Nor is it paradoxical that good soldiers should have been good Christians, although one or two fourth-century moralists would have us think so. St Paulinus of Nola, who abandoned his great estates and a worldly career for the cult of a small-town martyr in Campania, wrote to a soldier he had never met, urging him to leave the army: to serve the sword was to serve Death; but a Christian cannot serve two masters, God and Mammon, that is, Christ and Caesar. A soldier might hope to be promoted to *protector*, but if he enlisted in God's service, God would be his protector. The rank of *comes* would then be his starting-point, not a 'general', but literally the 'companion' (of Christ).[135] Another letter, to the Bishop of Rouen, told Victricius the circumstances of his (Victricius') own conversion. He had been a soldier first, but to the astonishment of the others on parade, he 'changed his weapons of blood for the weapons of peace'. He resigned publicly; and when a beating did not break his resolution, his officer took him before the *comes*, who ordered him to be beheaded; but his life was saved at the last moment when the executioner was miraculously blinded, and the *comes* pardoned him.[136] This dramatic story – was Victricius its source, or did he need to be reminded of it? – is an exercise by Paulinus in the Sulpicius Severus 'St Martin the military martyr' mode, and is about as authentic.[137] The Council of Arles (314) actually excommunicated soldiers who threw down their arms in peacetime.[138]

Military service was not inherently bad, or at least it was a necessary evil – this concession to common sense was part of the price the Church paid for the conversion of Constantine – and instead we find what may be called the Good Soldier. Like the Just War, this idea is eloquently expressed by Augustine. When Bonifatius as a tribune in Africa thought of resigning from the army after the death of his first wife, to become a monk, Augustine and his fellow bishop Alypius persuaded him to soldier on for the sake of protecting the local churches from barbarian raids. By wearing the belt of Chastity with his physical armour, they told him, he would be protected by spiritual armour more strongly, more safely.[139] Basil of Caesarea had already conceded that to kill in war was not murder, although he thought that three years' excommunication would be appropriate.[140] Augustine allowed the killing of others in self-defence, if one is a soldier doing one's duty.[141] But when Bonifatius returned to Africa as the *comes*, Augustine was disappointed at his worldliness and his lack of military success. He offered him spiritual advice. For the salvation of his soul, Bonifatius should give alms, pray, and fast without actually doing himself an injury.[142] Ideally, he should practise complete chastity and should withdraw from warfare, joining instead the fight of Christ's soldiers against, not men, but the Devil. However, this advice is grudgingly qualified. Since Bonifatius has married again, he owes a duty to his wife, and he should withdraw only 'without risking the peace of mankind'. If he must engage in warfare, he should keep to the Faith and seek peace.[143]

Augustine was an old man and sorrowful, and he was making the best of indifferent material: Bonifatius' second wife was a superficially converted Arian – their daughter was baptized an Arian – and he was keeping mistresses.[144] But the principle was there: the generals of Valens and Theodosius, with their personal devotions, had known that one could both be an active soldier and serve God. Their models were the faithful centurion whose servant Christ healed, and the centurion Cornelius at Caesarea, 'a devout man, and one that feared God with all his house'.[145] Even Maximus, Bishop of Turin in the early fifth century, an able advocate of moral rearmament while north Italy was being invaded, commends a general who has built a church: 'He has killed the enemies of our earthly king, and pursues the adversaries of the Lord of Heaven. He vanquishes barbarians – and demons.'[146] So generals should also be good men. Whether this made them better generals is not for us to judge, as Ammianus would say, but it prompts a snide comment from a contemporary of Maximus. The poet Claudian prays tongue in cheek for the Master of Cavalry, that St Thomas will be his shield, and St Bartholomew his comrade; that the Saints will bar the Alps, and invaders who swim the Danube will be drowned like Pharaoh's horsemen.[147]

When Pope Liberius was exiled by Constantius, he was given 1,000 *solidi* for his expenses which he returned, saying the emperor needed the money to pay his troops.[148] War is the father of taxes, after all.[149] Liberius' dignified self-denial was childishly parodied by Julian when he confiscated the funds of the church at Edessa for the benefit of the army, on the grounds that Christians were commanded to sell all that they had and give it to the poor.[150] What Liberius was really doing, with a sarcastic tone, was to echo the fourth-century consensus, that the empire had the right and duty of visible self-defence which the Church comple-mented by resisting mankind's invisible enemies. The first Christian emperor was a highly successful general – no doubt there was a connection – and Eusebius praised him for both physical and spiritual achievement: the barbarians were attacking civilization like wolves, or rather, like the demons which had ensnared the whole human race in polytheism; and Constantine had conquered them both.[151] Augustine told Bonifatius that it was the clergy's duty to pray for the soldier, and to 'fight against your invisible enemies; while you, in fighting for them, contend against the barbarians, their visible enemies'.[152] Ambrose, in reviewing the marvels of Creation, praised the Rhine and Danube for being 'the Empire's wall against savage nations', the sea 'for shutting out the frenzy of barbarism'.[153] In discussing Duty, he wrote that Fortitude is a truly Christian virtue, seen in its highest form in the martyr, but also to be commended when 'defending one's country against barbarians in time of war'.[154]

> Natural affection persuades us to watch over others. It is glorious for an individual to risk himself for the common peace. Anyone would rather save his country from destruction, than himself; and he would think it better to serve his country, than to lead a life of pleasure in retirement.[155]

Contemporaries might choose between these arguments, and what Paulinus sang in Nola, in February 402 about as far from a barbarian as it was possible to be:

> Others, who do not trust in Christ's salvation
> May trust in legions and refurbished walls;
> *We* sign ourselves with the Unconquered Cross.
> We may seem unarmed, but we are armed against
> Spiritual enemies.
>
> (Paulinus, *Carmen* 26: 103–14)

My sermon began with a text from Ambrose, and it may as well end there. Here he is again, urging the hapless Gratian against the Goths: 'Go forward, armed with the Shield of Faith and having the Sword of the Spirit, go forward to the victory promised in former times by the Prophet.' The Goths are equated with Gog, which falls upon Israel out of the north, and is utterly destroyed.[156] The eastern empire survived not least because of its religious faith combined with diplomatic and military expertise, and even over-confidence is better than despair. Here is what those Frankish chieftains replied to Arbogast, when he told them that he knew Ambrose: 'No wonder you win battles, Count, if you are a friend of that man, who says to the sun "Stand still", and it stands still.'[157]

ACKNOWLEDGEMENTS

This chapter has benefited from the discussion which ensued, but remains largely as delivered as a paper, with the addition of footnotes. Translations of Ammianus Marcellinus, Julian, Libanius, Eusebius, Sozomen, Socrates and Theodoret are as enumerated in the List of Abbreviations others as specified, or in my own translation. A systematic collection of all the evidence, archaeological and epigraphical, as well as literary, would be very welcome, but lies beyond the scope of this chapter.

NOTES

1 *De fide* 2.16, 142, written at about the time of Adrianople (9 August 378): see Homes Dudden 1935: 189.
2 Jerome, *ep.* 107.1–2, *vexilla militum crucis insignia sunt.* Kelly 1975: 273 n. 1, dates the letter to 401 or early 402, but this partly depends on when the Temple of Marnas at Gaza was destroyed (see below, note 76).
3 von Harnack 1905: 86–7, quoted by Odahl 1976.
4 Claudian, *De tertio consulatu Honorii Augusti* 77–82.
5 Paul., *V. Amb.* 34. It was illegal to execute a Christian in the arena (*CTh* 9.40.8, 365), but in practice atrocious criminals were still condemned *ad bestias* (Augustine, *Contra Faustum* 22.79). In seizing Cresconius the soldiers were acting legally: Theodosius had recently ordered (*CTh* 9.45.1, 392) that public debtors who sought sanctuary were to be dragged out of hiding; otherwise their debts would be transferred to the bishop. Ambrose was more circumspect: when Stilicho failed to punish a secretary who had been forging commissions, the man was arrested by Ambrose's order as he left church. After interrogating him and finding that he was guilty, Ambrose consigned him to Satan, and at once an unclean spirit tore him apart (Paul., *V. Amb.* 43).

CHRISTIANITY AND THE LATE ROMAN ARMY

6 Ignatius, *Letter to the Romans* (*ep.* 4.4–5) (trans. in M. Staniforth, *Early Christian Writings: The Apostolic Fathers*).

7 John Moschus, *Pratum Spirituale* 163, *panem et cicer infusum*.

8 Sozomen, *HE* 4.16. It was all in the stars: Mars in the fourth house inflicts 'difficulties' on soldiers, either a desert posting or the charge of wild animals (Firmicus Maternus, *Mathesis* 3.4.9). Arsacius would have been one of the Christians dismissed by Licinius, whom Constantine allowed to choose between reinstatement and honourable discharge (Eus., *VC* 2.20).

9 John Chrysostom, *Letters to Olympias* (trans. A.-M. Malingrey, SC 13, 1947, 1(11) and 9(14)).

10 *P. Abinn.* 6 (translation of *editio princeps*).

11 *P. Abinn.* 19 (translation of *editio princeps*). This Egyptian clergyman did not assume that service in the *comitatenses* was superior to that in the *limitanei*. According to Jones 1964, II: 649, there was 'no radical difference' in the fourth century.

12 *S. Pachomii vitae graecae*, vita prima 4–5, ed. Halkin and Festugière 1982. See Chitty 1966: 22.

13 The classic synthesis of the army's religious cults is von Domaszewski 1895, which devotes only five and a half lines (on p. 114) to 'Die Heeresreligion der christlichen Kaiser'. But I owe much to Nock 1952, especially 223–9 on 'Pagans and Christians in the Roman Army'; see also Gabba 1974; and Odahl 1976.

14 Epiphanius, *Panarion haeresium* (GCS Epiphanius III) 66, 1, 1.

15 There is a well-documented survey (*Christians and the Roman Army from Marcus Aurelius to Constantine* by J. Helgeland in *ANRW* II 23.1: 724–834), who sees early Christian pacifism as random comments rather than a consistent ideology. See also Windass 1964 and Crescenti 1966.

16 Luke 3.11. Virtuous centurions: Matthew 8.8–10; Acts 10.4.

17 Tertullian, *Apologeticum* 37.4; compare *Apologeticum* 5.6 (the Rain Miracle was due to the prayers of Christian soldiers), and 30.4 (Christians pray for 'brave armies'). But in *De Idolatria* 19, Tertullian sees Christianity and military service as incompatible. For this change in attitude see Barnes 1971: 99 and 132ff.

18 Tertullian, *De corona*, especially 1.1–4.

19 Eus., *HE* 7.15 = Musurillo 1972 no. 16, *Martyrdom of St Marinus*.

20 Musurillo 1972 no. 18, *Acts of Marcellus*.

21 Musurillo 1972 no. 17, *Acts of Maximilian*.

22 'Early' Christian soldiers' epitaphs are collected in *ILCV* 393–435, to which others can now be added from *AE*. But Helgeland in *ANRW* II 23.1: 791–3 follows Henri Leclerq in identifying only thirteen as pre-Constantinian, six of them being Praetorian Guardsmen at Rome.

23 *AE* 1981: 777, which also summarises the ample commentary by the stone's editor, T. Drew-Bear.

24 Eus., *HE* 8.4.2.

25 Barnes 1981: 18.

26 Libanius, *Or.* 30.6.

27 Eus., *VC* 1.16.

28 Lact., *De mort.* 15; compare Optatus Milevitanus, *De schismate Dona-tiano* 1.22 (according to the Donatists in 313, only Gaul escaped persecution), on which see Lieu in this volume, Chapter 8. Eusebius claims (*VC* 1.12–27), some thirty years after the death of Constantius, that he was actually a Christian, which has now been argued largely from silence by Elliott 1987.

29 Jones 1963, especially 23ff.

30 Hoffmann 1969: 131ff.

31 Eus., *VC* 1.28; Lact., *De mort.* 44.4–5. See, further, Barnes 1981: 43.

32 The remains of a shield made of coloured leather with gilt ornament were found in the grave of the *chef militaire* at Vermand, but only the silver-gilt iron boss was actually drawn: see Pilloy 1895 II: 38f. For a sceptical treatment of shield devices, see Grigg 1979, especially 108–12 with note 31.

33 Kent and Painter 1977: 25, no. 11 = Delbrueck 1933, pl. 57.

34 Fremersdorf 1952; summary in Fremersdorf 1967 VIII: 174ff.

35 Fragments survive of Theodosius' Column, and the base of Arcadius' Column was drawn before it became illegible: see Speidel 1995, Fig. 1 and pl. 48.1; and, further, *Archaeologia* 72 (1922), pls XVII and XX.

36 Kent 1994, under Honorius 1331 and 1332.

37 *ILS* 694, *instinctu divinitatis*. Constantine's own coinage omits the *Chi-Rho* almost entirely, and Magnentius is the first emperor to emphasise it: see Bruun 1962.

38 Speidel 1986: 253–62 with pls I–III; compare Eus., *HE* 9.9.6–7. Grigg 1979: 109, with pls II and III.

39 The Geneva *missorium* (Musée d'Art et d'Histoire, Inv. C1241) and the western *schola* shields are superbly illustrated in the exhibition catalogue *Gallien in der Spätantike* (R-G Zentralmuseum, Mainz 1980) 31 and 63. See also Delbrueck 1933, pl. 79 = *JRS* liv (1964), pl. VI; and Goodburn and Bartholomew 1976, pl. XXVIII.

40 Laubscher 1975: 148, n. 222; see pls 13, 32 and 42.2 (eagle); pls 38 and 56.2 (Hercules); pl. 32.1 (lion passant, unidentifiable here but still visible in Kinch 1890, pl. IV). Delbrueck 1952: 79–80. But Grigg 1979: 112 warns us 'not to expect from the illustrations of the *Not. Dig.* much more than a general idea of how late Roman insignia looked'.

41 Amm. 16.12.6, *scutorum insignia*. Vegetius (*Epit.* 2.18) confuses shield devices with ownership graffiti, as indeed does Cassius Dio (*Histories* 67.10.1). That shields are distinctive is taken for granted by Virgil, *Aeneid* 2.389–90, *mutemus clipeos Danaumque insignia nobis aptemus*. Various shield devices appear on Trajan's Column, but do not consistently distinguish army units.

42 Claudian, *de bello Gildonico* 1.423, *clipeoque animosi teste Leones*. For the lion shield on the Arch of Galerius, see note 40 above.

43 See above, note 39.

44 Jerome, *Vita Hilarionis* 21.

45 Delbrueck 1933, pls 94, 96 (detail) and 97 (detail). The 'chequered' shield looks identical to the one on the Cologne beaker: see Fremersdorf 1952 and Fremersdorf 1967.

46 Eus., *HE* 9.9.10 with Barnes 1981: 46 n. 18.

47 Sozomen, *HE* 1.4; Eus., *VC* 2.9 and 16.

48 The word *vexillum*, properly meaning the flag once borne by legionary detachments and cavalry, and still so depicted on the Arch of Galerius (see Laubscher 1975, pl. 31), is used by Vegetius only as a synonym for *signum*, in particular the standard of a century (*Epit.* 2.13). *Vexilla* is loosely used by Ambrose (*De fide* 2.16.142) and Jerome (*ep.* 107.1–2) to refer to the *labarum*.

49 Eus., *VC* 2.46 (the snake), with Bruun 1962: 21–2. Sozomen, *HE* 5.17 = Gregory of Nazianzus, *Or.* 4.66.

50 Eus., *VC* 1.8. For summary accounts see Jones 1964 I: 91, and Barnes 1981: 48. Goths, Ethiopians and Indians were typical far-flung converts: compare Jerome, *ep.* 107.2.

51 Sozomen, *HE* 1.4.

52 Eus., *VC* 4.18–20; compare Lact., *De mort.* 46 (Licinius' prayer).

53 Eus., *VC* 2.12. One was prepared for the Persian campaign (Eus., *VC* 4.56).

54 Sozomen, *HE* 1.8. Jones 1953 (= Jones 1964 II: 632–3) finds evidence only from the 450s, but to this should be added two letters of John Chrysostom (*epp.* 213 and 218 = *PG* 52: 729 and *PG* 52: 732) written in 404 to Philip and the presbyter Euthymius, respectively, consoling them both for being dismissed from 'the *schola*'. In Greek as in Latin, this word can mean either a (teaching) 'school' or a (Guards) 'regiment', but the latter sense is required here: see Palladius, *Dial.* 71, where Philip is said to be 'the ascete and presbyter of the *scholae*', the Guards clearly being meant; compare *Dial.* 72, where Provincialius is said to be 'soldier of the *scholae* attached to the Emperor'.

55 Jerome, *ep.* 107.2, *ecclesiarum tentoria*; but, as he later admits himself (*paene lapsus sum ad aliam materiam*), he has been carried away from his intended subject. Goths, Christianity and warfare made for facile moralising: when Ulfilas translated the Bible into Gothic, he omitted the Books of Kings because the Goths were already warlike enough (Philost., *HE* 2.5); Valens, who sent Arian missionaries to the Goths, for which they will burn in hell as heretics, was himself burnt alive by them (Orosius, *adv. pag.* 7.33); when the Goths sacked Rome, they behaved responsibly by respecting nuns and church property (Orosius, *adv. pag.* 7.39; Jerome, *ep.* 127.13).

56 *De vocatione omnium gentium* 2.33 (= *PL* 51: 717–18).

57 Amm. 15.5.31. Silvanus took refuge in a chapel (*aedicula*) in the palace, but he was *ad conventiculum ritus Christiani tendentem*.

58 Amm. 17.10.1–2, *praesidiis vacuam*. This should mean that there was no garrison, exceptionally (compare *Not. Dig. Occ.* 41. 21), or possibly that the new walls had not yet been built. Within the period 350–75, the legionary fortress was abandoned and the civilian suburb fortified instead; so there is no direct evidence of a 'garrison chapel', only that a church was available for the garrison.

59 P. D. C. Brown 1971: 225–31, citing evidence for Cologne and the three Rhine forts. These three 'garrison chapels' are also noticed by von Petrikovits 1971: 203, with the comment that securely dated

examples are not known before the end of the fourth century. For Saldum and Zanes on the middle Danube see Petrović 1980.

60 A statue of Nemesis was still standing in Abinnaeus' headquarters building near those hunting nets: see the editors' introduction to *P. Abinn.*, p. 20. It would be worth tracing the army's residual paganism – or rather, its religious inertia – by the survival of altars in their original position (despite *CTh* 16.10.19, *arae locis omnibus destruantur*), notably the Fortuna altars frequent in military bath houses. Another interesting criterion would be the date and circumstances of the end of individual temples, those of Mithras in particular.

61 Amm. 21.2.4–5, compare Thdt., *HE* 3.1.

62 Sulpicius Severus, *Chronica* 2.38, 5 (ed. C. Halm, *Sulpicii Severi libri qui supersunt*, Vienna 1866).

63 Thdt., *HE* 4.31.

64 Ruf., *HE* 9.32; Palladius, *Proem.* in *HL* 35.

65 Thdt., *HE* 5.24.

66 Orosius, *adv.pag.* 7. 36.4–7; Paul., *V. Amb.* 51. Mascezel reported his vision to some African bishops before his return to Italy, and they told Paulinus.

67 Thus Octavian after Actium bought a raven which said 'Ave Caesar, victor imperator', but the trainer had hedged his bet by training another raven to acclaim Mark Antony: see Macrobius, *Saturnalia* 2.4.

68 Philost. *HE* 3.26. See Bidez and Winkelmann's edition, p. 51, for the other testimonies, especially Cyril of Jerusalem, *epistula ad Constantium* (*PG* 33: 1166–76). That Magnentius was a pagan is inferred from his defeat, whereas in fact his coinage is the first to emphasise the *Chi-Rho.*

69 *Pan. Lat.* VI (7) 21.4, with commentary by Nixon and Rodgers 1994: 248–50. Barnes 1981: 36 observes that the story is 'brazenly' guaranteed by an appeal to the local hot springs which punish perjury. For the *topos* of Constantine's visit to the Capitol see Zos. 2.29.5 and the translation by Ridley 1982: 157 n. 64.

70 *CTh* 7.20.2, *Auguste Constantine, dii te nobis servent*. In *CJ* 12.46.1, the acclamation has become *deus te nobis servet*. The inference is drawn by Jones 1964 I: 81, but the transmitted place Beauvais cannot be reconciled with 1 March 320, since Constantine was then in Illyricum, and indeed does not seem to have returned to Gaul after 316. Barnes 1982: 69 n. 102 (summarised in Barnes 1981: 309, n. 42), emends the date elegantly to 307, but this would mean that Constantine, aged about 35, was addressing Gallic Army veterans as 'fellow veterans' (*conveterani*) after less than two years in the West; in *CTh* 7. 20.4, he assumes that a 'veteran' serves 24 years, or 20 years at least.

71 Eus., *VC* 3.54.

72 Eus., *VC* 3.55–7. See, further, Barnes 1981: 247.

73 Julian 379B, *ep.* 21. In general see Fowden 1978.

74 Thdt, *HE* 5.21 (quoted); Sozomen, *HE* 7.15; Libanius, *Or.* 30, especially *Or.* 30.46. Marcellus subsequently raised irregular troops of his own to attack shrines in the countryside, but by mishap he was

caught and burnt alive by a rustic mob. Gibbon pointedly refrains from drawing any moral: see Gibbon [1776] 1909 III: 207–8.

75 Eunapius, *vitae sophistarum* 472; Sozomen, *HE* 7.15.

76 Mark the Deacon, *Life of Porphyry* 70. T.D. Barnes has demonstrated (in his Syme Lecture at Oxford, 19 October 1995) that the Life is not, as it purports to be, a contemporary document; arguably, it is edifying fiction of the sixth century. That the Temple of Marnas survived until *c.* 400 is admitted by Jerome, *ep.* 107.2.

77 Thdt., *HE* 3.1.

78 Thdt., *HE* 3.2 (the bishops) and 3.3 (overt paganism). Ammianus likewise connects the two and places them both at Constantinople: see Amm. 22.5.2 (the first reference to Julian's overt paganism) and 22.5.3 (his audience for the various bishops), although it is certain from Julian, *ep.* 8 (LCL), that he first revealed his paganism at Naissus once he had heard that Constantius was dead. Ammianus omits this detail in his haste to get Julian from Naissus to Constantinople (22.2), but 22.5.1–2 is partly retrospective: Julian had been a closet pagan since childhood, but came out 'after the removal of his fears' (*abolitis quae verebatur*), i.e. when Constantius was dead. The formal edicts (*planis absolutisque decretis*) were evidently issued at Constantinople, part and parcel of the new policy of religious toleration extended to Christian bishops of all sects. Libanius (*Or.* 18.121), a contemporary witness but not there in person, dates Julian's overt paganism after the funeral of Constantius.

79 Thdt., *HE* 3.1.

80 Zos. 3.3.2, but the actual words are not found in the parallel passage in Julian, *Letter to the Athenians* 277D; Libanius applies them instead to the few Gallic soldiers who would have been left to him at Paris in early 360, if Constantius' agents had had their way.

81 Libanius, *Or.* 18.167.

82 Ephrem the Syrian, *Hymns against Julian* iii 10–12, translation in Lieu 1989: 119. Ephrem in his turgid, allusive way insists that Constantius' army was already pagan before Julian led it to defeat. In his joy at Julian's death, he ignores Constantius' Arianism as an explanation of Roman failures.

83 Amm. 21.5.10, compare 17.12.21 (and compare 16).

84 Vegetius, *Epit.* 2.5; compare Servius, commenting on *Aeneid* 7.614 (oath not to desert). The invocation of the Trinity is a Christianizing addition.

85 Sozomen, *HE* 5.1.

86 Julian, *ep.* 8 (LCL).

87 Eus., *VC* 1.27; Libanius, *Or.* 18.167.

88 Libanius, *Or.* 18.167.

89 Greg. Naz., *Or.* 4.64–5, τοῦ καίρου δοῦλον καὶ τότε καὶ πρότερον.

90 Ibid., *Or.* 4.82–3.

91 Ibid., *Or.* 4.84; repeated by Sozomen, *HE* 5.17.

92 The evidence is collected in Bidez and Cumont's edition of Julian *ep.* 50, at p. 57; in particular Ruf. *HE* 10 33, and Socrates, *HE* 3.13.1ff. John Chrysostom, *Homily on SS Iuventinus and Maximinus*

(*PG* 50: 571–8) points out that Julian avoided making martyrs because he knew the Church was strengthened by them. Julian would not have seen his policy in quite those terms, but the cults of Georgius and Artemius show how easily this could happen.

93 John Chrysostom, *Homily on SS Iuventinus and Maximinus* (*PG* 50: 571–8), worked up by Thdt., *HE* 3.15.4–9. See Franchi de' Cavalieri 1953.

94 Malalas, *Chronographia* 13.327.

95 *PLRE*: 933–4 under Valentinianus 7 collects the references, and tries unnecessarily to reconcile the various stories.

96 Augustine, *Enarr. in Psalm*. 124, 7 (CSL 40: 1841), citing Ephesians 6.5–6; compare *Contra Faustum* xxii 75 (*CSEL* 25: 673): a soldier is innocent who obeys the orders even of a pagan ruler. Optatus' rejoinder (iii 3) to Donatus' question '*Quid est imperatori cum ecclesia?*' is to cite 1 Timothy 2, 2, our duty to pray for kings and for all that are in authority even if (he adds) the Emperor is a pagan.

97 Sulpicius Severus, *Vita Martini* 20. In a cruder form, that the Catholic Maximus defeated Valentinian II because he was an Arian, this argument reappears in a letter attributed to Theodosius by Theodoret (*HE* 5.15). But Theodoret sees no illogic in Theodosius' decision to intervene none the less: the suppliant Valentinian would thereby be converted to Catholicism. A source favourable to Maximus would have credited him with telling his troops not to pursue Valentinian too closely, in hopes that he might repent and mend his ways: this is what Eusebius says of Constantine, in his defeat of Licinius (Eus., *VC* 2.11).

98 Amm. Marc. 22.12.6; 14.1–3.

99 Amm. Marc. 23.5.11.

100 Socrates, *HE* 3.21 (Callistus' epic poem). Libanius, *Or*. 24.6 (the Arab): see Bowersock 1978: 116–18.

101 Amm. Marc. 25.5.6.

102 Thdt., *HE* 4.1.

103 Thdt., *HE* 3.1 (quoted above p. 31).

104 Athanasius, *ep. ad Iovianum,* appendix i (*PG* 26: 820), trans. Coleman-Norton 1966 I: 294, no. 124.

105 Amm. Marc. 25.8.11; compare 26.6.3, Jovian murders one rival and drives another into hiding. St Agricola's church: *CIL* XIII 3256.

106 The praetorian prefect Salutius Secundus, a leading pagan, refused the throne in 363 on the excuse of being too old and ill; in 364 he supported the Catholic Valentinian. See *PLRE*: 814–17 under Secundus 3.

107 Zos. 5.46. *CTh* 16.5.42, a fragment of the directive, refers only to 'service within the palace' (*intra palatium militare*), but since it was addressed jointly to the *Magister Officiorum* and the *Comes Domesticorum*, it would have concerned both civilians and soldiers.

108 Socrates, *HE* 7.29. Firmicus Maternus (in *De errore profanarum religionum* 29) had already taken the Persians' failure as evidence

of God's favour, which could be conciliated further by executing apostates.

109 *CTh* 16.5.56 (428), excluding *militia castrensis* from the ban on heretics; Sozomen, *HE* 5.5.

110 Augustine, *De civitate Dei* 5.26 (Jupiter); Thdt., *HE* 5.24.4 (Hercules). Like Paulinus (in *V. Amb.* 31), they see the working of divine favour in the course of the battle and its outcome, but Christian soldiers from both armies probably contributed to the cemetery at Concordia (see Hoffmann 1969: 61ff.), and it would be simplistic to see the army of Arbogast as 'pagan'. Its behaviour illustrates rather the late Roman soldier's tolerance of his leaders' religious eccentricities.

111 *Not. Dig. Or.* 5.3 (*Ioviani iuniores*) and *Not. Dig. Occ.* 5.2 (= *Ioviani seniores*); compare Laubscher 1975, pls 13, 32 and 42.2. But note that the accompanying *Herculiani iuniores* and *seniores* also have eagle shields, not Hercules shields (contrast Laubscher 1975, pls 38 and 56.2), which looks like religious censorship. Victory might easily become an angel, but Hercules with his club was difficult to assimilate.

112 Sozomen, *HE* 6.6.

113 See the index to Seeck's *Not. Dig.* edition. Almost all the *Notitia*'s 'theophoric' units are Tetrarchic: legions like *Legio I Iovia* (*Herculia, Martia*) whose titles were formed by analogy with the old legions *I Minervia* (now only *Minervii*) and *XV Apollinaris*; and new-style infantry units of *Iovii*, *Martenses* and *Solenses* (but not the *Dianenses* which, like the two *auxilia Herculensia* explicitly from *Ad Herculem*, probably derived from the place name *Ad Dianam*). The Christian cemetery at Concordia attests Christian soldiers in the *Ioviani*, *Iovii* and *Martenses*. Iovinus, a *protector*, who buried his soldier son there, simply named him Iovinianus. The only instance of a Christian soldier deliberately avoiding a theophoric name seems to be Flavius Iovinus, sometime *praepositus* of the *milites Histrici*, who named his son Paulus (*ILS* 2787).

114 *Not. Dig. Or.* 38. 34. According to Seeck, other Egyptian forts with theophoric names are Apollo superior, Diospolis, and Hermoupolis Speos Artemidos. Note also the missionary–bishop Amantius, whose see was Iovia (*CIL* V 1623).

115 For example the *Atecotti*, the *Anderetiani*, and the numerous 'Theodosian' units and *Honoriani*. But in the fifth century, during the Persian siege of Theodosiopolis (Erzerum) in the reign of Theodosius II, note Thdt., *HE* 5.36. An obnoxious enemy officer was singled out by the local bishop, who killed him with a stone-throwing catapult. Its name was 'St Thomas the Apostle'.

116 Hercules has been displaced by Jupiter's eagle on the *Herculiani* shields in the *Notitia* (see above, n. 111), a somewhat limited piece of religious censorship. Two other instances have been offered, but neither is convincing. First, von Petrikovits 1971: 182–3 infers censorship from the omission of the title *Primigenia* by Legio XXII when it stamped bricks for Constantine's fort at Deutz; sometimes C.V. for *C(onstantiniana) V(ictrix)* (?) was added to the

numeral instead. But although *Primigenia* is an epithet of Fortune, it is not exclusively so; and it is not certain that a reference to Fortune was intended when the legion was formed, let alone still understood in the fourth century. Second, Hoffmann 1969: 68 and 78 has suggested that the *Regii* (*Not. Dig. Or.* vi 49; *Not. Dig. Occ.* v 229) are not Ammianus' *Reges* (16.12.45) but the sometime *Regii Emeseni Iudaei* instead (*CIL* V 8764, Concordia), their title being abbreviated after Jews were banned from military service in 418 (*CTh* 16. 8.24). But the Concordia stone is defective at this point, and Mommsen's restoration and expansion of the reading are both far-fetched.

117 C. Lang's useful *index verborum* in the old Teubner edition of Vegetius (Leipzig 1885) is not retained by Önnerfors in the new edition: *Deus* is found on 6 pages, but *antiquus* on 23 and *vetus* on 26.

118 Nock 1952: 226.

119 Socrates, *HE* 2.13 and 16.

120 Ibid., 2.38; Sozomen, *HE* 4.21.

121 *PLRE*: 812 under Sebastianus 2, citing the testimony of Athanasius.

122 Sozomen, *HE* 4.24.

123 Ambrose, *ep.* 20.12 and 26. Ambrose distinguishes 'Goths' from 'soldiers' in the besieging troops (ibid., 16 and *Sermo contra Auxentium* 27), as if distinguishing Arians from Catholics.

124 Palladius, *Dial.* 9.177ff., 192.

125 *PLRE*: 812 under Sebastianus 2.

126 This might explain why two of Valens' most senior civilian ministers command troops in his half-hearted persecution of the orthodox: the praetorian prefect Modestus at Edessa (Sozomen, *HE* 6.18) and the *comes sacrarum largitionum* Magnus, assisted by the prefect of Egypt, at Alexandria (Socrates, *HE* 4.21)

127 *PLRE*: 957 s.v. Victor 4; *PLRE*: 104 s.v. Arinthaeus.

128 Socrates, *HE* 4.36; Amm. 31.16.5–6.

129 *PLRE*: 921–2 under Traianus 2. Palladius, *Lausiac History* 57.

130 Amm. 30.1.2; compare 17.7.7 (Sabinianus). The Armenian historian Faustus (5.32) blames Traianus, not Terentius, for the assassination of King Papa; but 'it was probably a concerted plot' by them both, as Baynes rightly says (Baynes 1955: 204). Faustus accuses Papa of murdering the Armenian patriarch Nerses and of negotiating with Persia.

131 Ambrose, *ep.* 57.3.

132 *PLRE*: 765–6 under Richomeres.

133 Zos. 4.53.

134 Paul., *V. Amb.* 30. But Sulpicius Severus did not approve of Ambrose, as a bishop, entertaining high officials (compare his *Dial.* i 25, on Postumianus). Not that dinner with Ambrose was without its risks: some very Christian army officers were there when a clergyman of Milan started criticising his bishop, only to suffer a fatal stroke. When Paulinus told this story to an African bishop also critical of Ambrose, this man too had a stroke soon afterwards and died (*V. Amb.* 54).

135 Paul., *ep.* 25. Similar arguments including 'military' imagery are used by Jerome in *epp.* 14, 60 and 145, to persuade civil servants to abandon their *militia*, but these men are civilians, not soldiers.

136 Paul., *ep.* 18.

137 Martin's defiance of the tyrant Julian is a topos: see Fontaine 1963. Barnes has also proved (in his Syme Lecture at Oxford, 19 October 1995) that the transmitted chronology of Sulpicius Severus' *Vita Martini* 2–5 is impossible: Martin cannot have served in Julian's army for almost five years before he became a disciple of St Hilary (exiled in 356).

138 Canon 3, *qui arma proiciunt in pace.*

139 Augustine, *ep.* 220. 3, *accinctus balteo castissimae continentiae et inter arma corporalia spiritualibus armis tutius fortiusque munitus.*

140 Basil, *ep.* 188, 13.

141 Augustine, *ep.* 47.5.

142 Ibid. 220.6–11.

143 Augustine, *ep.* 220.12, *quantum rerum humanarum salva pace potuisses, ab istis bellicis rebus abstraheres* and *ut in ipsis bellis, si adhuc in eis te versari opus est, fidem teneas, pacem quaeras.*

144 Augustine, *ep.* 220.4.

145 Matthew 8.10: 'I have not found so great faith, no, not in Israel'. Acts 10.2; exemplary for John Chrysostom, *Baptismal Instructions* 7.28ff.

146 Maximus of Turin, *Sermones* 87.2 (ed. A. Mutzenbacher, *Maximi Épiscopi Taurinensis: Sermones*, CCSL 23, 1962). There is an unsympathetic account of these elegant sermons and their context in Casey 1979: 253–9.

147 Claudian, *Carmina minora* 50.

148 Thdt., *HE.* 2.13.

149 Greg. Naz., *Or.* 19.14.

150 Julian, *ep.* 40 (LCL). Honorius riposted in kind (*CTh* 16.10.19 (407), published at Rome): temple revenues are to be confiscated for the benefit of the army, *expensis devotissimorum militum.*

151 Eus., *Tric. Or.* 7.1.

152 Augustine, *ep.* 189.5.

153 Ambrose, *Hexaemeron* 2.12; 3.12.

154 Ambrose, *De officiis* 1.27, 129.

155 Ibid. 3.3, 23.

156 Ambrose, *De fide* ii 16, 136 (citing Ezekiel 38). Putting on the Armour of God (from Ephesians 6.11–17) is a favourite topos in sermons; the metaphor is developed at great length by Victricius in *Liber de laude sanctorum* 12, but disappointingly his language is entirely conventional and unspecific; one would never deduce that he had been a soldier.

157 Paul., *V. Amb.* 30.

4

THE CITIES OF ASIA MINOR IN THE AGE OF CONSTANTINE

Stephen Mitchell

In 327 Constantine founded the city of Helenopolis in honour of his mother Helena at the village of Drepanum, 'The Sickle', on the south side of the gulf of Nicomedia and close to the famous hot springs of Yalova, which had been part of the territory of Byzantium for centuries and now served as a natural resort for the court of Constantinople.[1] She had chosen the site herself since it harboured the remains of one of the most famous martyrs of the Great Persecution, St Lucian of Antioch. This was no guarantee of its suitability as a future urban settlement and, indeed, little more than two centuries later John Malalas punningly renamed it Eleeinoupolis, City of Misery, its last appearance in our surviving sources before it disappeared from history.[2] The foundation, according to Sozomen,[3] was designed to perpetuate Helena's memory, and Constantine thereby followed in the footsteps of any number of other rulers who had named or renamed cities after their wives and female kin, the Apameas, Laodiceas, Stratonicaeas, and probably most appositely of all Faustinopolis, formerly the village of Halala in the northern foothills of the Taurus near the Cilician Gates, which Marcus Aurelius had founded to commemorate his wife Faustina, who had died there.[4]

Constantine, like any ancient ruler, operated within a traditional framework and this trivial episode illustrates him in a traditional role. It was an emperor's task to promote cities, and the doctrine was crisply enunciated in Constantine's own answer to the petition of Orcistus in Phrygia, that it be promoted to the status of an independent civitas: *quibus enim studium est urbes vel*

52

novas condere vel longaevas erudire vel intermortuas reparare, id quod petebatur acceptissimum fuit (that petition found most ready acceptance from those who have the task of founding new cities, reviving ancient ones, and repairing those that are dying).[5] The former *vicus* of Orcistus had already flourished like a city: it had annual magistrates, was well known for its *curiales*, and had a numerous population of free men. Not only was it a well-sited *mansio* in the central Anatolian road-system, endowed with streams and watermills, but it had a forum decorated with the statues of old emperors, as well as public and private bath houses. Most importantly, its inhabitants were all Christians.[6]

Similar sentiments were expressed in Constantine's rescript of 326–7 addressed to the people of Umbria, that every city should not only retain its former rank but be advanced to higher status by the exercise of imperial beneficence. However, the actual substance of this decision, which released the Tuscans from their previous obligation to send a priest and contributions to the *ludi scaenici* and gladiatorial games at Vulsinii in Etruria, and allowed them instead to erect an *aedes Flavia* in their own town of Hispellum, henceforth to be named Flavia Constantia and to be the centre of the Tuscan community, has been interpreted by modern commentators as an illustration of 'the gradual substitution of the provinces for the municipality as the political and social unit of the empire', a message which was also implicit in several other Constantinian constitutions, which were addressed not to particular cities but to entire provinces or even to the provinces in general.[7]

The points made in Constantine's reply to Orcistus are also to be found in the rescript sent by an unnamed emperor, perhaps in the time of the tetrarchy, to Tymandus in south Phrygia, in which the ruler saw it as incumbent upon himself that the esteem and number of cities throughout the entire world be increased. Tymandus too offered a sufficient number of would-be decurions and could thereby claim the rights of a city, namely to hold curial assemblies (that is to have a council), to draft decrees, and to carry out the other functions to which a city was legally entitled, including the election of municipal magistrates, aediles, and quaestors.[8]

It is necessary, however, to ask what all this really meant. Within five years of the original decision about Orcistus Constantine was obliged to send its *curiales* another letter, which assured them that his grant was not intended merely as a nominal honour but as a real privilege. In the meantime, the people of Nacolea, to whom Orcistus had previously been subordinate, still insisted on collecting dues from the place, including a tax *pro cultis*, to maintain its pagan cults.[9] The writ even of Constantine had limited carrying power in the remoter corners of Asia Minor. This very sparse direct evidence for Constantine's involvement with cities in Asia Minor leaves entirely open the question whether he, or the members of his family, or his immediate predecessors and successors introduced any substantial changes to the cities of the region, or indeed to other parts of the Mediterranean world.

There is, in fact, an acute problem of evidence and its evaluation. The explosion of city life in the Roman world during the second century CE is well known from an abundant, probably over-abundant, documentation:[10] buildings, inscriptions, coins, to say nothing of contemporary writers, tell an unambiguous story of urban growth and prosperity which need not be retold here. The problems of these cities during the third century, under increasing pressure from requisitions and tax demands as well as under physical threat from barbarian invaders and from the indiscipline of Roman troops, also need no rehearsing. The history of the cities in this period, however, remains well documented. Inscriptions are rarer after the 220s, but coins from local mints were produced on an ever larger scale, and their types and legends provide ample information about city cults and festivals, about relations with the emperors and their armies, and demonstrate the evolution of civic values and ideology, which was highly responsive to the changing world of the third century, until the last of these civic mints, that of Perge in Pamphylia, ceased in the short reign of the Emperor Tacitus in 275.[11]

The surviving evidence from the cities of Asia Minor and the other Eastern provinces in the time of Diocletian and Constantine offers a bleak contrast. As a source for regional history, the products of the central imperial mints are no substitute for the locally minted bronze coinage; the thin trickle of mid-third-century inscriptions hardly increases in the early fourth, and archaeological investigation has been largely unhelpful in providing specific information or defining new trends during this period. If Asia Minor in the Hadrianic period offers a plethora of evidence for city life, under Constantine there is a complete contrast. It is extraordinarily difficult to gain any direct idea of what was going on in the early fourth century at Side or at Ephesus, at Sardis, Ancyra, or Aphrodisias.

The question, nevertheless, is of some importance. Much scholarly attention has been devoted to the broader question of the survival of classical city life in Late Antiquity.[12] Much of the debate on this topic has been obscured by problems of definition, and specifically by the question of what we are to understand by the term 'city'. If the word is defined simply as an urbanised population centre, whose inhabitants practised various forms of craft specialisation and developed or maintained a market economy, then no one will deny that cities, or better 'towns', survived in all parts of the empire through Late Antiquity, and even beyond. However, as the rescripts to Orcistus and Tymandus from the early fourth century show, ancient notions of a city were a different matter and liable to juridical definition. A city ought, no doubt, to be an urban population centre, although the case of Drepanum–Helenopolis may call even this into question, but it must more critically have magistrates, a curial class, and (perhaps optionally) certain material fixtures, like the forum and bath buildings of Orcistus. Such specific features of civic organisation could and did change, but it was essential that some form of independent organisation or constitution be preserved, if a community was to retain any trace of its origin as a classical city. This alone could preserve or sustain a city's identity, autonomy and financial viability in the face of the other chief sources of power and authority in the Roman world of the fourth to the sixth centuries, namely the wealthy rural landowners, the agents of the imperial government, and Church leaders.[13]

However these large questions about the survival of the city in Late Antiquity may be answered, the problem of how to approach the surviving evidence must be faced. In particular, we have to come to terms with the fact that most of the available information no longer focuses directly on the cities, but on the other elements in the late Roman state. The patristic literature is concerned with the ever-widening affairs and influence of the Church, although by no means exclusively with matters of doctrine. Meanwhile, the inscriptions and coins, which form the main documentation for the institutional history of the second- and third-century cities, are superseded by sources which turn the spotlight away from the cities and on to the imperial authorities, namely the Theodosian and Justinianic Codes, the huge collection of late Roman imperial legislation. The cities, the crucial administrative cogs of the earlier imperial system, hardly feature at all in the hundreds of fourth- and fifth-century imperial decisions and rulings that make up the

Theodosian Code. The emperors directed their attention at their subjects under a variety of headings: whole provinces, classes of the population, soldiers, officials, clergy, or members of trades and professions, but scarcely ever at civic communities.[14] It is rare for cities to be mentioned at all, and one exceptional example, concerning Asia Minor, simply helps to confirm the rule. In 388 Valentinian and Valens issued a rescript concerning the decurions of four communities in Bithynia: Claudiopolis, Prusias, Tottaus, and Doris, described as 'towns and public post stations'. This formulation in itself contrasts with the practice of the early Empire, and blurs the hierarchical division of status between earlier cities, namely Claudiopolis and Prusias, and subordinate villages, for Tottaus and Doris had hitherto been dependent on Nicaea.[15] The current conspicuousness of all four communities depended not on their status as cities but on the fact that they were stations of the imperial transport system, precisely the point emphasised by Orcistus, when it had presented itself for Constantine's approval as a *mansio*.

The substantial content of Valentinian and Valens' rescript, as in innumerable other cases, concerned the flight of decurions, who were attempting to avoid compulsory public services. The emperors' first recourse was to publish edicts summoning them back to their home towns. Were this, as seemed likely even to the emperors, to fail, they were simply to be replaced 'from any suitable groups, and preferably from groups who have completed approved imperial service in the office of the Praetorian Prefect, and who will take over the patrimonies of the fugitives and fulfil their obligations'.[16] The towns themselves had ceased to be important; only the availability of decurions able to fulfil their duties to the state was of any concern.

It is important to be clear on the point at issue here. The curial class of the empire's cities, the decurions, remained essential to the state's well-being between the fourth and sixth centuries, but their importance was as providers of taxes and services and not as the organised driving force of civic communities. Our best evidence for the curial class in fourth-century Asia Minor comes from the correspondence of Basil of Caesarea in the 370s and 380s. They are revealed as powerless in the face of demands from the imperial authorities, relying on the protection offered by their bishop. In a letter addressed to a governor of Cappadocia, Basil pleaded on behalf of an old man, himself exempt from public service, who was expected to discharge the financial obligations of his 4-year-old grandson, who had been drafted onto the council of Caesarea. The circumstances in themselves reveal that councillors in political terms were no more than straw men, but a later phrase of the letter is even more revealing: οὐ γὰρ δήπου τὸ παίδιον εἰς βουλευτὰς συντελέσει, ἢ ἐκλέξει τὰς εἰσφορὰς, ἢ στρα– τιώταις χορηγήσει τὸ σιτηρέσιον (It was not to be supposed that the child in person would make his contribution to the *curiales* (that is, fulfil civic liturgies), raise taxes, or dispatch grain to the soldiers.) These three functions amounted to a virtual definition of the role of the city councillor, whose sole *raison d'être* was to maintain the flow of income in cash and kind to the state.[17] The same realities are demonstrated by the best known episode in Cappadocian politics in Basil's time, the decision of the Emperor Valens in 371–2 to divide the province into two parts. Cappadocia Secunda lacked substantial towns and was short of *curiales*, so the emperor simply decided to transfer substantial numbers of the councillors of Caesarea to the miserable way-station of Podandus.[18] The council of Caesarea itself was powerless to resist, 'now that we have no more debates, no more gatherings of the wise men in the Forum, nothing more of all that made our city famous'.[19] The result, said Basil in a letter to Sophronius, the *Magister Officiorum*, was that no city shattered by an earthquake or engulfed by a flood was so swiftly ruined as Caesarea by this new constitution.[20] The rhetoric of Basil's appeal is doubtless overstated, but the point was a central one. The concern of the state with the *curiales* was not that their community flourished, but that they could be called upon to deliver their taxes. Defaulting councillors in Bithynia could have their property confiscated and be replaced, at the stroke of an administrator's pen, by substitutes; the *curiales* of the great city of Caesarea could be moved like pawns on a chess board to the miserable village of Podandus if it suited imperial needs. City status was not a matter for concern. Imperial priorities were no longer with the foundation and maintenance of autonomous cities, but with the organisation of their subjects as tax-payers.

It is a scholarly commonplace to locate the watershed between the civic world of the early Roman empire and the state and Church domination of the fourth and fifth centuries on the chronological cusp, say in 300 or, to avoid such an obvious nonsense, over the period of the tetrarchy and the reign of Constantine, the half-century between 285 and 337. As we have already seen, direct evidence that this period was critical in the transformation of the classical city is extremely sparse. A frontal approach to the actual remains of the cities themselves, documentary or archaeological, leads to disappointingly inconclusive results. Charlotte Roueché introduces the section of her study of Aphrodisias in Late Antiquity concerned with the period of Diocletian and Constantine, with the remark that 'there is frustratingly little evidence for the way in which the city developed during what must have been a critical period in its history'.[21] The sentiment is applicable throughout Asia Minor. Clive Foss' detailed surveys of the history of Sardis, Ephesus, and Ancyra in Late Antiquity offer no evidence of substantial activity during this period in any of these cities, apart from road building (see below).[22] Claims that the great Roman market building of Ephesus was transformed into the Cathedral Church of St Mary under Constantine have been refuted by detailed architectural study.[23] The observation of a later source that the cities of Asia Minor – Nicomedia, Cyzicus, Caesarea, Tralles, Sardis, Mocissus, Sebasteia, Satala, Smyrna, Seleuceia, Tyana, Iconium, and Nicaea – were stripped of statues and steles to adorn the Hippodrome at Constantinople, is much more revealing of the realities of this period.[24] However, it is of course possible that other changes to the cultural and political patterns of the Empire in the early fourth century had major consequences for the cities, and that the fate of the latter, whatever it was, was determined by these wider changes. Some of these need to be examined and I shall select for scrutiny six topics which have, at one time or another, been picked out as representing significant new developments of the age of Diocletian and Constantine, and which may be presumed to have affected the life of the provincial cities. These are:

1   the division of the empire into smaller provinces;
2   the growth in the number of imperial officials;
3   the construction and maintenance of the road system;
4   the transformation of the imperial taxation system from one where revenues were usually collected in cash to one where levies in kind predominated;
5   the relationship between cities and rulers embodied in the imperial cult;
6   the development of Christianity.

Since it would obviously not be difficult to write an entire book on each of these topics, my aim is simply to cite a sample of the evidence from Asia Minor relevant to each question. This is to show that, where new developments and changes can be discerned, they began far earlier than the last quarter of the third century. It is, therefore, either false, or at least misleading, to attribute a decisive role in these developments to the period of the Tetrarchy or to the regime of Constantine.

It is convenient to take the first two topics together, if only because they were explicitly linked by Lactantius at the beginning of the *De mortibus persecutorum* and identified as a major source of the miseries inflicted on their subjects by Diocletian and his colleagues.[25] It is now clear from the epigraphic finds published by Charlotte Roueché from Aphrodisias and from numerous third- and fourth-century milestones from Asia Minor discovered by David French, that the splitting of the empire into smaller provinces, although fully confirmed for the early fourth century by other sources, notably the Verona List, began, in Asia Minor at least, at a significantly earlier date. During the early principate, provincial boundaries had in fact been much more fluid in Anatolia than in other parts of the empire, but the tendency to favour smaller subdivisions was palpably accelerated in the Severan period. Under Severus Alexander Pontus, previously attached to Cappadocia, became an independent province and, apart from being briefly reunited with Galatia around 250, remained so through the fourth century.[26] Isauria, previously part of the so-called 'Three Provinces' since the time of Antoninus Pius, was a separate province by the time of Gordian III.[27] Proconsular Asia was carved up around 250, when the new unit of Phrygia and Caria was created.[28] It is clear from many inscriptions that the term *provincia* or *eparchia* was widely used also in the first and second centuries to denote parts of the larger provinces governed by proconsuls and *legati Augusti*: the combination of Lycaonia, Cilicia, and Isauria was officially designated the *Tres Eparchiae;* the constituent parts of Galatia– Cappadocia, including Phrygia, Pisidia, Lycaonia, Isauria, Pontus Galaticus, Pontus Polemoniacus, and Armenia Minor in the Flavio- Trajanic period were labelled as *provinciae*, and procurators were designated to several regions, named provinces, which did not correspond to the larger units administered by governors, among them the Thracian Chersonese, Hellespontus, Phrygia, and Lycia.[29] Given the inadequate third-century documentation, it would be no surprise to learn in the future that other small provinces, such as Pisidia and Paphlagonia, had been created before the time of Diocletian. He may have addressed the issue of provincial division more systematically than his predecessors, but he certainly did not begin the process. The reason for this policy is doubtless that hinted at by Lactantius, that the creation of smaller administrative units, with a correspondingly larger number of officials, meant that provinces could be more intensively supervised, or rather, that taxes and other dues could be exacted from them with greater efficiency. The motive to do so existed a hundred years before Diocletian.

The same is obviously true of the multiplying official presence in the provinces. The change in the nature of the evidence between the third and the fourth centuries is surely largely responsible for disguising the similarities between the oppressive hordes of minor officials, especially concerned with tax collection, revealed by the Theodosian Code, and perhaps even more vividly by the letters of Libanius, concerning Syria and the hinterland of Antioch,[30] and of Basil of Caesarea concerning Cappadocia,[31] and their third-century predecessors. The counterparts of these fourth-century imperial agents and soldiers were already present in strength across Asia Minor from the Severan period, as we know from the numerous petitions of Asian communities which complained at their abusive behaviour.

Many of them were of course simply soldiers, as in the earliest document of this type known to date, a letter of Aemilius Iuncus, the proconsul of Asia in 193, who published a decision taken during the three-month regime of Pertinax to protect the people of Lydian Tabala from bands of soldiers, wandering about intent on extortion, who had left the military highway, and extracted a recruitment tax from them.[32]

In fact the whole of Lydia, a zone of prosperous small towns and villages which had hardly been directly touched by Roman administration before this period,[33] was virtually overrun with soldiers and officials in the following half century. The unholy trio of oppressors, named singly or in combination in every inscription, were the *stationarii*, the soldiers from the gendarme-posts along the main roads who were to be found the length and breadth of Anatolia throughout the Principate, the *frumentarii*, and the *collectiones*, who, in the words of one group of petitioners, were in the habit of treating the peasant population like war-time enemies.[34] It is surely beyond question that the purpose of these officials was to collect levies and taxes, either in kind or in cash. It is worth emphasising how widespread their activities were. *Stationarii* not only guarded the roads of Isauria, and provoked the complaints of the peasants of Lydia and Phrygia, but were responsible for collecting fines payable for tomb violation at Tium on the Black Sea coast, at Lydian Apollonis, and at Olympus in Eastern Lycia, none in any way part of a military zone.[35] *Frumentarii* emerged not only as oppressors but as helpers and patrons of communities, doubtless in return for a consideration. Aragua's petition was presented to the Philips at Rome by a centurion and *frumentarius*.[36] Aurelius Gaius, holding precisely these ranks, was praised for his decency (perhaps rather for his restraint) at Aphrodisias around the 250s, and a centurion of the region called Aurelius Gaius was active around Pisidian Antioch in the mid-third century.[37]

These junior officials, while on the one hand free to behave as they pleased with the local population, were also virtually the only people with access to higher authorities, and they automatically assumed the double role of oppressors and patrons, creating the relationship described in detail for late fourth-century Syria by Libanius in the *de patrociniis*.[38] The origins of this 'military patronage', in which soldiers interceded for or protected a community against the predations of higher officialdom, are not difficult to trace to the circumstances of the earlier third century. A fine example comes from a village in the territory of Nicaea, whose inhabitants in 263–4 honoured as patrons a group of centurions and their families in return for unspecified benefactions.[39] It should be noted in passing that the same categories of officials and soldiers retained not only their functions but also their names and titles from the third to the fourth century. The *frumentarii* evolved notoriously into part of the imperial 'secret service' of the later empire, although they surely continued to supervise the collection of tax grain, as their title implies,[40] while *stationarii* are attested by numerous constitutions of the Constantinian period, behaving exactly as they had done a hundred years earlier, as a police force more inclined to take the law into their own hands than to maintain order and justice.[41]

In one of the surviving early third-century petitions the peasant inhabitants of Güllüküy in Lydia reported that they had turned in vain to eirenarchs to protect them from criminal abuse by soldiers and imperial officials.[42] They were appealing to the standards of a former age. The move away from reliance on cities and local magistrates to officials and soldiers was already in full swing a century before the laments of Lactantius on the subject.

The transformation in the relationship between masters and subjects, at the expense of the independent functioning of the cities, would have been impossible without the existence of Roman roads, the next topic for consideration. It is a text-book commonplace that the essential road system of Anatolia, linking the military area of the Balkans with Syria and the north-eastern frontier of the empire along the upper Euphrates, was created in the Flavio-Trajanic period. What happened during the third century has received much less attention. Certainly the extensive road system of central and eastern Asia Minor was maintained, but it was now supplemented by a much increased network in the West, especially in the province of Asia. The overwhelming majority of milestones from Asia date to the third and fourth centuries. There were notable bursts of activity under Septimius Severus and his colleagues, during the Tetrarchy, and under Constantine, but the role of shorter-lived emperors during the rest of the third century should not be overlooked.[43] Moreover, construction seems to have broken new ground, especially in the heart of West–Central Anatolia, Lydia and Phrygia, where the only direct evidence for earlier road-building comes from the area around Synnada, the *conventus* city for Eastern Asia as well as the administrative centre for the imperial estates and marble quarries of Phrygia, and from around Thyatira, where, by the Flavian period, a route cut across the hinterland leading from Ionia to the Hellespont.[44] In northern Phrygia, around Aezani and in the upper Tembris valley, for instance, which has now been very thoroughly explored epigraphically, no milestones are known from before the Severan period, and almost all documented activity belongs then or in the early fourth century.[45]

Arguments from silence are always suspect, but at least we should conclude that only in the early third century were roads being built and repaired on a large scale in the hinterland that linked the agricultural towns of these hitherto isolated and unconsidered regions. The construction of these *leophoroi hodoi,* to use the language of the contemporary petitions, was the fundamental precondition for the vastly increased presence of soldiers and officials in these regions during the Severan and later periods. In this case the continuity between the third and fourth centuries has not been disguised by any change in the nature of the evidence, for milestones continued to be set up or re-inscribed in the traditional manner without interruption until the end of the fourth century.[46] They are the clearest evidence for the continuity between the Severan and the Constantinian age, and they symbolise, more tellingly than any other type of document, the decreasing emphasis on the cities and the rising importance of a new world of roads, *mansiones*, travelling soldiers, and tax collection.

Taxation is another critical topic in the appraisal of the fourth century. It is indisputable that in the fourth century a large proportion of tax revenue was extracted from the provinces not in cash but in kind, overwhelmingly, no doubt, in the form of grain requisitions. So universal was the practice, that imperial officials were themselves often paid in grain rather than in cash, being expected to realise their assets by selling this themselves.[47] The question at issue, however, is how far this tax regime differed from earlier practice. It is a widespread assumption, canonised by Keith Hopkins' famous article on 'Taxation and Trade in the Roman Empire', that most state revenues of the early empire were levied in cash.[48] In fact there is very little direct evidence for this and from Asia Minor, at least, a good many significant contrary indications. If we look back as far as the late Republic it is evident that revenues largely took the form of a tithe on crops. Otherwise Mark Antony's speech to the cities of Asia in 43 BC, which promised to alleviate their troubles by asking them not for fixed totals but for specific proportions of their harvests, would make no sense (Appian, *Bellum Civile* V. 4).[49] The newly published Ephesian inscription containing the regulations for the Asian customs dues demonstrates two relevant points: first, that methods of assigning and collecting tax did not change significantly between 75 BC when it was first drafted, and AD 62 when it was published in this revised form; second, that in the time of Nero *publicani* still collected a tithe of crops produced, or, in appropriate cases, a tenth part of oil harvests and vintages.[50] In confirmation, Dio Chrysostom indicates that the produce of Nicaea was normally tithed,[51] and R. Duncan-Jones has produced an ingenious interpretation of a first-century CE inscription from Cibyra suggesting that it paid a fixed proportion of its harvest from arable land as a tax to Rome.[52] Writing in the early second century Hyginus emphasised the need for careful land-surveying to prevent under-estimation of land values, which had occurred in Pannonia, where dues were paid in cash, and also in Phrygia and throughout Asia, where by implication levies were raised in kind.[53] He indicates that sometimes as much as a fifth or a seventh of the harvest was collected in this way.

This specific evidence needs to be placed in the wider context of land ownership and land usage in Asia Minor. Here I must forego detailed examination and simply state the bald fact that under the

Roman empire much of land-locked central Anatolia was used by large landowners for cereal cultivation.[54] This would only have made economic sense if the means existed to transport the grain out of the region. In a pre-mechanised world this was only possible by a system of state transport. The state could, and did, oblige its subjects to deliver their produce, which was levied or compulsorily purchased from them, to consumers, the main customers naturally being the armies and Roman officials.[55] Hence the fundamental importance of the whole apparatus of the state transport system of the Roman empire: the all-embracing road system, the growing network of *mansiones* which, as van Berchem saw (1937) years ago, functioned not only as relay stations for official travellers but as collecting points for tithes (the *annona militaris*), and the solution of the overland transport problem by requiring the inhabitants of the provinces, as part of their tax obligations, to shift agricultural produce from the place where it was grown to a destination required by the state.[56]

None of these observations, of course, is in any way novel, but their implications are rarely fully grasped. The empire was always run on these lines, from the period of the late Republic to Justinian. Asia Minor had met most of the demands of its Roman masters by contributions in kind and in services, not with cash payments. The latter could only be extracted from the monetised economies of the cities, which never accounted for more than, say, 20 per cent of economic activity under the empire. The relative unimportance of the cash contributions of the cities to the state treasury is highlighted by the fact that until the time of Diocletian most urban inhabitants were exempt from paying the poll tax. The attempts of Diocletian and Galerius to collect taxes from the city dwellers aroused a storm of protest in the provinces, as well as in Rome itself, and Maximinus backed down by offering urban inhabitants tax remission if they declared their hostility to the Christians; Julian was later to do the same. None of these political manoeuvres would have been conceivable, if the sums involved had been of substantial significance to the state budget.[57]

If there was a moment when provincials might have noticed a significant change in the system of levies and taxation, it was surely not in the time of Diocletian and Constantine but in the Severan age, when more roads were built and larger numbers of soldiers and officials were sent to the provinces. This led to more systematic collection, but also to much more widespread abuse and corruption.[58] The forms of service to the state and of taxation sometimes acquired new names as the screw was tightened: *annona militaris, cursus publicus,* and the like. But the phenomena which these terms described had been common and widespread practice for centuries. Moreover, the deployment of increasingly numerous state representatives reduced the reliance on help from city magistrates, who had hitherto been largely responsible for collecting taxes and levies, and organising such services. The decline of the cities was intimately linked to the process.

Beside such large-scale economic activity and taxation regimes, one small but familiar example of imperial ritual, the *adventus* ceremony, no doubt seems a small matter, but it too can be singled out to illustrate a significant change which overtook city life in the late empire, and whose origins belong not in the age of Constantine, but at least a century earlier in the cities of the provinces during the Severan age. As Simon Price has so well shown,[59] the imperial cult of the early principate played a critical role in articulating the relations between emperors and cities, to the benefit of both parties. Cities simultaneously came to terms with imperial power and bolstered their own prestige by building temples for the emperors and instituting festivals in their honour. What Price's study does not reveal is the way the relationship developed in the third century. During the civil wars and Parthian expeditions of Septimius Severus and throughout the third century military activity on Rome's Eastern frontier increased, caused both by Rome's own revived ambitions to conquer Mesopotamia and by the stirring of a formidable adversary, the Sassanians.[60] No major military expedition could take place in the ruler's absence, and so the emperors appeared with increasing frequency in the cities of the Eastern provinces, usually leading armies from the hinterland to the front, or between campaign stations and winter quarters. This activity transformed imperial ceremonial and the imperial cult. No longer was the emphasis on devising forms of worship to honour an absent, but universal and all-powerful ruler, but on his actual arrivals and departures, which were celebrated with new games and festivals, hosted by the cities for the benefit of the 'sacred armies', but also frequently in order to lavish attention on the emperor in person.[61] *Adventus* and *profectio* became the high points of public activity, no longer a regularly predictable event in the annual civic calendar, but on dates determined by the edicts which announced the itinerary of imperial journeys and the movements of campaigning armies, and which required cities to make appropriate arrangements to host the visitors.[62] Here too the initiative, which had been with the cities, passed to the emperor.

The practice set the new style for the later empire. Under Diocletian and Constantine *adventus* and related forms of imperial ritual became the central means by which the emperors presented themselves to their subjects.[63] The origins of these rituals should not be sought in the triumphs and imperatorial processions of early imperial Rome, but in the passage of campaigning emperors through provincial cities, especially of the East, throughout the third century. Here was another aspect of Constantinopolitan culture with Eastern provincial roots.

So finally to the undeniable novelty of the Constantinian age: the official promotion of Christianity as the central form of religious activity in the empire. How did this affect the communities, and in particular the cities of Asia Minor? The question of how far the Christianization of the Empire was a consequence of, and how far a precondition for the Constantinian revolution remains controversial. I range myself on the side, for instance, of Harnack and Barnes, against, say, MacMullen and Lane Fox, in believing that a very significant proportion of the population of the Eastern provinces was already Christian by the end of the third century.[64] The evidence from Asia Minor, especially from Phrygia, which has produced more documentary evidence for pre-Constantinian Christianity than the rest of the empire outside the city of Rome put together, must play a significant part in this wider argument. It is worth noting in passing that the surviving evidence for Christianity from central Asia Minor, randomly preserved by inscriptions, contains no direct indication that the open profession of Christianity by Constantine, or even the pro-Christian measures which he subsequently promoted, had any impact on local beliefs and practices. Substantial groups of Christian inscriptions, like the 'Christians for Christians' texts of the upper Tembris valley, the early Christian inscriptions from Isauria and Lycaonia, which can be dated between the early third and the late fourth century, or those from the heretical centre of Laodicea Catacecaumene, indicate no identifiable change of style or practice before and after the Constantinian watershed.[65] As one might have inferred from Orcistus' experience, whose Christians were still forced to pay pagan dues to Nacolea round 330, central imperial decisions were not a decisive factor in determining local religious practices.

In the cities, however, one would have expected Constantine to have offered some material encouragement to the Church, just as he enlarged the powers and privileges of the clergy. But the compensation which the Edict of Milan of 313 offered to those who had unwittingly acquired confiscated Church property, thereby enabling Christians to recover their former places of worship, was not followed by any other forms of material support, at least not in the Asia Minor provinces.[66]

Archaeologists have been no more successful in identifying ruined churches of the Constantinian period in the Anatolian provinces than they have been in finding examples from the third century. A detailed survey of Constantinian church building in Rome and the Eastern provinces reveals no activity at all in Asia Minor, to set alongside church building in the Holy Land, Constantinople, and Rome.[67] The only epigraphic example of Constantinian church construction in Asia Minor is the epitaph from Laodicea Catacecaumene of Eugenius, which owed everything to the energy and patriotic ambition of this Novatian bishop, and nothing to imperial patronage.[68] In general, neither the state nor individuals and communities seem to have had the cash to spare for grandiose church construction before the last third of the fourth century. Although Cappadocian Nazianzus had had a bishop since 327, its first public church was not built until 374. It is only towards the end of the fourth century that earlier public buildings, in particular pagan temples, were converted for Christian use into basilicas.[69]

Of course, this cannot be the whole story. The religious issue has always been the central item on the agenda of Constantinian studies, and none of the evidence from Asia Minor suggests that this judgement is mistaken. The introduction, spread and establishment of Christianity, and the interaction between Christian and non-Christian groups were the critical social developments in Anatolia, as elsewhere in the empire. Closer study of the archaeology of the cities of Asia Minor in the first half of the fourth century will certainly throw more light on such developments, and places of worship should reveal the most telling information. One of the most radical studies of precisely this type is the recent, highly cogent re-analysis of the evidence from the Sardis synagogue by H. Botermann, which suggests that none of the Jewish material should be dated before the fourth century, and that the creation of a synagogue within the buildings of the former city gymnasium took place not between 170 and 200 but between 330 and 350.[70] The original publication of the finds from the Sardis synagogue, reinforced by the more recent find of the Jewish

inscription from Aphrodisias, have provoked a thorough reapprai-
sal of the evidence for Jewish communities in second- and third-
century Asia Minor.[71] Much of this effort, although it has been
immensely stimulating, may have been chronologically misdir-
ected. The reasons for dating the Aphrodisias inscription itself
to the early third century are far from compelling. Many of the
names of the 'donors' which it lists fit more comfortably in a
fourth- than a third-century context, and the designation of individuals either as *bouleutai* (i.e. *curiales*) or by their professions, is
also typical of the later empire.[72] The redating of the Sardis
evidence to the fourth century, and perhaps that from Aphrodisias
also, should lead to further investigation of the role of Jewish
communities in Asia Minor after the Constantinian religious
transformation, a topic which has attracted far less attention
from recent scholars.[73]

ACKNOWLEDGEMENTS

The invitation to contribute to the Warwick Symposium on
'Constantine and the Origins of Christian Europe' came precisely
as I was completing my large-scale study of Asia Minor in antiquity (now Mitchell 1993). It has prompted me to ask specifically
how far the age of Constantine brought significant changes in the
history of what was to become the Byzantine heartland, Asia
Minor. In fact, as the entries for Constantine in the index show,
those volumes pay relatively little attention to what is traditionally seen as a period of crucial importance. This chapter attempts
to make some amends, but also offers some reasons why, in this
area at least, talk of a Constantinian Revolution is wholly inap-
propriate. I am enormously grateful to Sam Lieu for the suggestion
that I write this chapter, and to the other Symposium participants,
whose discussion stimulated much further reflection.

NOTES

1 See Robert 1949.
2 Malalas *Chronographia* 13.323; for the sources for Helenopolis see F.
  Ruge, *RE* V: 1697 under Drepanon 4; and O. Seeck, *RE* VII: 2810–12,
  under Helena. See also *Chron. Pasch.* 327, with the indispensable notes
  and commentary of Whitby and Whitby 15 n. 51. Procopius, *De aed.*
  5.2, and other writers reported the belief that Helena had been born at

Drepanum, but this was presumably no more than a guess, inferred from the later name. He also indicated that Justinian had built or repaired an aqueduct, two bath houses, and other buildings associated with the imperial court and administration, which contrasted with the meagre input made by Constantine to the place when it was founded. See now Mango 1994: 143–58.

3 Sozomen, *HE* 2.2.5.

4 See *SHA* (*Vit. M. Aur.* 26. 4); Ballance 1964.

5 *MAMA* VII 305.13–16. See the recent discussion by Chastagnol 1981, who places the petition between 8 November 324 and the middle of 326. Constantine's second rescript, discussed below, is dated to 30 June 331 (see panel III, lines 1–8). There is an English translation and discussion of the *MAMA* text in Coleman-Norton 1966 I: 95–8, no. 43.

6 The earlier status of Orcistus is discussed by Chastagnol 1981. The interesting foundation inscription of 237, published by Buckler 1937: 1–10, which refers to its *pandemos ekklesia* and *geraioi*, led him to believe that Orcistus was then a city. But crucially there is no mention of a *boulê* in this document, and Orcistus should be seen as a well-developed and well-organised village community, which had not yet acquired city status; cf. Mitchell 1993 I: 181–3.

7 Text of Constantine's rescript:

> Omnia quidem, quae humani generis societatem tuentur, pervigilium curarum cogitatione complectimur; sed provisionum nostrarum opus maximu(m) est, ut universae urbes, quas in luminibus provinciarum ac regionum omnium species et forma distinguit, non modo dignitatem pristinam teneant, sed etiam ad meliorem statum beneficentiae nostrae munere provehantur.

See also *CIL* III 5265; *ILS* 705; Abbott and Johnson 1926: 496–9, no. 156. The quotation is from Abbott and Johnson's commentary, repeated by Roueché 1989: 34. The discussion of Mommsen 1905–13 VIII: 25–45 is still fundamental.

8 *CIL* III 6866; *ILS* 6090; Abbott and Johnson 1926: no. 151; *MAMA* IV 236; lines 33–5 indicate that the author was a pagan emperor, the only clue, apart from the general style of the text, to date and identification.

9 *MAMA* VII 305.17–42. Eus., *VC* 4.37–9 refers to an unnamed Phoenician community and to Maiuma near Gaza, which was renamed Constantia and elevated to city status by Constantine, apparently because of the fervent Christianity of its inhabitants. Julian was to demote it again, after they had destroyed a pagan temple (Julian, *ep.* 56; Sozomen, *HE* 5.3,6–7; Eusebius, *HE* 4.1–5).

10 MacMullen 1990: 3–12.

11 See now K. W. Harl 1987. The coinage of the cities of southern Asia Minor has been intensively studied recently; for agonistic motifs and legends in the Cilician coinage of this period, Ziegler 1985: 127–43. Nollé 1986 illustrates how the ideology of imperial victory in the

wars with the Sassanians was taken over by the Pamphylian cities of Perge and Side. For Pisidia see now Weiss 1992: 143–65.

12 See Liebeschuetz 1992; Barnish 1989.

13 Whittow 1990 rightly emphasises that the decline and disappearance of the *curiales* in the later fifth and sixth centuries need not in itself imply the end of the classical city. But surely the other sources of authority which emerged in this period rendered the cities them- selves, as organised political centres, redundant. Moreover, the extent to which the *curiales* themselves had been masters of their own and their cities' destinies is highly questionable. The material collected by Peter Brown 1992 in support of this view comes overwhelmingly from the provincial and imperial capitals of the eastern empire, and reveals little about conditions in smaller cities.

14 Jones 1964 I: 347–65 offers a survey of the individuals and groups who petitioned the emperor and the imperial authorities, leading to the imperial constitutions of the fourth and fifth centuries. Indivi- dual provincial cities are not a large group.

15 For Claudiopolis and Prusias see Robert 1982: 11–146. For Tottaus and Doris see Şahin II: 1, 19 and II: 3, 117 T. 51. Tottaus is a station on the Pilgrim's Road leading from Nicaea to Ancyra (*RRMAM* I: 31). According to the Acts of the Council of Chalcedon of 451, Doris was a *regio* of Nicaea. Şahin suggests that it was identical to the road station Dablis.

16 *CTh* 12.1.119, 21 June 388.

17 Basil, *ep.* 84.

18 Basil, *epp.* 74–6; Kopecek 1974; van Dam 1986: 53–76.

19 Basil, *ep.* 74.

20 Basil, *ep.* 76

21 Roueché 1989: 15.

22 Foss 1976 and 1979; Foss 1985 and 1987. Note also Nollé 1993 I, especially 127–35 on Side in Pamphylia, who argues in general for 'die fortgesetzte Lebendigkeit und Bedeutung der Stadt' (p. 127 with n. 3). Side, like Sardis, Ephesus and Ancyra, was a major provincial centre and enjoyed advantages which were not available to the majority of cities. Elsewhere, Nollé stresses the continuity between the third and fourth centuries:

> Mit der Tetrarchie des Diocletian wurde in Side keineswegs der Beginn einer neuen Epoche faßbar; vielmehr setzten sich die meisten Entwicklungen, die im Laufe des 3. Jhdts., beson- ders in seiner zweiten Hälfte, schon sichtbar geworden waren, kontinuierlich fort und gaben – nun sich allerdings verfesti- gend oder in institutionelle Formen gebracht – der Stadt allmählich im Laufe des 4. und 5. Jhdts. ein neues Gesicht.

23 Restle 1968.

24 *Origines Constantinopolitanae*, in Th. Preger (ed.), *Scriptores Originis Constantinopolitanorum* (repr. 1975) 189, cited by Foss 1976, under sources 6.

25 Lact., *De mort.* 7,4:

> et ut omnia terrore complerentur, provinciae quoque in
> frusta concisae, multi praesides et plura officia singulis
> regionibus ac paene iam civitatibus incubare, item ratio-
> nales multi et magistri et vicarii praefectorum . . .

26 Mitchell 1993 II: 158–9.
27 *CIL* III 6783.
28 Mitchell 1993 II: 158 n. 1 for bibliography.
29 C. Naour and T. Drew Bear, *ANRW* II.18.3: 1974–6.
30 Liebeschuetz 1961.
31 Mitchell 1993 II: 73–84.
32 Malay 1988; *SEG* 38 (1988) 1244; Mitchell 1993 I: 229.
33 This aspect of Lydian culture is emphasised by W. Eck, *BJb* 183
    (1983) 853–6 in a review of P. Herrmann and J. Keil (eds), *Tituli
    Asiae Minoris* V.1
34 *Tam* V 1.319. See Herrmann 1990.
35 Ameling 1985, commentary on no. 92.
36 I accept Rostovtzeff's reading *cen(turionem) frum(entarium)* in l. 3,
    where the text was read *GENERUM*.
37 On all this, see Roueché 1981: 113–16.
38 Libanius, *de patrociniis (oration* 47).
39 Sahin II.2 1552; cf. *Tituli Asiae Minoris* V.1 758.
40 The recent bibliography is gathered by Herrmann 1990: 41–2 n. 41.
41 For abusive behaviour by *stationarii* in the fourth century see *CTh* 4.
    13. 2–3 (July–Aug. 321, against illegal requisitioning of transport
    by *stationarii*); 6. 29. 1 (22 June 355, forbidding *stationarii* and other
    officials to try persons without referring them to judges); 8. 4. 1 (10
    May 315, against illegal extortion). *CTh* 7. 20. 2, 8. 5. 1, and 16. 2.
    31, by contrast, refer to their legitimate duties. These fourth-century
    legal texts tell exactly the same story as the second- and third-
    century epigraphic references to *stationarii* in Asia Minor, on which
    see Mitchell 1993 I: 233.
42 *SEG* 19 (1963) 718.
43 D. H. French (*ANRW* II.7.2: 720, diagram 7) shows this graphi-
    cally; the numbers of texts, but not the proportions have been altered
    by his own subsequent researches, which have raised the total of
    milestones known from Asia Minor from around 600 (1980) to
    1,000 (*RRMAM* II.1 and 2), and by now to over 1,200.
44 *RRMAM* II nos 39 (Hadrianic) and 37 (?Domitianic), *RRMAM* II
    nos 288, 689 (Flavian).
45 See *MAMA* X, xxiii–xxvii.
46 See *RRMAM* II 2, 428–87 for the distribution of milestones by
    emperors' reigns.
47 Liebeschuetz 1961: 242–56 explains the system very clearly.
48 Hopkins 1980. The thesis has provoked much discussion. On the
    point at issue here, the proportion of money taxes to levies in kind,
    see Duncan-Jones 1990: 187–98.
49 Appian, *Bellum Civilum* V. 4.

50 Engelmann and Knibbe 1989: lines 72–4; Nicolet 1991; *SEG* 39 (1989) 1180, paras. 31–2.

51 Dio Chrysostom, *oration* 38.26.

52 Duncan-Jones 1990: 187–98, commenting on the text now edited by Nollé 1982: 267–74 (*SEG* 32 (1982) 1306).

53 Hyginus, *De limitibus constituendis*, in *Gromatici Veteres* I, ed. C. Lachman, Berlin 1848: 205.

54 Mitchell 1993 I: 143–7, 149–58, 245–50.

55 The decisive direct evidence for the fourth and early fifth centuries is provided by numerous constitutions in the *CTh*, notably *CTh* 8.5.34.2: 'It is contrary to reason that the stables should be furnished at state expense, since we consider that they can be more expeditiously and advantageously furnished at the charge of the provincials'; *CTh* 11.1.2: 'The tax–payer shall deliver to the several municipalities each month from his own storehouse the actual supplies that are due'; *CTh* 11.1.11, on delivering produce to frontier areas; *CTh* 11.1.15 interpretation, on delivery of wheat in instalments to public stations; *CTh* 11.1.21, allowance made for distance of transport; *CTh* 11.17.4, all people (of whatever station) required for the (compulsory) purchase and transport of supplies in kind for the needs of Illyricum; *CTh* 13.7.2, all men in common, if necessity should so demand, must be at the service of the public welfare and must duly undertake transportation, without appeal to the special privilege of rank; *CTh* 16.2.5, clerics liable to all compulsory services including transportation. See also I.4.4; 7.5.2; 7.17.1 (end); 8.4.11; 8.5.16. 18, 20, 33 (clothing for soldiers); *CTh* 11.1.9, 13, 22; *CTh* 11.10.10; *CTh* 11.16.15, 18; *CTh* 13.5 (ship transport); *CTh* 14.6.1–3 (of lime for public building); 14.21.1 (timber by boat); 15.1.49; 16.2.40. For the second and third centuries AD see in particular Modestinus, *Digest* 26.7.32.6 (trans. in B. Levick, *The Government of the Roman Empire* (London 1977) 217, n. 212), discussed by Herz 1988: 181–4.

56 van Berchem 1937.

57 Barnes 1982: 227–32 for the poll tax; Mitchell 1988: 121–3 for Maximinus (Barnes 1989d: 257 does not convince, see Mitchell 1993 II: 64 n. 68); Sozomen *HE* 5.4 for Julian.

58 MacMullen 1988 is almost invigoratingly depressing!

59 Price 1984.

60 Dodgeon and Lieu 1991 is now of course fundamental. For the resurgence of Roman aspirations to conquer Mesopotamia see Millar 1989: 145–7 and Lightfoot 1990: 115–26.

61 Harl 1987: 255; Ziegler 1985: 112 n. 281 and index under Adventusdarstellungen.

62 Millar 1977: 32–6.

63 MacCormack 1972: 721–52; MacCormack 1981; McCormick 1986; other bibliography in Millar 1977: 31 n. 21.

64 In general, recent studies have tended to take a minimal approach to the numbers of Christians in the Roman world around 300: e.g. Grant 1977: 1–12; MacMullen 1984: 32, 82 ff.; Lane Fox 1986:

589–91. But for arguments against the last two see Barnes 1989c: 306–10, and specifically for Asia Minor, Mitchell 1993 II: 57–64.

65 The chronology of the introduction of the *Chi–Rho* symbol (the *Constantinianum*) would bear further detailed investigation: see Tomlin above, pp. 25–8.

66 Lact., *De mort.* 48,2–12; Eus., *HE* 10.5.2–14; Millar 1977: 583–4.

67 Klein 1990 (my thanks to Dr Engelbert Winter for this reference).

68 *MAMA* I 171.

69 For a full recent survey see Vaes 1984–6; further bibliography in Mitchell 1993 II: 66 nn. 82–3.

70 Botermann 1993.

71 Trebilco 1991 renders excellent service in making the dispersed epigraphic and other documentation readily accessible, and providing level-headed interpretation.

72 Reynolds and Tannenbaum 1987; *SEG* 36 (1986) 970. See now Williams 1992, an important discussion, which follows hints in M. Goodman's review of the *editio princeps* in *JRS* 78 (1988) 261–2. Williams argues that the persons listed by the text were probably members of a burial society, and the stone itself could have stood by the doorway of a communal dining chamber. She points out that the absence of Aurelii from the text is no evidence for a date before 212, since no Roman *gentilicia* occur in the list of names at all, and draws attention to the occurrence of several Jewish names in their indeclinable Hebrew forms, a feature more characteristic of Late Antiquity than of the imperial period. Many of the other names in the text, on Reynolds and Tannenbaum's own admission, are barely attested before the third century, and some not until the fourth (Amachios, Eusebios, Heortasios, Eugenios, Praoilios, Acholios, Eutychios, Gorgonios, Paregorios, G(r)egorios, Polychronios, Politianos, Leontios, Procopios, and others). That so many names typical of the fourth and fifth century should occur in an early third-century document seems incredible. For the use of professions to indicate status in Late Antiquity, see Mitchell 1993 II: 120. I would take the *bouleutai* as an indication for a fourth- rather than a fifth-century date. These doubts about the proposed dating are shared by Botermann 1993.

73 See now Millar 1992.

5

THE ILLEGITIMACY OF CONSTANTINE AND THE BIRTH OF THE TETRARCHY

Bill Leadbetter

The *Origo Constantini Imperatoris*, the first part of the text usually known as the *Anonymus Valesianus*, is a document of uncertain origin which nevertheless remains of considerable importance as an account of the early years of Constantine. Its importance lies in its freedom from hagiographic legend about its subject, despite a significant degree of devout interpolation.[1] The opening sentences of the document, then, vouchsafe some signal pieces of information:

> Constantius, a grand-nephew of the divine Claudius (Gothicus), best of princes, through his brother first became protector, then tribune, and afterwards governor of the Dalmatias. Then he was made Caesar by Diocletian, along with Galerius. Having left Helena, his previous wife, he took to wife Theodora, daughter of Maximianus, by whom he subsequently had six children, the brothers of Constantine.
>
> (*Anon. Vales.* 1.2)

This affords us a great rarity: the ancestry, early career and family of Constantius I, an emperor of the tetrarchic period and best known for having fathered Constantine (see Figure 5.1). But testimony about the father is, as König has pointed out, tainted by the propaganda needs of the son.[2] The genealogical link with Claudius II Gothicus has long been recognised to be fraudulent;[3] the career of Constantius remains plausible and often accepted, but incapable of proof. The last item pertaining to the divorce and

74

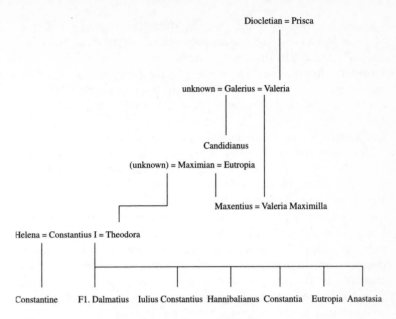

Figure 5.1 The family of Constantine the Great

remarriage, however, has engendered uncertainty. Some scholars accept this testimony as genuine.[4] Most do not, but there is no consensus amongst such scholars as to what did happen, and why the story arose in the first place.[5]

What is generally agreed is that the date of 293 for the marriages of both Constantius and Galerius is most unlikely. In all likelihood, the marriage of Constantius took place some years earlier. The evidence for this is indirect, resting upon an allusion by an imperial panegyrist. In the year 289, a Gallic rhetorician (sometimes identified by the name Mamertinus) delivered a speech in praise of the Emperor Maximian.[6] In the course of this, he referred to a happy occasion upon which Maximian had bound the holders of highest office to himself by bonds of kinship.[7] This has long been understood to refer to a marriage alliance between Maximian's family and that of his praetorian prefect, although the nature of this match has remained elusive.

The evidence itself is therefore both vague and ambiguous, which has led to a variety of interpretations being advanced. One old and influential suggestion, for example, deriving from no less a scholar than the great Otto Seeck, is that the panegyrist was alluding to a marriage between Maximian himself and Eutropia, the former wife of his praetorian prefect, Afranius Hannibalianus.[8] Although this is an attractive suggestion, it is also inherently improbable. The context of the panegyrist's own comments make it clear that Maximian inspires loyalty by such rewards for faithful service as alliance with the imperial house. His servants therefore did not obey him out of fearful obsequiousness (*timoris obsequia*) but out of proper devotion (*pietas*).[9]

The marriage of Maximian and Eutropia cannot have been recent in 289. Of their children, Maxentius and Fausta, Fausta may have been born before then;[10] Maxentius certainly was. Estimates of his date of birth vary from 277 to 287.[11] The latter date would (only just) be consistent with a marriage recent in 289, but it is more likely that Maxentius was born somewhat earlier than 287. Eutropia was without doubt his mother[12] and the boy is described in the Panegyric of 289 in terms which would indicate that he was not yet 7.[13] Lactantius, however, describes Maxentius as 'a baleful man' (*homo perniciosus*) in 305, which would seem to indicate that he was a grown man by that time.[14]

There are also other indicators that he was by then an adult. He had married Valeria Maximilla, daughter of Galerius and had fathered his son Romulus upon her.[15] Maxentius and Valeria Maximilla must have been married by 304, at which time Galerius is described as Maxentius' father-in-law (*socer*) by Lactantius.[16] In 306, Maxentius successfully usurped the purple. Barnes also adduces a circumstantial detail in order to argue that Maxentius was born in 283/4. In 312, Eutropia was obliged to claim that Maxentius had not been the offspring of Maximian, but the fruit of her adultery with an unnamed Syrian. Maximian was naturally in Syria with Carus' army in 283–4, and presumably, Eutropia was with him.[17] However attractive, this view is not compelling. Syrians could be found in parts of the empire other than Syria. Nevertheless, whenever he was born, Maxentius was a grown man by 305–6 with a child of his own. This must push the date of his birth backwards, into the early 280s. Thus, the panegyrist's propitious match cannot be found in a marriage between Eutropia and Maximian.

The link with the Hannibaliani, highlighted by Seeck, must therefore be found elsewhere, perhaps in the person of Constantius' imperial bride, Theodora. Although she is described as Maximian's step-daughter (*privigna*) in the sources, she may well have been the daughter of Maximian by an earlier marriage.[18] Herein may lie the elusive connexion with the Hannibaliani. If she is regarded as Maximian's daughter rather than Eutropia's, then it is perfectly plausible that her mother, Maximian's first and presumably deceased wife, was of the Hannibaliani.

Furthermore, Hannibalianus was in all probability not Maximian's praetorian prefect in 288–9. He was certainly someone's praetorian prefect at some stage, but neither the date nor the emperor is secure. Barnes suggests on good grounds that the emperor is likely to have been Diocletian.[19]

An alternative match must be found to make sense of the panegyrist's reference. Scholars have found a solution to this in redating the marriage of Constantius and Theodora to 289. There is some good evidence for this. Prosper Tiro gives the date for the marriages and elevations as 288, the only tetrarchic date in his chronicle which might otherwise seem to be badly wrong.[20] Constantius was certainly eminent enough to be Maximian's praetorian prefect in 289, as *Anon. Vales.* 1.2 (translated above) makes clear: *protector primum, exin tribunus, postea praeses Dalmatiarum.*[21]

This reconstruction is somewhat strengthened by the evidence for the match which was linked in the sources to that of Constantius and Theodora: that of Galerius and Valeria. The daughter of that marriage, Valeria Maximilla, was married to Maxentius at some time prior to 304.[22] If Valeria and Galerius married in March 293, the earliest that any child of theirs could have been born would be December of that year. This would make her 9 or 10 at the time of her marriage. She was also a mother before Maxentius' usurpation on 28 October 306, when she would still have been younger than 13.[23] On this basis then, it is unlikely that Valeria Maximilla would have been born as late as the end of 293 – the very earliest possible date for her birth if the marriage of her parents took place in March 293. If she was born before 293, then 289 presents itself as a possible year of birth. This would link Galerius' marriage to that of Constantius, and make Valeria a bride at 15 and a mother before she was 17; both are reasonable propositions.[24] It may also, therefore, be the case that Galerius was Diocletian's praetorian prefect in 288.[25]

Thus, when Diocletian and Maximian met in 288, they conferred about Carausius and devised a method to deal with him. They also determined to join their daughters in wedlock to their praetorian prefects, lest they also be too successful.[26] In all likelihood, then, the marriages of the Caesars long preceded their promotion to imperial rank.

The tradition which links the marriages with the promotions of 293 is therefore in error, although it is also clear that the error was an early one and possibly deliberate. The association of the story of the divorces and remarriages with other matters known to be fraudulent (Constantine's invented ancestry) invites suspicion, particularly since it is clear that this story is what Constantine wanted posterity to believe.

A number of sources (according to König, the majority) reject the proposition that Helena was Constantius' lawful wife and instead call her a *concubina*.[27] They also agree, without dissent, upon the fact of her humble birth. Eutropius calls her origin 'quite humble' (*obscurius*); the *Anon. Vales.* labels it 'most base' (*vilissima*); Ambrose testified that she was a tavern-girl (*stabularia*).[28]

She did not remain in such circumstances. When Constantine became emperor she became a great lady. After 306 she may have lived in Trier,[29] where there are local traditions about her, and she was certainly resident in Rome after 312, where she seems to have owned considerable property, including the Sessorian Palace.[30] In 325, along with Constantine's wife Fausta, she was accorded the title of Augusta.[31] In the following year, she played a role in the death of Crispus,[32] after which she went on her famous pilgrimage, returning to Rome to die, aged nearly 80.[33]

The sources have, however, presented us with something of a problem. There is no essential dissent amongst the relevant sources on the question of Helena's social origin. Later tradition compensated for this by depicting her as of more noble birth, including the entirely fabulous story repeated by Geoffrey of Monmouth that she was a British princess, indeed, the daughter of Old King Cole.[34] Constantius, on the other hand, was a person of rank. The introductory passage to the *Anon. Vales.* already quoted, which speaks of his divorce from Helena, also gives his career as *protector*, *tribunus*, and *praeses*. As Barnes himself has pointed out, the offices of tribune and *praeses* carried with them equestrian rank and the title of *vir perfectissimus*, tenure of which precluded legal marriage to a woman of infamous profession, as indeed a *stabularia* was.[35] Furthermore, the *lex Julia de maritandis ordinibus* and the *lex Papia Poppaea* both established that certain unions were forbidden to men of particular status including, according to Ulpian, marriage between any free-born man and a woman of low repute (*famosa*).[36] Barnes' solution to this conundrum is that the two were married before Constantius' ascent to higher office. This is plausible, although it stretches possibility to its utmost, and begs the whole question of why an ambitious young officer (as he surely was) would make a marriage so socially disadvantageous to him, especially when the expedient of concubinage was open to him.

Concubinage was frequent enough amongst the Roman military élite. Constantius' colleague Galerius is described as having a son, Candidianus, by a concubine.[37] Constantine himself fathered Crispus upon his concubine Minervina.[38] Constantine's colleague and rival, Licinius, is generally believed to have fathered a son on a slave woman and then sought to legitimise him by imperial rescript.[39] Furthermore, Jane Gardner has pointed out that at least three emperors of the high empire resorted to concubinage rather than remarriage.[40] It was thus a common enough resort, and it is therefore unsurprising to find sources referring to Helena as Constantius' *concubina*.

The good sense of this proposition, however, is vitiated by epigraphic evidence to the contrary. A number of inscriptions of the 320s refer to Helena as the wife (*uxor*) or spouse (*coniunx*) of Constantius.[41] For Barnes, at least, this evidence is decisive. However, it should be noted that the inscriptions all postdate Helena's assumption of the title *Augusta* and seem to reflect, to some extent, her local patronage of senatorial class men. In such a situation, the truth of Helena's concubinage needed to be deflected. It neither added dignity to the elderly dowager and patroness, nor did it reflect well upon her son, the emperor, for whom legitimacy was an important matter.

There is no doubt that Constantine was devoted to his mother, perhaps as much as he was devoted to the pursuit and tenure of power. He had also been troubled, ever since his acclamation as Augustus in July 306, with the problem of legitimacy. Constantine's initial claim to power was based upon an hereditary claim. While he accepted Galerius' nomination of him as Caesar in 306, this was a tactical move. His marriage, in 307, to Fausta, the daughter of the rebel Augustus Maximian, underscores the fact that Constantine was never loyal to Galerius' tetrarchy. This was in contrast to his contemporary tetrarchic emperors, whose legitimacy was based on their nomination by more senior colleagues and the *concordia* which existed within that college.

What this signified for Constantine is that he could never regard himself as immune from the challenge of those who wished to assert their own claim to rule, whether based upon the legitimacy of tetrarchic nomination, or that of a reasserted dynasticism. The Panegyric of 310 elucidates Constantine's strategy for dealing with such claims. First, it emphasises his filial relation to Constantius, and Constantius' approval of his accession;[42] second, it reports a vision of Apollo, providing divine sanction for his assumption of the purple;[43] third, it asserts Constantine's descent from Claudius II Gothicus.[44] These are all quite specific assertions of legitimacy, their stridency reflecting their necessity. In 310, Constantine was regarded elsewhere in the empire as a usurper, a matter made clear by the consular nominations.[45] This view of Constantine was not necessarily ameliorated by his defeat of Maxentius in 312. Indeed, his dynastic assertions were so successful in establishing a claim to legitimacy that they may have been mimicked by his rival, Licinius, who, it is attested, claimed descent from Philip the Arab.[46]

After the defeat of Licinius, and his assumption of sole rule, Constantine was still not without potential rivals. His father's marriage to Theodora had been very productive. Although Constantine was content to make use of his half-sisters for dynastic matches, his half-brothers were conspicuously relegated. They lived in the provinces, far from the temptations of office.[47] Their continued existence constituted a clear alternative to Constantine's claim to dynastic legitimacy. According to Julian, it was Helena herself who kept Constantius' other sons away from power.[48] Certainly, they did not receive even its appearance until Constantine was an old man beyond challenge, and his sons were all Caesars.

The strength of Constantius' sons' claim to the succession is illustrated by events after the death of Constantine. At this point, there was a stand-off about the succession between the two branches of the family. Although Constantine's sons were all Caesars, none of them felt immediately powerful enough to assume the title of Augustus. Rather, the impasse continued for some months, with the sons of Constantius asserting their own claims to legitimacy through the posthumous acclamation of their mother Theodora as Augusta, and the striking of commemorative issues in her name.[49] It is significant in this context that Constantine's sons reacted in this propaganda war by the striking of commemorative issues for Helena Augusta.[50] The crisis was ultimately resolved by the massacre of Constantius I's descendants and adherents. Even then, an attempt to justify their deaths may have been made through a claim that Constantine had been poisoned by his brothers.[51]

When Constantine saluted his mother as Augusta, therefore, he had more in mind than a simple act of *pietas*. It was a political act in which he asserted his legitimacy over his half-brothers who otherwise could exercise a powerful dynastic counter-claim to his tenure of imperial office. The coins and inscriptions from the period make clear just how important dynastic links were in the Constantinian assertion of legitimacy. This position would have been decisively undermined by any perception that Helena had not been Constantius' wife, and, worse, that Constantine was Constantius' bastard and not his legitimate son. There was, therefore, a political necessity to identify a marriage between Constantius and Helena, and to do so earlier rather than later in Constantine's reign. That is why inscriptions dated to the late 320s refer to Helena as the wife of Constantius. The dedicators, grateful to Augusta for her exercise of patronage, had every reason to repeat official history, obediently accepting that Helena had been married to Constantius, and, by extension, that Constantine was their legitimate son.

In this context, an item of Constantine's legislation makes one pause: an edict against the recognition of the children of morganatic marriages by the élite. In it, he lists a number of unsuitable mothers, including daughters of tavern-keepers.[52] The law is not a new formulation, but a reaffirmation and extension of principles which had been in existence since the time of Augustus.[53] Ironically, in another law, he emphasises the low status of tavern-girls by excusing them from accusations of adultery explicitly because of their quasi-servile occupation.[54] These edicts reflect Constantine's official regard for the values enshrined in Roman family law, values he was not going to subvert by publicly legislating his own legitimacy. He asserted it instead, and legislated as if his assertion were the truth.

How much did it matter? Constantine's claim to power, after all, was not based upon his parentage, but upon victory in war. Clearly, however, it *did* matter to Constantine himself. His initial seizure of power in 306 had been justified by a public rhetoric of legitimate inheritance. Such a claim, once made in the public arena, could not be readily discarded. But it could be complicated by the maturity of others with better claims of dynastic propinquity to Constantius I. Thus, the fiction was compounded and canonised by the promotion of the elderly Helena to the status of Augusta. Like the claim to have been descended from Claudius Gothicus, the invention of Helena's marriage to Constantius swiftly became history within the canonical narratives of Constantine's reign.

This, in turn, has, by its insistence on a prior marriage for Constantius, distorted the source tradition on the origin of the Tetrarchy. It has resulted in an assertion that both Constantius and Galerius had prior wives, put away for the sake of empire. This has, in turn, implied that Diocletian and Maximian promoted Galerius and Constantius to imperial rank, a promotion subsequently sealed by marriage. What is clear from the foregoing, however, is that the Caesars were not chosen to be the sons-in-law of the Augusti, but that the existing sons-in-law of the Augusti became the Caesars. The implications of this for the origin of the tetrarchy are considerable, implying, as it does, that the network of power relations which the tetrarchy established was already in place before 293, and that the nomination of the Caesars in March of that year reflected the end, rather than the beginning, of a political process.

NOTES

1 The *Anon. Vales.* was recently re-edited, with commentary, by König 1987. The issue of the document's provenance has never been satisfactorily resolved. Den Boer 1972: 167 regards it as the work of a Christian, although it was pointed out over a century ago that the Christian content of the work bears sufficient resemblance to parts of the text of Orosius to have been interpolated by a later, pious editor. See here Klebs 1889: 53–80. On this basis, Pätzig (1898) considered that the *Urtext* might be a fragment of Ammianus Marcellinus, although this view has not found acceptance. König 1987: 19–28 dates the work to the end of the fourth century, accepting the argument that an earlier text was tampered with by a Christian editor. On the problems of the text generally, see *FCJ* 39–42.
2 König 1987: 17.
3 For discussion, see Syme 1974.
4 Jones 1948: 28; MacMullen 1969: 21; Elliott 1987: 422.
5 Some scholars accept the fact of at least one divorce, that of Galerius (Seston 1946: 236; Stein 1959: 68); Williams 1985: 64 accepts both divorces but dates them before 293; Vogt 1973: 112 accepts Constantius' divorce of Helena, but dates it before 293; Barnes 1981: 8 and 288 n. 55 rejects both divorces and remarriages; Kolb 1987: 71 is certain that Galerius and Valeria were married before 293; for Piganiol 1932: 32, Helena is clearly a concubine, in which consideration, he agrees with Seeck 1921: 47. Pasqualini 1979: 14 evades the question, simply stating that in order to marry the daughter of Maximian, 'Costanzo Cloro . . . fu constretto ad abbandonare Elena, la madre di Costantino'. Nixon and Rodgers 1994: 70 leave the question open.

6 On the date, occasion and authorship see Nixon and Rodgers 1994: 41–3.

7 *Pan. Lat.* 2.11.4.

8 O. Seeck in *RE* IV: 1041. The argument with respect to the name 'Hannibalianus' is a strong one. Constantius I and Theodora had a son to whom they gave the name, as did another of their sons, Dalmatius (*PLRE*: 407 under Hannibalianus 3). A second item is of circumstantial value. Gallus Caesar, grandson of Constantius I and Theodora, spent a part of his youth relegated to Tralles, before being sent to join Julian in internal exile in Cappadocia (Julian, *ep.* 271 B). The family of Hannibalianus had a hereditary connexion with Tralles (see Groag 1907: 288; Barnes 1982: 34). If Gallus' time in Tralles had been spent at a family estate, as would seem likely, then might not such a property have come into the family's possession via Hannibalianus?

9 *Pan. Lat.* 2.11.4.

10 She was born in Rome (Julian, *Oration* 1.5c). Maximian was perhaps in Rome at this time (Barnes 1982: 34, 58). She was certainly no longer an infant by 293 (Barnes 1982: 34).

11 Barnes 1982: 34 n.20.

12 The context of *Anon. Vales.* 4.12 makes it plain that Eutropia is meant.

13 *Pan. Lat.* 2.14.1 describes him as 'child' (*progenies*), a word with no age-specific nuance. Moreover, as Barnes 1982: 34 points out, the phrase 'for whom some fortunate teacher waits' (*felix aliquis praeceptor expectat*) should mean that by 289 Maxentius was not yet 7.

14 Lact., *De mort.* 18.9.

15 Lact., *De mort.* 18.9, also *ILS* 666–7. The inscriptions pre-date the usurpation of Maxentius, who is described in *ILS* 666 as *clarissimus*.

16 Lact., *De mort.* 18.9.

17 Barnes 1982: 34.

18 *Anon. Vales.* 1.2; Barnes 1982: 33.

19 *ILS* 8929 is the evidence for Hannibalianus' prefecture. It exhibits problems. It dates from between 285, when Diocletian first took the victory title Germanicus Maximus which appears on the inscription (see Barnes 1976c: 178), and 292 when Hannibalianus was consul with Asclepiodotus. On the basis of the victory title, Chastagnol 1962: 28 prefers a *terminus ante quem* of 290 (followed by *PLRE* 407 under Hannibalianus 3). Given that the only victory title in the inscription is Germanicus Maximus, it ought properly to belong quite early in Diocletian's reign, and Howe 1942: 51 n. 67 argues that it belongs to the first twelve months; but his argument is weakened by his assumption that Diocletian's *tribunicia potestas* was not renewed until November 285, whereas it was augmented on 10 December 285, nineteen days after he seized power. This inscription cannot date from so early in Diocletian's reign, when his titulature was still uncertain (see *AE* 1973, 540; *P. Oxy.* XLVI 3055), and in any event, its provenance (Oescus, on the distant Danube, which news might not reach so swiftly) should settle the matter. On the matter of whose prefect Hannibalianus was, his primacy in the

inscription would indicate Diocletian, rather than Maximian (Barnes 1982: 124).

20 It is worth noting that Prosper's account of the tetrarchy differs from that of Jerome in significant particulars. Most noteworthy is his omission of the catalogue of woes in connexion with the creation of the Caesars.

21 See *CIL* III 9860, which also attests him as *praeses* of Dalmatia. The *SHA* (*Vit. Car.* 17.6) also states that Constantius was a governor under Carus. If the date is correct, a doubtful proposition when the evidence is from the *SHA*, most likely he was governor during the civil war between Diocletian and Carinus. If so, his loyalty to Diocletian had already been of crucial importance.

22 For the date, see Lact., *De mort.* 18.9.

23 For the date of the usurpation, Lact., *De mort.* 44.4. Maxentius had held power for six years exactly when he was defeated at the Milvian Bridge (*CIL* I^2: 274).

24 Two objections to this proposition must be overcome. First, it is possible that Valeria Maximilla was the child of a first wife, as Constantine and Theodora apparently were. Lactantius' statement (*De mort.* 50.2) that Valeria, Galerius' wife was incapable of bearing children lends support to such a view. The evidence of the nomenclature, however, suggests otherwise. The name of Valeria Maximilla contains elements of both Galerius' name ('Maximilla' – Galerius may have been called Maximinus before his elevation to the purple [Lact., *De mort.* 44.1]), and that of his wife Valeria. As to the issue of the elder Valeria's sterility, Lactantius, strictly speaking, is referring to the mid-290s when Candidianus was born. Such a reference does not preclude an earlier child, with Galerius' resort to concubinage a subsequent development as a result of his desire for the son whom his wife could not give him. Lactantius shows no sympathy for Valeria, and finds peculiar satisfaction in her later execution at the hands of Licinius (*De mort.* 51). His gibe at Valeria's sterility might then be another piece of rhetorical nastiness, as was his reference to Diocletian's cowardice (see Barnes 1982: 38). *ILS* 674 gives the immediate imperial ancestors of Valeria Maximilla's son, Romulus. Unfortunately, the text breaks off with the word *ac*, after which the fact that the deceased boy was also the great-grandson of Diocletian might well have been added, thereby clinching the matter.

25 As conjectured by Barnes 1982: 136.

26 Barnes 1982: 38 on the date of the wedding of Galerius and Valeria.

27 König 1987: 61.

28 Eutropius 10.2; *Anon. Vales.* 1.2.; Ambrose, *oratio de obitu Theodosiani* 42 (*PL* 16: 1463).

29 This has been recently doubted by Drijvers 1992: 22–33, who argues that Helena the mother of Constantine has become confused in the tradition with Helena, the wife of Crispus.

30 Drijvers 1992: 32.

31 For discussion of the date and sources, see *PLRE:* 410, under Helena 3.

32 *Epitome de Caesaribus* 41.12.

33 Eus. *VC* 3. 46–7.
34 Drijvers 1992: 12, 22–30; cf. Geoffrey of Monmouth, *Histories* 5.6.
35 Barnes 1982: 36 n. 37.
36 Ulpian, *Institutionum et regularum iuris* 16.2; see Treggiari 1991: 50.
37 Lact., *De. mort.* 50.2.
38 On Minervina's status, *Epitome de Caesaribus* 41.4; Zos. 2.20.2; *PLRE*: 602 under Minervina asserts for no good reason that she was Constantine's first wife, and not a concubine.
39 *CTh* 4.6. 2–3; *PLRE*: 510 under Licinius 4; this identification has been recently called into question by Corcoran 1993: 117.
40 Gardner 1986: 58; on concubinage generally, see Treggiari 1991: 51–2.
41 On *CIL* VI 1134 (= *ILS* 709), Helena is called *genetrix* of Constantine; on *CIL* X 678, she is called the *uxor* of Constantius; and on *CIL* X 517 (*ILS* 708), his *coniunx*. For discussion of the inscriptions, see Drijvers 1992: 45–52.
42 *Pan. Lat.* 6.3–4 and 10.1.
43 Ibid. 21.5–6.
44 Ibid. 2.2.
45 Bagnall *et al.* 1987: 154.
46 *SHA* (*Vit. Gord.* 34.6). This, given the context, may have been one of the author's witty falsifications. If Licinius did claim descent from Philip, he was far quieter about it than Constantine was about his putative ancestor. Constantine, for example, minted a number of commemorative issues for Claudius II (see Kent 1994 VII: 27), whereas Licinius minted none in the name of the Philippi. The point here, however, is not whether Licinius did or did not actually claim descent from the Philippi, but that the author of the *SHA* considered it at least a plausible falsification.
47 Iulius Constantius lived for many years in Gaul and Achaea (Ausonius, *Professores* 16.11–12; Libanius *Or.* 14.29–31, *PLRE*: 226 under Constantius 7); his brother Dalmatius, later granted an official career, also lived in Gaul, where his son was educated by Exsuperus at Narbo (Ausonius, *Professores* 17.11–12). Dalmatius was consul in 333, at which time he was also granted the title of censor (*PLRE*: 240 under Dalmatius 6). While resident at Antioch, he suppressed the rebellion of Calocaerus in 334 (Barnes 1982: 15). Hannibalianus may have died young. He had no official career and was evidently dead by 337 (*PLRE*: 407 under Hannibalianus 1).
48 Libanius *Or.* 14.30.
49 Kent 1994 VIII: 3–7.
50 Ibid. VIII: 3–7.
51 A tradition reported by Eunapius and repeated by Philost., *HE* 2.4: see Blockley 1983 II: 15.
52 *CTh* 4.6.3.
53 See Evans-Grubbs 1993: 130–3.
54 *CTh* 9.7.1.

6

SOME CONSTANTINIAN DOCUMENTS IN THE *VITA CONSTANTINI*

Stuart G. Hall

I

We begin with a well-known letter. After his account in *Vita Constantini* 2 of the victory over Licinius, the lifting of persecution and the Letter to the Provincials, Eusebius reports that Constantine became aware of what we call the Arian controversy: envy crept in to disturb the prosperity of the churches,

> openly flaunting itself in the very assemblies of the saints. Indeed it set even the Bishops against each other, imparting divisive quarrels with divine doctrines as the excuse. Then it broke out like a great fire from a little spark. It began from the summit of the Alexandrian church and spread through all Egypt and Libya and the further Thebaid. It had already reached the other provinces and cities, so that it was possible to see not only the leaders of the churches sparring with words, but the multitudes also fragmented, some inclining to one side, some to the other. The spectacle of these events reached such absurdity that sacred points of divine doctrine were now subjected to disgraceful public mockery in the theatres of the unbelievers.
>
> (Eus., *VC* 2.61.4–5)

At the same time, he writes, upper Egypt and the Thebaid were divided by a longer-standing quarrel (what we know as the

Melitian dispute), which also reached other provinces. The emperor, taking this bitterly to heart,

> despatched one of the godly men of his court, one whom he knew well to be of proven moderation of life and faithful virtue, a man very famous for his religious confessions in earlier times, as a mediator to reconcile the disputants in Alexandria. By him he sent those responsible for the quarrel a most apposite letter, which, as itself providing evidence of the emperor's concern for the people of God, could well be presented in our account of him. It reads as follows:
> Victor Constantinus Maximus Augustus to Alexander and Arius . . .
>
> (Eus., *VC* 2.63–4)

There is no question who were the persons ostensibly addressed, though the devout postman is not named. Alexander and Arius are also addressed separately in the middle of the letter:

> I understand then that the first stages of the present dispute were as follows. When you, Alexander, demanded of the presbyters what view each of them took about a certain passage from what is written in the Law, – or rather about some futile point of dispute, you, Arius, thoughtlessly replied with that opinion which either ought not to have been conceived in the first place, or once conceived ought to have been consigned to silence. The dispute having thus arisen between you, fellowship was repudiated, and the most holy people was divided in two and forsook the concord of the common body. Accordingly, let each of you extend pardon equally, and accept what your fellow-servant in justice urges upon you. It is this: It was neither right to ask about such things in the first place, nor to answer when asked.
>
> (Eus., *VC* 2.69.1–2)

It is my purpose to argue that the heading of the letter, and the circumstances of its despatch, are not those which Eusebius states. Rather, it is addressed to Antioch early in 325, and related to the council which met there. Even if the address at the head of the letter itself, 'to Alexander and Arius', were correct, one would be reading a sort of open letter, with the wider audience in mind. But the evidence points to the address in fact being misleading.

In the first part of the letter we find, after general reference to Constantine's twin religious and secular policies, an account of the dispute in Africa known to us as the Donatist Schism.[1] His troubles over Africa lead him to address his audience directly:

> When I personally desired to put right this disease [the Donatist schism], the only cure sufficient for the affair that I could think of was that, after I had destroyed the common enemy of the whole world, who had set his own unlawful will against your holy synods, I might send some of you to help towards the reconciliation of those at variance with each other.
>
> (Eus., *VC* 2.66)

'Some of you' (ἐνίους ὑμῶν) is at best rather odd, if the letter is actually addressed to Alexander and Arius. I suppose they could be taken as representing a larger church than the two of them constituted. But the oddity is increased when their location is indicated:

> For since the power of the light and the law of holy religion by the beneficence of the Supreme were issued, as one might say, from the bosom of the East, and lit up the whole world at once with a sacred lantern, it was reasonable that, believing that you would be a kind of pioneers of the salvation of the nations, I should try to seek you, both by the intention of my heart and by actual sight.
>
> (Eus., *VC* 2.67)

It is perhaps possible that Constantine would so fulsomely (and mendaciously) describe his intention of travelling to Egypt to interview Alexander and Arius. But what of 'from the bosom of the east' (ἔκ τινων τῆς ἀνατολῆς κόλπων; v. l. οἷον ἔκ τινων τῆς ἀνατολικῆς κόλπων) from which the message and scriptures of Christianity might be said to have issued? The Eastern Prefecture indeed included Asia, Pontus, Thrace and Egypt as well as Oriens, and it is reasonable to assume that Constantine's letter 'to the eastern provincials (ἐπαρχιώταις ἀνατολικοῖς)' included them;[2] another letter was also distributed ἐν τοῖς

ἡμετέροις ἀνατολικοῖς μέρεσιν.³ In this broader sense, however, Constantine is himself already in the East: he writes from
Nicomedia or thereabouts. The more natural reference of 'bosom of
the east' is to Syria, as when Antioch is described by Eusebius as
τῆς ἀνατολικῆς μητροπόλεως,⁴ though he could also describe
a Persian war as stirred up by τῶν ἐπ' ἀνατολῆς βαρβάρων.⁵
More particularly here the expression most naturally refers to the
administrative area based on Antioch, the Diocese Oriens, which
included Palestine, since that is where the faith originated. With
this we should take the first paragraph of the letter:

> To let you appreciate how much this distressed me, when
> I recently set foot in the city of Nicomedia, my intention
> was to press on eastward straight away; I was already
> intent on visiting you and a large part of me was already
> with you, when the news of this business put a stop to my
> plans, so that I might not be obliged to see with my eyes
> what I had not thought it possible I would ever hear
> reported verbally. By the accord among you open to me
> now the road to the East, which you have shut by the
> controversies between you, and make it quickly possible
> for me to look with pleasure both on you and on all the
> other congregations, and in pleasing terms to express to
> the Supreme my debt of thanks for the general concord
> and liberation of all.
>
> (Eus., *VC* 2.72.2–3)

Here the terms are 'eastward' (πρὸς τὴν ἑῴαν) and 'the road to
the east' (τῆς ἑῴας τὴν ὁδόν). The word ἑῴα used here is the
one technically used for Diocese Oriens, and therefore a journey
East from Nicomedia to Syria is the natural meaning. Were it not
for the address naming Alexander and Arius, no one would ever
have thought otherwise.

The same passage gives a clue to the further identification of
those addressed. 'Make it quickly possible for me to look with
pleasure both on you and on all the other congregations' (ὑμᾶς τε
ὁμοῦ καὶ τοὺς ἄλλους ἅπαντας δήμους) suggests that he is
addressing a church or synod of churches rather than individuals.
It is in fact rather ludicrous to suggest that the reconciliation of
the two individuals who began the dispute would itself so dras-
tically affect the imperial travel plans.

I think we may find a further clue near the beginning of the letter. We quoted the comment on Donatism:

> When I personally desired to put right this disease, the only cure sufficient for the affair that I could think of was that, after I had destroyed the common enemy of the whole world, who had set his own unlawful will against your holy synods, I might send some of you to help towards the reconciliation of those at variance with each other.
>
> (Eus., *VC* 2.66)

Licinius' ban on episcopal synods is in *VC* the first and direst of his crimes.[6] But why should it be mentioned here? Precisely, I suggest, because while Licinius reigned, no synodical notice could be taken in the East of the Donatist controversy. With the victory over Licinius an assembly has been called, and one which can be asked to supply mediators for Africa – or could have been, but for the dreadful news of the divided East:

> Immediately upon my great victory and my veritable triumph over my enemies, I chose to make the subject of my first enquiry that which I considered to be of first and greatest importance to me.
> But, (O best, divine Providence) what a deadly wound my ears suffered, or rather my very heart, – the information that the division arising among you was much graver than those I had left behind there, so that your regions, from which I had hoped medicine would be supplied to others, were now in greater need of healing.
>
> (Eus., *VC* 2.67–68,1)

What confronts Constantine therefore is a synod in the East, hard on the heels of the victory over Licinius, itself torn by dissent, which prevents him travelling there from Nicomedia. The tense of γιγνομένην 'now arising', indicates a fresh controversy, even if on an old topic, and not one pre-existing, like that of Arius and Alexander.

We should consider the gathering of bishops at Antioch early in 325, which condemned Arius and supported Alexander, issued a credal statement, and excommunicated three leading defenders of Arius. This council is known from the synodical letter of its president, probably Ossius of Corduba, to 'Alexander, Bishop of New Rome'. This exists in two modern Syrian manuscripts. Syriac text and Greek retroversion are conveniently reprinted in Eduard Schwartz;[7] James Stevenson translated most of Schwartz's Greek into English.[8] The first paragraph, not included in Stevenson's English version, invites this Alexander to participate spiritually in the proceedings, explaining that:

> when I came to Antioch and saw the church much troubled by weeds (ζιζανίοις) through the teaching and rebellion of certain people, I decided not to remove and drive out such a thing by myself, but that over so urgent a matter I shoud rather summon our supporters and fellow-bishops nearest to hand.

If this introduction is genuine, and if Ossius went at the behest of Constantine, he presumably reported in comparable terms to the emperor as well as to the Bishop of Byzantium. One is reminded of the later events in Antioch which involved the deposition of Eustathius, the champion of the anti-Arians, and drew further letters from Constantine. Eusebius refers to the public disorders, but draws a veil over most of the proceedings.[9] Until it was eclipsed by Constantinople, Antioch was to remain, throughout the religious controversies of the fourth and fifth centuries, the prize to win. More than any other city it had, from apostolic times, been the centre from which the gospel spread, and could fittingly be saluted as its nursery or cradle, the bosom from which it was issued.

It is possible that Constantine's letter was addressed to the episcopal synod at Antioch which Ossius superintended, the proceedings of which are reported in the surviving Syriac letter. If so, one can see why Eusebius distorts its true destination. That synod was not one he cared to remember: he was perhaps the chief of the three bishops excommunicated on that occasion for their support of Arius. He regards the synod as just one of the many controversial meetings which were held in the wake of Licinius' defeat. It is also possible, however, that it preceded the main episcopal synod. It might fit an earlier gathering of the local church with a few bishops from neighbouring sees, which elected Eustathius in opposition to an Arianizing party.

The word σύνοδος occurs six times in this letter. Unfortunately it is difficult to interpret relevantly. Licinius 'had set his own unlawful will against your holy synods',[10] where apparently the word is used technically of Christian, particularly episcopal, assemblies. After apostrophising Alexander and Arius and describing their argument, Constantine says, 'The dispute having arisen between you, fellowship was repudiated (ἡ μὲν σύνοδος ἠρνήθη), and the most holy people was divided in two.'[11] Lampe's *Patristic Greek Lexicon* cites this as its sole example of the meaning 'intercourse' for σύνοδος, which I have improved as 'fellowship'. Here I am tempted to suggest that the 'you' is no longer Alexander and Arius, but already the church or assembly in Antioch, so he means, 'the dispute having arisen among you at Antioch as a result of this Alexandrian quarrel'. Similarly, such intellectual disputes should not be aired: 'It is our duty to shut them up inside the mind, and not casually produce them in public meetings nor incautiously commit them to the hearing of the laity.'[12]

Twice the phrase τὸ τῆς συνόδου τίμιον occurs: 'through a few futile verbal quarrels between you, brothers are set against brothers and the honourable synod divided in ungodly variance' (τὸ τῆς συνόδου τίμιον ἀσεβεῖ διχονοίᾳ χωρίζεσθαι);[13] and, second, 'It is possible for the honour of the synod to be preserved intact by you, and one and the same fellowship to be kept generally (τὸ τῆς συνόδου τίμιον ὑμῖν ἀκεραίως σῴζεσθαι).[14] In both cases the phrase is difficult to interpret except as a reference to a specific synodical gathering. Nor does either sentence make easy sense if the 'you' addressed is Alexander and Arius. The same is true of 'so that I may lead back his congregations themselves by my own address and ministration and earnest admonition to your synodical fellowship' (τὴν τῆς συνόδου κοινωνίαν ἐπαναγάγοιμι).[15]

Constantine uses this term so often, because the effect of the Arian dispute is to make it impossible for the churchmen of Antioch, or for the bishops assembled at Antioch, to sit down together. That in turn is the ghastly spectacle he cannot bear to see, being pained enough by the very report of it.[16]

Other parts make better sense if we read them in this way:

> As I considered the origin and occasion for these things, the cause was exposed as extremely trivial and quite unworthy of so much controversy. Being driven therefore to the need for this letter, and addressing myself to that discretion which you have in common, and calling first on the divine Providence to support my action, I offer my

modest services as a peaceful arbitrator between you in your dispute.

(Eus., VC 2.68.2)

The dispute has originated elsewhere, and it is trivial: Constantine offers to reconcile the bishops in Antioch, as he would later do at Nicaea.

We must therefore avoid being talkative in such matters; otherwise, whether because by our natural limitations we cannot explain properly what is propounded, or because with their slower intellect the audience is incapable of reaching a correct understanding of what is said, one way or the other the people may be brought inevitably to either blasphemy or schism.

(Ibid. 2.69.3)

It is the leaders of churches outside Alexandria who are clearly in his mind:

Both unguarded question therefore and incautious answer require a mutual exchange of pardon equal on both sides. For the impulse of your quarrel did not arise over the chief point of the precepts in the Law, nor are you faced with the intrusion of a new doctrine concerning the worship of God, but you have one and the same mind, so that you should be able to come together in compact of fellowship. That so many of God's people, who ought to be subject to the direction of your minds, are at variance because you are quarrelling with each other about small and quite minute points, is deemed to be neither fitting nor in any way legitimate.

(Ibid. 2.70–71.1)

The bishops have direct responsibility for 'so many of God's people'. It is not Alexander and Arius who are in his mind:

For since, as I have said, there is one faith in us and one understanding of the belief we hold, and since the commandment of the Law in its every part throughout confines its totality to a single disposition of the heart, this which has raised a slight quarrel between you, since it does not refer to the meaning of the Law as a whole, must surely not import any division or faction among you.

(Ibid. 2.71.5)

Here the reference at the end to χωρισμόν τινα καὶ στάσιν is more appropriate to a large assembly than to two individuals.

Finally, one might note some of Constantine's appeals for peace:

But let the excellence of general love, and faith in the truth, and reverence for God and the religion of the Law, remain undisturbed among you. Return to mutual love and kindness, restore to the whole people the proper bonds of affection, and you yourselves, as having purified your own souls, recognise each other again. Often love becomes sweeter when it returns again in reconciliation after hostility is set aside.

(Ibid. 2.71.8)

Give me back therefore peaceful days and undisturbed nights, so that I too may still have some pleasure left in the clear light and happiness of a quiet life. Otherwise I must weep and constantly break down in tears, and not even face the rest of my life with equanimity. If the peoples of God, my own fellow-servants I mean, are so divided by wicked and damaging strife between themselves, how can my thoughts be any longer collected?

(Ibid. 2.72.1)

These sentiments fit the dispute at Antioch more naturally than the past quarrel of Arius with Alexander.

Why, then, is the letter presented in *VC* with a false address? One reason is that the documents in *VC* are chosen for what they reveal about Constantine. Here the chief point is Constantine's 'concern for the people of God'.[17] No doubt Eusebius is also interested in his pacific analysis of the original Arian dispute: it is an argument about words and ideas which do not touch the substance of Christian truth, a question which it was improper to ask and an answer which it was wrong to give, permissible only in private argument, if at all, and not to be aired in public or allowed to divide the churches. That is a view in which Eusebius himself would heartily concur. I quote Frances Young:[18]

For Constantine and Eusebius, the primary issue was Christianity's claim to be the truth in the face of the pagan majority. It was this fact which made the church so vitally important to both. Internal struggles undermined their overall purposes.

Hence it was precious and relevant.

The letter contains much which is expressed in the second person plural, and can plausibly be read as addressed to the two originators of the schism. I hope I have shown enough reason for reading most of the 'you's as the churchmen at Antioch. If this is correct, the naming of Alexander and Arius is, as things stand, a curious kind of apostrophe. Eusebius perhaps found the letter without address (as he appears to have done the letter or fragment to Šapor);[19] or someone else may already have put on the false heading. He certainly writes as though he had found it so headed, and states that the emperor:

> despatched one of the godly men of his court, one whom he knew well to be of proven moderation of life and faithful virtue, a man very famous for his religious confessions in earlier times, as a mediator to reconcile the disputants in Alexandria. By him he sent those responsible for the quarrel a most apposite letter, which, as itself providing evidence of the emperor's concern for the people of God, could be well presented in our account of him.
>
> (Eus., *VC* 2.63)

Eusebius says that the messenger went to Alexandria. B. H. Warmington has plausibly argued that the messenger is to be identified with the bearer of a similar mission to Jerusalem described in *VC* 4.44, who in the Capitulum is called 'Marianus the *notarius*'. Socrates, however, identified the bearer here as Ossius of Corduba.[20] One might think that my argument favours Socrates against Warmington, but it is not necessarily so. Allowing that Ossius was involved at Antioch, and chaired the synod which condemned Arius and Eusebius, it is still quite possible that the emperor sent a letter to that synod by another agent. It is even possible that the same notary went on at some later stage to Alexandria, thus helping create the confusion in Eusebius' mind. There are further possibilities which may exculpate Eusebius of the lie direct. Perhaps Constantine sent his letter to Arius and

Alexander supposing them to be themselves at Antioch (which might even have been true); or perhaps copies of a letter addressed to the Bishops assembling in Antioch had been 'personalised' not very thoroughly and carried to Alexander and Arius in Alexandria. Such things remain speculation.

To my main argument I add two minor points. First, Robin Lane Fox was wrong when he placed Constantine's *Address to the Assembly of the Saints* at Antioch and at Ossius' Council there,[21] for three reasons. First, it is impossible to interpret the Letter to Alexander and Arius as discussing a journey to Egypt from Antioch: 'to the east' cannot bear the meaning which Lane Fox gives it. Second, he perhaps crams too much into the period between 25 February 325, when Constantine was in Nicomedia, and June, when he welcomed the bishops at Nicaea, to have Constantine in Antioch for Easter. I notice, however, that Timothy D. Barnes[22] is prepared to envisage a winter visit to Antioch between his attested presences at or near Nicomedia on 8 November 324 and 25 February 325. Third, even if Constantine could have addressed his speech to an assembly at Antioch, it could not have been an episcopal council. He refers clearly to the occasion: it is the morning which ushers in the resurrection (προοίμιον μὲν ἀναστάσεως, κτλ); it is 'the day of the passion' (ἡ τοῦ παθή–ματος ἡμέρα). Both Barnes and Lane Fox follow numerous other historians in taking this as 'Good Friday'; but that is an anachronism. There is no recorded ritual observance of Good Friday until the Jerusalem Holy Week connected with the church of the Anastasis, which was not yet built. The early church kept one united observance of the Passover or Pascha (our Easter), which recalled both the suffering and the resurrection. The most likely day for the speech is the Saturday, the eve of Easter, when a long vigil was kept, with scriptures, preachings and baptisms. It could, however, also be the morning of Easter Sunday. But whichever it is, it excludes the possibility of an episcopal synod. The paschal festival is the one weekend of the year when bishops must be in their own churches (as the eastern bishops were to plead at Ephesus in 431 to excuse their late arrival). So whatever the date of Ossius' council, it was not at Easter; and whatever the circumstances of Constantine's speech, it was not to a synod of bishops.

Second, a textual footnote. In *VC* 2.73 Eusebius apparently refers to Constantine and to his agent:

The Godbeloved thus provided for the peace of the Church through the letter which he issued; while he (?) gave honourable and noble service by assisting not only with the letter, but with the purpose of its sender, and was in all respects a godly man, as has been said.

Ὁ μὲν δὴ θεοφιλὴς ὧδε τὰ πρὸς εἰρήνην τῆς ἐκκλησίας τοῦ θεοῦ διὰ τῆς καταπεμφθείσης προὐνόει γραφῆς. διηκονεῖτο δὲ οὐ τῇ γραφῇ μόνον συμπράττων, ἀλλὰ καὶ τῷ τοῦ καταπέμψαντος νεύματι καλῶς κἀγαθῶς (v.l. καλὸς κἀγαθὸς MSS JNAB), καὶ ἦν τὰ πάντα θεοσεβὴς ἀνήρ, ὡς εἴρηται.

The difficulty of the subject of the second sentence is not relieved by the variant reading, which might be rendered: ' . . . while an honourable and noble person gave service by cooperating'. My tiny suggestion is that we should add the definite article before οὐ to read:

while the one who assisted not only with the letter but with the purpose of its sender gave honourable and noble service, and was in all respects a godly man, as has been said.

διηκονεῖτο δὲ <ὁ> οὐ τῇ γραφῇ μόνον συμπράττων, ἀλλὰ καὶ τῷ τοῦ καταπέμψαντος νεύματι καλῶς κἀγαθῶς, καὶ ἦν τὰ πάντα θεοσεβὴς ἀνήρ, ὡς εἴρηται.

II

Our second passage concerns the documents in *VC* 2.20–21 and 2.30–41. Pasquali begins with the discrepancies of these passages to demonstrate that there were two editions, or else a dislocated composition, of *VC*.[23] I believe they can be accounted for within Eusebius' own rather involved purposes.

One passage describes, the other presents, a law restoring rights and property to Christians. There is undoubtedly some repetition between his account in the summary of *VC* 2.20–21 and the detailed provisions of *VC* 2.30–41: the return of exiles, restoration of property, release from forced labour and from mines, and so on. Eusebius usually summarises the effect of a document before he quotes it, but if he does so here, *VC* 2.20–21 seems unnaturally long and precise, and there is no reference back when the document finally appears. This might suggest clumsy or incomplete editing of a half-finished piece. There is the further evidence of dislocation in the description of two letters, one to the churches and one to those outside, in *VC* 2.23.2, of which Eusebius decides that only the latter is relevant.

Before accepting this analysis the following two points might be considered. First, the summary and the text of Constantine's letter are cited for expressly different purposes. The summary is the factual evidence for the generalisation that 'there were now promulgated among us, as previously among those who occupy the other half of the civilised world, decrees full of the beneficence of the emperor'.[24] Hence the list of personal benefits to disgraced Christians, and the restoration of property to Christians and churches, in *VC* 20.3–5 and 21, illustrate the emperor's generosity. Eusebius then tells us that the same happened to the non-Christians,[25] but gives no particular evidence here for the immediate period after the victory over Licinius. I think that he is saving it up for Book 4.

Second, the letter of *VC* 24–42 is cited, not to demonstrate the emperor's beneficence, but to make a theological point:

> When everything had fallen under the Emperor by the power of the Saviour God, he began to make it plain to everyone who it was that supplied good things to him, and he would insist that he considered him to be the cause of his triumphs, and not himself; and he proclaimed this very thing in both Latin and Greek in a document sent to every region. The excellence of his statement may be observed by looking at the actual texts. There were two of these, one sent to the churches of God, the other to the outsiders in each city. It would in my opinion be relevant to our present theme to include the latter, both so that the actual text of this decree may survive through our history and be preserved for those after us, and in order to confirm the truth of our narratives.
>
> (Eus., *VC* 2.23.1–2)

It is in this context that Eusebius states that there are two letters, and he will cite the one to the outsiders, both to preserve the text of the decree to posterity, and 'to confirm the truth of our narratives (διηγημάτων)'.[26] The document is therefore chiefly cited for the religious confession it contains (VC 2.24–28 and 42): this is the proof that Eusebius' narrative is correct in saying that Constantine made it plain that the Saviour God was responsible for his victory. But even without pressing the plural 'narratives', a reference back to the account of VC 2.20–22, which is confirmed by VC 2.29–41, is also possible.

This difference of purpose at each point might in itself account for the apparent doublet: the same document is cited twice for two different purposes, first summarised to demonstrate the emperor's beneficence, and then quoted in full to exhibit Constantine's witness to God. But there is a further possibility. One might suppose that the letter to the churches referred to in VC 2.23.2 contained more or less a duplicate of the legal provisions of VC 2.29–41. In view of the benefits to churches and church members such a copy in the same or similar terms would probably be sent to bishops. The similarity of content could itself explain why Eusebius does not cite it as well as the one to the outsiders. If that were so, it is also possible that Eusebius did not want to abandon the letter altogether, so he used it as the basis of his evidence for Constantine's generosity in VC 2.20–21. In that passage it is explicitly a measure for benefiting the churches; it is not like the document of VC 2.24–42, however much they may overlap in content. While this is a combination of suppositions, it does account for one intriguing detail. Eduard Schwartz identified the Latin technical legal terms behind the document and the summary, and Pasquali reports them.[27] Unsurprisingly there are more such legal terms in the document than in the summary. But there is one in the summary at VC 2.21 which does not appear in the equivalent passage in the document about the *fiscus* in 2.39: ἡ κατὰ πρᾶσιν ἢ κατὰ δωρεὰν ἐκποιηθέντα (= *per emptionem vel donationem alienata*). If Eusebius were working with the same document in both places, it is strange that he introduces such a technical phrase into the summary, when it is not in the document. But if he were using a similar but not identical legal document it is easy to understand.

III

We turn to the Sabbath question in *VC* 4.18.2. It illustrates the policy of Constantine towards the Jews, which was in part favourable. We know a severe law against stoning converts to Christianity, dated 315 (the date should probably be 329).[28] In 330, however, those who serve the synagogues and (or, as) patriarchs or presbyters, and those who personally preside over the law in that sect, are relieved of all personal and civil *munera*.[29] In 331 this is confirmed for *hieros et archisynagogos et patres synagogorum et ceteros qui synagogis deserviunt*.[30] This is closely comparable to the reliefs allowed the Christian clergy in Constantine's letter to Anulinus,[31] though with nothing like the reference to the advantages which Christian worship brings to public affairs. In 321 a substantial relief, one Jew only to be called to the local *curia*, had been decreed for Jews.[32] When we find Constantine sharply attacking Jews in an ecclesiastical context (as in *VC* 3.18.4), we should bear this in mind.

I suggest that Constantine reaffirmed the long-standing right of Jews to keep the sabbath. The evidence of earlier times from Josephus is well known. Roman policy was to preserve the rights already conceded under Hellenistic rulers.[33] In 412 Christian emperors reaffirmed this, making clear the vital point, that without it Jews could be summoned or prosecuted on the sabbath and their cases fall by default.[34] Interestingly, Justinian's text adds the same protection for Christians against Jewish action on Sunday.[35] We have only fragments of Constantine's legislation. He banned litigation on Sundays except manumission; and he permitted farm-work on Sundays to take advantage of God-given weather. This is reaffirmed and developed by later emperors (e.g. *CTh* 2.8.25), but invariably with reference to the *dies dominicus/dominica*, whereas Constantine refers only to the veneration due to the day of the sun. It is notable that Eusebius nevertheless puts upon the Sunday observance a clear Christian interpretation.[36]

In the same place Valesius altered the text to change Saturday observance into Friday. The MSS read:

> Therefore he decreed for all those living under Roman government that they should rest on the days named after the Saviour, and similarly honour the sabbath days, in remembrance, I suppose, of the things done by the Saviour on those days.

διὸ τοῖς ὑπὸ τῇ ʿΡωμαίων ἀρχῇ πολιτευομένοις
ἅπασι σχολὴν ἄγειν ταῖς ἐπωνύμοις τοῦ σωτῆρος
ἡμέραις ἐνομοθέτει, ὁμοίως δὲ καὶ τὰς τοῦ σαββά–
του τιμᾶν, μνήμης ἕνεκα μοι δοκεῖν τῶν ἐν ταύταις
τῷ κοινῷ σωτῆρι πεπρᾶχθαι μνημονευομένων.

Christ was crucified on Friday, rose from the dead on Sunday, and
did nothing in particular on Saturday. Sozomen, *HE* 8.11–12,
takes Eusebius to refer to Sunday and Friday, associating the
rest with Constantine's cult of the cross of Christ. Valesius, followed by Winkelmann, brings Eusebius' text into line by adding
<πρὸ> before σαββάτου: 'the pre-sabbath days'.

Certainly, Friday is observed as a fast day among Christians. But
Saturday had always been observed in a modest way as a feast in
eastern Christianity. More important, the rest of Jesus in the
tomb, doing nothing, is precisely what the Sabbath is about in
Christian exegesis. Gregory of Nyssa uses it in his sermon for the
paschal vigil *De tridui spatio*[37] and again at the beginning of his
Easter Sunday address *In sanctum et salutare pascha*.[38] It is clearest
illustrated in another document, an anonymous pre-paschal homily, dated with assurance to 387 because of its remarks about the
Easter cycle:[39]

> Scripture has taken the Sabbath to mean rest, in these
> words, 'And God rested from all his works on the seventh
> day and hallowed it.' So also the Lord having wrought the
> consummation, having suffered on Friday and finished his
> works for the restoration of fallen man, rests the seventh
> day and abides in the heart of the earth, having finally
> given to those in Hades the release his passion affords (*or*
> from suffering). As to the fact that he rests now from all
> his works, when the fall of man became apparent as a
> result of his transgression, there remained a further work
> for God, which he had yet to achieve and restore. When
> he had done that in his passion, and made safe again the
> lost man, whom he saved, on the day of the paschal
> sabbath he 'rested from all his works', no work any longer
> remaining for the achievement of our salvation.

All this suggests that Eusebius also could quite well understand
Saturday rest as referring to what Christ did on that day, and
might so interpret the law of Constantine. But no legislation of

the Christian emperors enjoins Saturday rest, except where reliefs are extended to the Jews. I therefore surmise that the legislation which Eusebius knew of in fact reiterated the old reliefs to the Jews, while Eusebius gives it a Christian interpretation. Note the μοι δοκεῖν of Winkelmann's edition of the *VC* (126.20): the Christian interpretation is on his own testimony Eusebius' own theory. This applies to the Sunday legislation too, inasmuch as (notoriously) Constantine's decrees on this subject refer only to the *dies solis*, as in *CTh* 2.8.2 cited by Winkelmann, while Eusebius praises them as Christian.

The nut then, which this sledgehammer has now cracked, is this: Winkelmann is wrong to add with Valesius <πρὸ> before σαββάτου and Sozomen was wrong to read the text of Eusebius as though it were there. Constantine reaffirmed the Jews' right to keep Sabbath, and Eusebius forced upon his action a Christian interpretation.

NOTES

1 Eus., *VC* 2.64–66.
2 Ibid. 2.48.1 cf. *VC* 2.55.1.
3 Ibid. 2.42.
4 Ibid. 3.50.2.
5 Ibid. 4.56.1.
6 Ibid. 1.51.
7 Schwartz 1959: 136–43.
8 Stevenson 1987: 334–7.
9 Eus., *VC* 3.59–62.
10 Ibid. 2.66.
11 Ibid. 2.69.1.
12 Ibid. 2.69.2.
13 Ibid. 2.71.3.
14 Ibid. 2.71.6.
15 Ibid. 2.71.4.
16 Ibid. 2.72.2.
17 Ibid. 2.63.
18 Young 1983: 16.
19 Eus., *VC* 4.9.
20 Warmington 1985: 95–7; Socrates, *HE* 1.16.5.
21 Lane Fox 1986: 627–53.
22 Barnes 1981: 212.
23 Pasquali 1910: 369–77.
24 Eus., *VC* 2.20.1.
25 Ibid. 2.22.
26 Ibid. 2.23.2.

27 Pasquali 1910: 370–4.
28 *CTh* 16.8.1.
29 Ibid. 16.8.2.
30 Ibid. 16.8.4.
31 Eus., *HE* 10.7.
32 *CTh* 16.8.3.
33 See R. Goldberg in *ANRW* II 19.1: 414–47.
34 *CTh* 2.8.26.
35 Justinian, *Corpus Iuris Civilis* 1.9.13.
36 Eus., *VC* 4.18.2; *CTh* 2.8.1 quoted in Winkelmann's footnote.
37 Greg. Nyss., *Serm.* I (p. 274 of Heil's edition).
38 Ibid. (p. 309 of Heil's edition).
39 Floëri and Nautin 1957: 145–7.

Part II

CONSTANTINE
Legend

7

BIOGRAPHICAL MODELS

The Constantinian period and beyond

Anna Wilson

Between the writing of Eusebius' *Vita Constantini* and Gregory of Nyssa's *Life of Moses,* it is possible to watch the emergence and evolution of Christian biographical panegyric as a confident major new genre that eventually crystallises out into a form which it is convenient to label 'hagiobiography', although the precise balance between the *bios* element and that of panegyric varies from work to work during the period.

As is usual in literature, nothing springs from nothing, and the literary householders of the fourth century regularly offer us 'the old' along with 'the new'. For the assimilation of familiar elements we may look both to the new genre's debt to the ideals and categorical divisions of secular biography and panegyric – increasingly we should probably be thinking in terms of a *rapprochement* between the two[1] – and to the major contribution of both Old and New Testament biographical narrative to the new constructs. New is the confidence to produce a thorough-going fusion of both secular and Christian tradition, so that the format, organisation and often even the content of a given life can be profitably compared with a wide range of forms, with imperial biography and panegyric, with philosophical *bioi* – with which the fourth century will see a Christian dialogue in progress – with the histories of certain patriarchs and with the gospel narratives. Crucial in all of this was the ease with which it was possible to align the lives of both Job and Moses with the secular formats. One reason why the origins of the new genre have been so heavily disputed in the past[2] was a failure to recognise the eclecticism of some fourth-century Christian authors who quite deliberately threw all the elements at their disposal into the melting pot with the express purpose of producing an alignment between them and a new Christian amalgam. If some of the initial results were not entirely generically stable, this has more to do with the novelty of the experiment and sometimes with the literary ability of the experimenter than with the actual process employed.

More important than chasing specific generic origins for their own sake is a consideration why these literary experiments were undertaken so consistently at this period, and of why their authors thought them useful. Politically (and there is much that will be political about this genre as a whole), there was no ducking the significance from the Christian religious viewpoint of Constantine's conversion and of his long and eventually stable reign. That Christianity had become not merely respectable,[3] but potentially part of the establishment, presented the Christian writer with a perhaps unexpected challenge. Ideal lives rather than ideal deaths were called for. *Martyrion* must give place to *bios* in more than one sense. Along with new possibilities came new problems, not least the possible takeover of Christianity by emperor or empire. Literary responses were called for, and a range of very different approaches to this question would characterise fourth-century writing.

Equally important for subsequent literary developments would be the long years of doctrinal confusion and dispute that ensued almost immediately. As far as our extant authors are concerned, the Arian dispute itself, the reigns of subsequent emperors with Arian or semi-Arian sympathies, not to mention the brief intrusion of Julian's actual apostasy, would go some way towards undermining the new trend, and reinstating the all too familiar perils. Here it is important to remember that after the *Vita Constantini* we can trace only the orthodox half of the biographical literary record, that of the side that presented itself as fighting and winning. There is considerable food for thought as to how hagio-biography might have been shaped had Arianism developed successfully and Cappadocian writings not come to occupy the pre-eminent position that they did. I would argue that, in the long run, the trials faced by those eventually judged orthodox, undesirable as they may have seemed at the time, offered a literary gold mine to the authors concerned, and contributed substantially to their ability to separate the interests of church and state, thereby mitigating some of the potential dangers to Christianity inherent within its own new supremacy. Harnessing emperor to church rather than church to emperor was a serious issue in the fourth century and beyond.[4]

Whether *bios* or panegyric, we are in most cases dealing with a narrative if often episodic response to events, usually largely chronologically arranged[5] and focused upon the activities and the character of a deceased[6] individual. None the less, that individual is employed as a model for the future behaviour either of a more or less limited range of similar individuals or of Christians *en bloc*. In this respect, like much other early Christian literature, all such works relate closely to the generic options available within the Bible as a whole and the gospels in particular. If most early *martyria* had concerned themselves chiefly with the narrative format of the Passion, the Bible provides the fourth century with a very different narrative framework, one which draws on the full-scale 'birth to death' account of the gospels as a whole as models for life as a whole. This aspect in particular facilitates the Christian assimilation of the formal topics and divisions of secular panegyric and biography, and it is noteworthy that particularly from the fourth century onwards, martyrs too begin increasingly to acquire something approaching a full-scale biographical background.

With the emphasis on the pattern of Christ's life as well as His death comes the opportunity for much greater attention to the interface between Old and New Testament as it was already known from typological exegesis. Moses, as an allegorical forerunner prefiguring Christ's life and crucifixion, was a long-familiar theme in Christian writing.[7] In a rather different manner Eusebius himself had underlined the identity of many of Moses' actions with those of Christ in book 3 of his *Demonstratio Evangelica*, possibly drawing on Ammonius Sakkas.[8] Increasingly, such aspects of Old Testament figures come to be handled as mimetic of Christ, and it is in a many-layered concept of *mimesis* that all the biographical writing of the fourth century is rooted. In this Old Testament sense, the idea blends well with the various types of *synkrisis* long associated with the secular genres of biography and panegyric, particularly those types most concerned with ethical topics.[9]

Rich material would be available to the Cappadocian fathers to fuel long lists of individual cameo-episodic or ethical comparisons between their subject and his or her Old and New Testament counterparts,[10] all of whom acquired saintly validation either through their typological association with Christ or their discipleship. But the implied *mimesis* of Christ gave such figures a new religious and ethical clout that was less readily available to a secular panegyrist providing a *synkrisis* with a Hercules, a Theseus or an Alexander.[11] The point is even stronger with the running narrative *synkrisis* based either directly on the gospel account of Christ, or far more commonly on that of Moses, that could, on occasion, serve to articulate the narrative of an entire life.[12] This is the earliest form that we meet and it will prove the most enduring.[13]

In such a construct, *mimesis* can function on as many as four levels, deriving like a chain from the particular *mimesis* of Christ which it is the ultimate purpose of the work to instil in its audience. Where *synkrisis* is involved, Christ may be seen successively imitated by one or more biblical characters, and their imitation of Christ will itself provide the model followed or often superseded by the contemporary subject who is then himself or herself, explicitly or otherwise, presented by the author as a potential model to his audience. On one level, the provision of intermediaries as models for imitation may prove more accessible for the addressees of the work than the awe-inspiring task of imitating Christ directly.[14] On another, the enormous authority accruing to a recently deceased contemporary through viewing him in terms of these overpowering biblical figures has its daunting aspects. Fourth-century figures are being grafted into a continuing biblical tradition and into the continuing saga of God's involvement in the affairs of His created world;[15] and they are grafted in such a way as to distance them from the more normal aspects of their humanity, to set them up on a stage of the visionary and the miraculous that separates saintly ideal figures from the ordinary run of mankind who must still strive to reach such heights.

At this period biblical-style miracles and visions are of course not to be scoffed at; they must be taken seriously as marks of divine approval that were accepted as readily credible.[16] At the same time, when they do occur they are not just two a penny, but major claims with a fundamental and validatory function in the role of literary saint-making. The more biblical, and so the more mimetic in both the literary or rhetorical and the theological sense the narratives are, the greater their effect. It is small wonder that one of the favourite images of hagiobiography is that of the coin or seal portrait impression from the genuine *typos*, whether applied to imitation of Christ or used of his true imitators, or suggested as a *modus agendi* to the recipients of the work.[17] One other literary aspect that may be a candidate for biblical *mimesis* is the early tendency to stress what might slightly tendentiously be called documentary reportage, particularly in writings where the *bios* aspect is strong.[18] *Ipsissima verba* have very clear associations both with Christ and Moses, *ipsissima acta*, especially in the sense of law-giving, particularly so with Moses, but also with much other Old Testament writing, and in both cases authority accrues. Without going overboard on the idea of Christianity as the religion of the book at this period, this feature should not be overlooked.

Other aspects of the biographical author's relationship to the text that he creates bring us back to the theme of power and politics. The writing of these Christian laudatory narratives, freighted with such a wealth of theological associations, is by no means the simple pious endeavour, adorned with a set of platitudinous moral exhortations, that it might fashionably be considered today, but something very much more ambitious. Far more ambitious, too, I believe, than the traditional secular panegyric as used for normative or protreptic purposes in the classical world. Fourth-century hagiobiography is almost a form of legitimised and legitimising piracy. The writer takes over his subject, moulds him according to the ideals and models that he himself favours, and uses the result to impose precisely those ideals on his audience. The legitimation resides in the praise of the subject as a major Christian or Christ-like figure, but this in no way reduces the fact that the genre is being hijacked from its overt purpose of praise and that the individual described is turned into a role model to serve the writer's own agenda. To a degree, this had of course been done in even the earliest secular panegyric,[19] but not with the revolutionary force of a proselytising religion and an omnipotent and providential deity behind it. To say that the development was quite natural for Christianity in no way reduces its impact.

In the fourth century, with the urgent need to frame normative models for a Christian *bios* rather than a Christian death, all the roles were available for definition. And defined they were: the ideal monk,[20] bishop,[21] Christian wife[22] and mother,[23] Christian virgin[24] and, first and definitely not least, the model Christian emperor,[25] all presented in terms of the lives of more or less contemporary individuals. At the same time, the prominence of many of the actual figures makes them desirable associates for Christian writers in an age of controversy and crisis, whether we are talking of Church–state relations, or of ecclesiastical politics.

The biographer, by writing the biography, claims his subject for his own side and as a legitimisation of his own agenda. Thus the subject's *kudos* and authority, itself enhanced, accrues to the writer and enables him to prescribe the more effectively exactly how the model presented should be followed. Factual veracity, though it may be lauded and very often observed, would not be permitted to conflict too much with the author's requirements, any more than it had been in secular precedents, but, to set scepticism aside for a moment, in the fourth century, the perceived benefits of something more than lip-service to the truth may often have been more substantial than had hitherto been the case, or indeed, would be in much later hagiography.

EUSEBIUS AND THE *VITA CONSTANTINI*

The complete list of the various traditional genres that the learned and enthusiastic Eusebius recast in a Christian forge, on occasion into a form almost beyond identification, is too long to enumerate here. But it is scarcely surprising that an author capable of turning much of what was presumably expected to be the basically panegyrical thrust of his *Tricennial Oration* into a mixture of a treatise on Christian kingship[26] and one on Christian/Pythagorean numerology,[27] had something rather special up his sleeve when it came to dealing with the deceased Constantine. Eusebius, like many of his fourth-century literary successors, found himself in the rather enviable position of being able to do either the expected or the unexpected, and he seems to have been only too happy to exploit that situation.

The precise chronological genesis within Eusebius' own œuvre of the particular mix of elements in the *Vita Constantini* is probably now irrecoverable,[28] and any reconstruction must be subjective. Certainly, we can point to verbal citations from, for example, the *Historia Ecclesiastica*[29] and from the *Tric. Or.*,[30] and assume that these are merely the tip of the iceberg, given Eusebius' general tendency to rewrite himself.[31] We cannot prove whether, when Eusebius heard of Constantine's death, he swiftly mounted his pulpit and preached a Christian funeral panegyric on the first Christian emperor, but it would be very surprising had he not done so, given the magnitude of the event. Some, indeed many, common elements between such a panegyric and the *VC* are overwhelmingly probable. But the likelihood is that in doing so

Eusebius would have drawn for his funerary panegyric on the more literary aspects of a work that he had probably had in hand for a considerable time.[32]

There are several reasons for proposing such a view, and these are for the most part connected with the length of Constantine's reign. Barnes has argued for a fourth edition of the *HE* in or after 324 with final modifications in or after 326.[33] This leaves a gap before the *VC* of at least eleven or twelve years. There seems to have come a point beyond which simply adding further updating bulletins and revisions to the *HE* no longer fitted the bill.[34] The work was too backward-looking. Restoration of the Church was not the issue any more. Rather, the relationship between Christian Church and Christian emperor provided a new focus. When opportunity arose, Eusebius would indeed address himself to this topic, most notably in the *Tric. Or.*[35] If such rhetorical occasions were hardly conducive to the documentary approach of the *HE*, there is no reason to suppose that Eusebius had at any point ceased his long-standing practice of gathering relevant documents as and when these became available to him.[36] Increasingly, it must have become clear that the occasion for any fresh 'historical'[37] response would be the moment of the death of the first Christian emperor, and that that response would have to be centred on the life of one man. Equally, as Constantine's reign went on, the question of what would happen after his death – particularly with regard to a satisfactory formulation of the desired relationship between Christian Church and Christian emperor on a permanent and systematic basis – must likewise have become increasingly acute.

In preparation for such an unprecedented occasion, the form that Eusebius chose was a hybrid, and, I would argue, deliberately conceived as such from the start;[38] a fusion of the *bios* in an authoritative documentary form that would evoke his earlier *HE*, together with funerary panegyric with all its traditional prescriptive and normative functions, the whole naturally adapted to the Church's needs as perceived by its author, and quite certainly intentionally resulting in a revolutionary form of hagiography. The close parallelism between the organisation of the content of the two secular genres in certain forms would facilitate such an approach, and give ample opportunity for the further exploitation of the biblical life of Moses as a running *synkrisis*, a patriarchal and a kingly model with which Eusebius himself had already experimented at one point in the *HE*.[39]

The accusation is not infrequently levelled against Eusebius that in the *VC* he fails consistently to fulfil his initial promise to deal with the Christian aspects of the emperor's career, to write, so to speak, *Christianos* rather than *basilikos logos*, but covers, for example, purely secular legislation as well as that relating to the Church.[40] This is to underestimate the 'have your cake and eat it' mentality of any Christian rewriter of genres, let alone Eusebius. He is celebrating the first ever Christian emperor and seeking to ensure that the tradition continues; if he says that a particular action is characteristic of the emperor qua Christian, then to a large extent it becomes so, in that the author has the authority within such an unprecedented work to legislate as to what does and does not fall within the sphere of Christianity. If the *VC* was, as I suggest, planned and in part composed over a considerable length of time, then certainly aspects might creep in that were less consciously orientated towards that idea, but this would scarcely affect one of its general concepts, which is surely to extend as widely as possible the area over which either Christianity's or the Church's writ will run in future. Certainly, the angle and the overall weighting of events will be different from those of a secular *bios*, but from a viewpoint that sets religion centre stage, there were few facts that absolutely had to be excluded on the grounds that their import was purely secular. Rather, Eusebius is giving himself *carte blanche* to select his material as he chooses.[41]

As author of the *HE*, Eusebius may well have felt he had almost a prior claim on this enterprise, and perhaps, given his own Arian sympathies, have viewed it as offering him considerable opportunity, even at his advanced age. His problems at the Council of Nicaea are well known. In the *VC* he may celebrate the occasion itself, the concept of such a council, and above all the emperor's initiatives for peace and unity with rapturous enthusiasm[42] – it fits well the role of Moses in which he casts the emperor – but as to the Arian issue and the council's enactments in this regard, those he glosses over with hardly a word.[43] The doctrines of Nicaea comprise one of the few areas in which he fails to prescribe imitation for Constantine's successors, unsurprisingly, for here an element of change may be more than welcome both to him and to them, if not already positively on the cards. The omission is the more striking given the documentary nature of the life as a whole. Had Eusebius wished at this late stage in his career to give his own ratification to Nicaea, he could without difficulty have justified inclusion of its main decisions as in some respect an achievement of Constantine. That he does not do so indicates one of two things: either an awareness of the inherent dangers to the Church in presenting doctrinal matters as in any sense imperial achievements, or the precise opposite and thereby a tacit invitation to Constantine's successors to imitate by reversal. The former is impossible in view of his extravagant praise of Constantine's role in the whole affair. This leaves one wondering uneasily about the latter. Nicaea as a symbol may have survived to the end of Constantine's reign, but its tenets and orthodox supporters were falling increasingly out of favour by then. It may be overstating the case to argue that Eusebius was biding his time, but the possibility cannot be dismissed out of hand. We know too little of his relationship with Constantine's successors, but it is possible that doctrinally speaking the *VC* should be viewed as a very delicate balancing act indeed.

The fact that Eusebius chooses to include so many Constantinian documents, both letters and decrees, within the *VC* has, I believe, a rather mixed background. I have already suggested that the documentary nature of the *HE* itself simply continues, despite the change in genre, and that at least to a limited degree there is the possibility of precedent within the genre of the *bios*.[44] As the self-appointed keeper of the record for his own time that both *HE* and *Chronicle* already demonstrate him to be, this is scarcely an approach that we should expect Eusebius to abandon for the sake of mere literary form. The documents – at least almost all the documents – were an important part of the genuine record and in they would go. This can be observed when in the *VC* he provides the fourth-century equivalent of a footnote, referring his readers to the proposed appendix of two of his own sermons and one of Constantine's, that were altogether too long for the main body of the text – perhaps even a touch of restraint or acknowledgement of generic propriety here. In revising book ten of the *HE* he had been content to leave the whole of his own panegyric on church building at the head of a dossier of documents which may well have begun as appendices to an earlier version,[45] but were left in the definitive version to be followed by a rather hasty narrative conclusion of the work. Additionally, in the *VC*, authority might accrue to what he had to say to Constantine's successors through the inclusion of the documents, and there was the opportunity to put his own interpretation on their significance.

But underlying Eusebius' passion for citing the evidence in full, both here and in the *HE*, the overwhelming biblical precedent must also be significant. As regards the New Testament, the determined preservation of Christ's words is complemented by the dossier of Apostolic Epistles as a record of the teaching of the early Church, and Eusebius had shown himself as interested as any in the identification and preservation of a genuine canon.[46] Equally with the Old Testament, the concern for the true and complete record, for *ipsissima verba* and *acta*, is everywhere, nowhere more so than in the accounts of Moses as law-giver. If Exodus can include a blow-by-blow account of the giving of the law, and do so more than once,[47] there is no earthly reason why Eusebius cannot present Constantinian decisions in a similar light as one aspect of the detailed *synkrisis*. Rather, there is every reason that he should do so.

The running *synkrisis* with Moses is fundamental to the organisation of the *VC*. Its genesis certainly dates back to the Constantinian material at the end of the *HE*, given that the Pharaonic handling of the Milvian Bridge episode against Maxentius, which is the longest and most explicit Moses sequence in the *VC*, is drawn directly from that earlier account.[48] Now, throughout large parts of the *VC*, the *synkrisis* is worked out in detail and matches a schema of Moses' life that aligns very neatly with basic panegyrical and biographical format. Family, birth and childhood function very well in terms of Constantine as a latter-day Hebrew equivalent brought up as a hostage at an Egyptian-style tetrarchic court.[49] 'Early promise' is evoked in the honour accorded the young Constantine at the imperial court, and for this young 'Moses' threatened with assassination at the hands of jealous emperors, flight to the wilderness, or at least to join his father, duly follows.[50] So also does the brief notice of the downfall of the persecutors, which seems designed to parallel the brevity of that on the death of the original Pharaoh at the equivalent point in Exodus.[51] Constantine's prayer, his perception of the world as bowed beneath tyranny, his desire to act as liberator and his active seeking of divine aid to this end through prayer[52] before he receives his own 'burning bush'-style vision,[53] whilst raising very similar issues, all present him in a superior light to the hesitant Moses, not at all an unusual feature of *synkrisis*.[54] In addition, the first of several attributions to Maxentius of sorcerous practices owes not a little to Pharaoh's magicians.[55]

Hereafter, matters become more complex. In their immediate context, Constantine's vision of a cross of light, its inscription 'Conquer by this', and, advanced out of its correct chronological sequence,[56] the making of the *labarum* in response to the subsequent dream[57] match successively the vision of the angel in the burning bush, Yahweh's promise to smite the Egyptians with the famous self-identification 'I am that I am', and the instructions to Moses on the powers of his rod, most notably the phrase 'and Moses took the rod of God in his hand'.[58] Certainly the *labarum* will continue to do duty as the rod in subsequent episodes,[59] but throughout it will be fused synthetically with several other Mosaic symbols, that fall outside the strict sequence so far. The early description eases this fusion by making the multiple symbolism clear from the start. In that it is to be followed by Constantine's armies, it will relate also to the pillar of cloud and flame as a symbol of God's preservation of his people and their rescue from their Pharaonic enemies.[60] Still more importantly, both as something to be followed[61] and as a rich and divinely inspired artefact that incorporates the name of Christ, it has unmistakable associations with the great series of articles that God commands Moses to make, namely the tabernacle,[62] priestly robes and breastplate, but above all the Ark of the Covenant which contains the Law.[63] Particularly significant in this respect is Constantine's calling together of craftsmen in gold and precious stone, much after the manner of Moses' identification of Bezaleel, Aholiab and other skilled workers to undertake the work involved.[64]

In Chapter 32, Eusebius signals his return to chronological sequence, both with regard to Constantine and to Exodus. Thus Constantine's instruction at the hands of priests which he accepts as 'knowledge taught by God' should primarily be linked to Moses' divine instructions at the time of the vision of the burning bush,[65] and the account of Maxentius' tyranny to the cruelty of Pharaoh to the Hebrews.[66] The wars against Maxentius and Licinius will occupy Eusebius from this point down to 2.17. In secular terms, they comprise the majority of the heading associated with 'External Wars'.[67] One option would have been to equate Maxentius with Pharaoh and link Licinius to the war against the Amalekites, and certainly any Amalekite elements are confined to the Licinius account,[68] but instead Eusebius chooses to distribute different aspects of Moses' struggle to liberate God's people from Pharaoh across the two wars, and this has the effect of stressing the identity of the struggle in both Western and Eastern Empire. Against Maxentius, it is the rod-like aspects of the standard that are uppermost as Constantine marches back towards Egypt, that is to a Rome in captivity to paganism, only to lead it out to freedom and the promised land of Christianity. As the 'Pharaoh' Maxentius goes down with his over-laden boats in the Red Sea of the Tiber at the Milvian Bridge.[69] A brief interlude more properly belonging to deeds of peace, but designed to take us up to Constantine's *Decennalia*[70] follows, before Book I concludes with the preliminaries to the war against Licinius. Again latter-day 'Hebrews' are persecuted but, in this 'Egypt' of the East, attacks on the Christian religion and Licinius' rapacity now receive the main emphasis.[71] One major element of the Exodus account, so far lacking, now finds its place as a dramatic conclusion to Book I. Incorporating the plagues of Egypt within the Constantinian account can have been no easy matter, but Eusebius is certainly game to try. Even the examples of Galerius' worm-infested ulcer and the horrific blinding of Maximinus Daia, both victims of the 'divine scourge',[72] fail to influence Licinius. For Eusebius that is the strongest evidence of his madness,[73] and of the 'dark night of error' in which his understanding is 'cloaked'.[74] It seems fairly clear that Licinius is here being portrayed as Pharaoh whose 'heart is hardened' during the plagues, and the phrase is used explicitly later.[75]

In Book 2, 'Moses' marches once more against a persecuting emperor who is once again given over to Egyptian soothsayers and magicians.[76] As always the *labarum* is at the head of Constantine's army, but in this sequence it is to be viewed both as the pillar of cloud and fire leading the people through the wilderness towards the promised land of a *pax christiana*, and as the Ark within the tabernacle. For Eusebius states explicitly that Constantine pitched the tabernacle of the cross outside the camp and prayed there in imitation of Moses' practice.[77] Finally, the death of Licinius and the universal religious celebrations with processions and hymns evoke for a second time the overwhelming of Pharaoh and the songs of Moses and Miriam.[78]

At this point the nature of the *VC* changes radically. Licinius duly dealt with, in panegyrical terms the deeds of peace follow,[79] together with any internal threats. As regards the latter, internal Christian dissension, particularly the Arian controversy, is attributed to that old secular chestnut, envy,[80] here masquerading in the guise of the devil: ὁ φθόνερος καὶ μισόκαλος δαίμων.[81] Whereas hitherto Eusebius has given us narrative, with next to no documentary evidence,[82] from now on, that is for more than half of the entire work, we will get almost nothing but documents, with the bare minimum of narrative to link them. Certainly, this can be easily accounted for in terms of Eusebius' likely access to documentary evidence. But at first sight, in a highly literary work, the result is one of crass imbalance. It would be unthinkable in secular panegyric. Although biography, after summarising legal enactments and diplomacy under the 'deeds of peace' that illustrate justice, temperance or wisdom in the hero, may before the account of the end of the reign frequently insert a section on literary endeavours, with occasional quotations,[83] documentation on this scale could scarcely be justified by that genre either.[84]

Certainly Eusebius had a literary problem, given the likely chronological distribution of documents in his possession that he wished to include. But he also had a ready literary model not just in Exodus alone, but in the entire Old Testament sequence of Moses' speaking of the law to Israel between his first ascent of Sinai in Exodus 19 and his departure onto the mountain to die at Deuteronomy 32.48.[85] As far as the narrative sequence of Exodus goes, three substantial categories remain: law-giving which is pre-eminent, dissension among the Children of Israel, most memorably in the disruption of the Golden Calf episode, and, intimately connected with the Law, the making of the tabernacle and its contents. It can fairly be said that Eusebius divides the rest of the *VC* among equivalent topics, albeit any sequential narrative parallels fade almost completely by the end of Book 3. The second half of Book 2, which opens with Constantine's imperial edicts on the peace of the Church and on toleration, and Constantine's letter to Eusebius, may be compared with the first law-giving to Moses.[86] Thereafter, the rumblings of the Arian controversy and the Easter dispute[87] take us through the disaffection of the Israelites which culminates in a Golden Calf episode, with Arius and the disaffected bishops doing duty for the unfortunate Aaron.[88] Constantine naturally plays Moses in all of this, but this is yet another point in which he excels his equivalent in the *synkrisis*; no furious outbursts or breaking of the tablets for him, rather, sweet reason and pleas for the *pax christiana*.[89] There can be little doubt that, given a rather different outcome, the Creed of Nicaea would have been enthusiastically celebrated as a new Decalogue, and in fact the *VC*'s description of the Council of Nicaea, whatever Eusebius' reservations, gives it that kind of build-up, unwittingly making still more obvious to later readers possessed of history's hindsight the yawning omission of the document *par excellence*, the new 'Decalogue' of the Nicene creed.

Thereafter matters quieten down, and borrowings from the

Moses narrative for the most part become far more schematic. Roughly correctly positioned both for the divine instructions about the tabernacle in the first giving of the tablets of the law and for its actual construction after the second, comes the long sequence on Constantine's role in the construction and adornment of Christian churches, a theme which gets major attention here, but will also recur later on.[90] The loss of most of Eusebius' orations and writings at the time is particularly galling in that he tells us[91] that he explained the symbolism of the new Church with reference to the prophets, but not explicitly that he used the Mosaic tabernacle. Origen certainly uses the tabernacle as a figure of the Church.[92] Gregory of Nyssa applies the heavenly tabernacle with its gold columns and silver capitals and bases to the incarnation,[93] and the earthly tabernacle to the Church, with the apostles as a group as its pillars and individuals among them represented as different items within the sanctum, notably John as a *louter*, a laver or basin for ritual washing.[94] Cyril of Jerusalem is still more explicit on the baptismal symbolism of the laver in the tabernacle.[95] Eusebius tells us that the Church of the Holy Sepulchre had twelve columns according to the number of the apostles and that their capitals were adorned with great silver bowls donated by Constantine.[96] Visualising the effect may be problematic, but we are certainly justified in arguing for links with the Mosaic tabernacle. Indeed, one may well take it further and suggest that Constantine's architects were the recipients of complex symbolical advice from his top-ranking theologians, one at least of whose names looks identifiable![97]

After this point in the *VC* it seems forced to try to go any further with details of the Moses narrative, for example to link Constantine's dealings with heretics with the various outbreaks of warfare between the Israelites and other tribes during the period in the wilderness.[98] At the most, one can perhaps say that the great occasion of the dedication of the Holy Sepulchre,[99] picking up from the description of the plan in Book 3 does mean that the *VC* offers some reflection of the two lengthy passages of instructions for building the tabernacle and its eventual construction in Exodus. Far more important for these final books is the consistency of the general range of topics and above all the further development of the emphatic portrait of Constantine as new Law-giver, Christian ruler, and guardian of the *pax christiana*. In the end Eusebius may run out of steam, but by and large he has succeeded in his object, a prescriptive imperial life that sets up Moses as the model for imperial *imitatio Christi*, and that argues for a harmonious cooperation between Church and state, based on the pre-eminent role of the emperor as God's vice-gerent in human affairs. Eusebius has provided the prototype, but like many prototypes, the *VC* is not the form which will eventually leave the production line in any quantity. It is a one-off and the circumstance that created it was not susceptible of repetition, even had ecclesiastical politics turned out differently. As it was, Eusebius had demonstrated only too clearly the perils inherent in the writing of a model Christian *bios* with an emperor as its subject.

THE ORTHODOX OPPOSITION: ATHANASIUS AND THE CAPPADOCIANS

It is the opposition who move the notion of the Christian *bios* down very different paths. What Athanasius and the Cappadocians have most fundamentally in common here apart from their Nicene orthodoxy is a shared experience of long periods in exile and opposition, together with a not unnatural coolness towards imperial interference in Church affairs. In addition, they are concerned with the problems of providing post-*martyrion* Christian models over a much wider area of human experience. The problem of excusing oneself for not being martyred remains more widespread in literature than the theological argument that martyrdom should not be actively sought might indicate. Even in Eusebius' case his personal autopsy of so many martyrdoms, whilst he did not himself suffer, presents a certain awkwardness throughout Books 8–9 of the *HE*. Given Athanasius' and the Cappadocian bishops' experiences of exile and persecution, they are certainly the last people we should expect to hear proclaiming a joyful *pax christiana* and an end of problems. What they do not share among themselves at all is similar views on the role of secular learning in any model form of *bios*.

Athanasius' choice for a model life is monastic; it is the obvious alternative to martyrdom and it is already by this period well established as a solution to the problems of the world. Certainly, Athanasius had a commission from monks abroad somewhere,[100] we only wish we knew where for sure, and clearly he was closely associated with the orthodox monks of Egypt: writing the work may well have been much to his taste; but there was also a practical spin-off. Writing the life of Antony[101] enabled him to confirm and establish a picture of monastic respect towards one's bishop[102] combined with a pretty cavalier approach to such things as even respectful letters from Constantine,[103] to underline how hierarchies and loyalties should run both within the Church and between Church and state, and it is a world away from Eusebius. It also enabled Athanasius to associate a major monastic figure with himself, and neither consideration was to be rejected.

That Athanasius' Antony represents not a peaceful monastic retreat into solitude, but rather a carrying of the warfare against the devil out of the city, particularly after the period of persecution, in order to continue the martyrs' struggle by means of something akin to a death in life is well known.[104] So also is the extensive and unacknowledged debt of the life's structure to the gospel narratives of Christ up to the time of his passion.[105] Again, the format is constructed in a manner comparable to secular or philosophical models, equally consonant of course with the gospel pattern of birth; training or *paideia* (in which fasting and temptation in the wilderness are naturally paramount from Antony's point of view); acts or *praxeis* (of teaching and miracles); and finally passion and death. For the Life of Antony the gospel model functions excellently for birth and *paideia*,[106] temptation, including repeated play on triplets in the grouping of the temptations, in Antony's village,[107] in the tombs[108] and finally as he sets forth for the fortress in the mountains[109] before the culmination of twenty years of struggle in the fortress itself.[110] As well as the idea of triple temptation, several of the temptations involved have close affinities with those of Christ. Then he emerges to preach a mini-treatise of twenty-seven chapters on temptation and demonology.[111] Set, as this sermon to disciples is, in the mountain wastes of Pispir, its resemblances to Christian apologetic or the discourses of Greek sages are less significant structurally than its associations with the Sermon on the Mount, and the earlier admixture of healing miracles[112] reinforces the link to Christ. However, it all falls apart in Chapters 46–47 when Antony fails to become a martyr and learns that one bears witness to Christ in imitation of his life rather than his death; he must return to his solitude, indeed, go even further into the desert and to the mixed life of asceticism, healing and teaching which he has already established for himself. Christlike behaviour it may be, but the gospel structuring is gone.

Further inspection reveals that whilst the gospel narrative patterns the first half, elements of the complementary narrative of

Moses are interleaved with the whole, taking over almost entirely in the second half: re-division is called for. The young Antony decides to leave home, fortuitously an Egyptian village.[113] Successive retreats into the wilderness cover Moses' years as a shepherd in the wilderness.[114] The heavenly supporting visions against the devil might do some kind of initial duty for the burning bush.[115] The descent to Alexandria to minister to the martyrs[116] equates with the return to Egypt to Moses' own people and is certainly intended to echo it, but the latterday Moses has received no explicit divine instructions, and this is in fact a false move. He is not cut out for defeating mortal Pharaohs – the episode is omitted entirely. Instead he receives his marching orders on his return to the desert which had[117] itself become a city; he is told to retire to the inner mountain rather than to the Upper Thebaid.[118] In that retreat we have a clear and deliberate parallel to Moses' period in the wilderness with the people of Israel and his withdrawal to commune with God on Mount Sinai. For law-giving and correction of the people after the Golden Calf incident, one may perhaps look among other episodes to that of the supposedly illiterate Antony's putting to shame of the philosophers in a learned discourse that is clearly familiar with sophisticated allegorical approaches to Greek legends.[119] What is not in doubt is that Antony's secret burial on the mountain is designed to recall Moses' ascent of a high mountain and mysterious disappearance from the eyes of men so that no man knew the place of his burial.[120] The biblical connotations of the incident are reinforced by a complementary implicit parallel between his bequeathing of his few garments to Bishops Serapion and Athanasius and the passing of Elijah's cloak to Elisha.[121]

We must leave Antony and turn for a few final details to the Cappadocian Fathers. Their agenda is again different from that of Athanasius and on an altogether more comprehensive scale. In the stress laid by both Gregories on cult and on the festal as well as the funerary panegyric, one can observe that those celebrated serve the Cappadocian and orthodox cause in every bit as ruthless a manner as can be seen in Basil's determined populating of every conceivable see with his own relatives and family friends. More goes into all this than just a chance literary reflection of what happened to be preached and survive; rather, these are grand public works. The addition of prominent bishops, pressed by their memorial into the service of Trinitarian orthodoxy is one notable feature: Gregory of Nazianzus on Athanasius; Gregory of Nyssa on

Gregory Thaumaturgus, with whom he claimed distant family associations, and on Meletius of Antioch; still more remarkable is the exploitation of Basil himself as the vehicle for major panegyric by both Gregories, not to mention almost every known member of his own family, father with mother, secular brother Caesarius, and married sister Gorgonia, by Gregory of Nazianzus, and his reclusive sister Macrina in a very striking generic variation by Gregory of Nyssa.[122] The manufacture of contemporary saints is the very clear object and the incidence of the miraculous, particularly in the family and friends category is noteworthy; in the episcopal group: Athanasius' triumphant return to Alexandria is painted in the light of Christ's Palm Sunday entrance into Jerusalem and scourging of the temple;[123] Gregory of Nazianzus' Basil is a new martyr fighting the unreasonable tyranny of an Arianising emperor and prefect, and the literary style of this part of the account is radically altered to evoke the flavour of the *procès-verbal* of an early martyrdom, a point picked up by Ephrem Graecus in his versification of the episode.[124] That Gregory of Nyssa systematically represented the subjects of his biographical panegyrics as a new kind of martyr, reclaiming the Pauline imagery of both martyr and athlete for those who struggled, whether against tyrants or as ascetics or both, and lived rather than died for their faith, has been well demonstrated by Monique Alexandre.[125] Likewise, Marguerite Harl has long since highlighted the importance of the three forty-year periods of the life of Moses for the Cappadocian development of the episcopal *bios*: despoiling of the Egyptians' secular learning; ascetic withdrawal as a monk; and then active engagement in the world of the Church as an ascetic and philosophical bishop.[126] If the last two categories may be reminiscent, with variations, of Athanasius' Antony, the early 'Egyptian' *paideia* that enables the Cappadocians so effectively to exploit at will and then frequently purport to reject entirely the rules of secular philosophy, panegyric and rhetoric in general, when in fact they are blatantly engaged in the now familiar practice of Christianising them,[127] is certainly wildly at odds with the proud claims of illiteracy made for Antony.[128] Indeed, the time spent by Gregory of Nazianzus on his own and Basil's Athenian period is as much a still slightly self-conscious defence of the effort that went into their joint acquisition of the most polished rhetorical skills as it is a boast of the closeness of the friendship they once shared.[129] Justification by Moses is implicit throughout the work, even though he figures as only one among

the cavalcade of biblical figures employed for *synkrisis*.[130] An even
stronger pre-eminence of Moses as the major model has again been
demonstrated by Marguerite Harl for virtually all the relevant
works of Gregory of Nyssa, most notably his wrongly neglected
panegyric on Basil, which is constructed almost entirely out of a
chiasmic series of massive *synkriseis* moving from Old to New
Testament and back to culminate in a full-scale biographical
and ethical *synkrisis* with Moses.[131] That work's opening, however,
is the key to what the two Gregories are up to. Basil is explicitly
made a saint with his festival set at the point in the Church's year
where one moves from the celebration of the birth of Christ to the
major patriarchs, prophets, and Basil himself, as the argument
builds that God provides saints in every age of the church as
teachers and shepherds of His flock.[132] As the collection of panegyrics mounted,[133] the Gregories were bolstering their authority
with the prestige of the famous outsiders they celebrate, with the
models for Christian life provided from within their own family
and above all with the cult of the one man on whose authority
their own ultimately rested, Basil of Caesarea.

I have left two of Nyssa's works to one side, those in which he
provides us with complementary models for the nun and for the
monk. Macrina is famously presented as yet another new martyr in
terms of her strength in the face of personal suffering,[134] her
asceticism and prayer,[135] and in the manner of her final illness
and death, where Gregory draws explicit parallels with Job.[136] She
is the offspring of a vision that underlines the dynastic element in
this kind of hagiography, the descendant of generations of holy
women going back to one instructed by Gregory Thaumaturgus.[137] Her philosophy and learning are Christian rather than
secular, built on a passionate love of the Bible,[138] she has been
the inspiration of a new Christian female community;[139] she has
received miraculous healing.[140] Like the Life of Antony, that of
Macrina too is cast in epistolary form. Conventionally, it is held
that there are no apparent links between the two works, or at least
that there is no internal evidence that Gregory knew the Life of
Antony. There are perhaps two small pointers. We have looked at
the use of Christ and Moses as models in that work, but those are
structural models and Moses at least is never made explicit there.
The one explicit *synkrisis* that we do get in Antony is with Job.[141]
The other pointer is even smaller; when Gregory praises his
brother Peter's help during a famine in the community, he says
that Peter was able to get hold of so many provisions that the

crowd of visitors made the desert a city.[142] This seems too close an echo of the famous phrase from *V. Ant.* 14 to be mere chance, and there may be more links to be picked up yet. It is certainly striking that Gregory too picks an epistolary framework for his Life of Moses, his own model for the ascetic *bios*, albeit a model far more intellectual and philosophically Neo-platonic than Athanasius would surely have approved, and it is perhaps better not to consider what he would have made of the predominance of the Phaedrus myth in Gregory's account of Exodus.[143] But this late great *bios* of Gregory is not as far from the main line as it may sound. Contemporary models are not left out altogether in favour of mainline typological exegesis in the *theoria* of the Moses story. Instead, you might say that finally the Moses *synkrisis* swallowed its subject. The roles reverse and the wheel comes full circle. Moses, the type for Christ, becomes the subject; but it is Basil the ideal ascetic who provides the *synkrisis* and in this work the true model for *mimesis*.[144] It is, in fact, Gregory's final tribute to his brother's life.

ACKNOWLEDGEMENTS

I am grateful to Prof. S. N. C. Lieu and Dr D. Montserrat at Warwick University for providing me with the opportunity to reformulate my ideas on this subject. Early drafts of some elements were given at seminars at the Queen's University of Belfast and at the Institute of Classical Studies in London and I am grateful to all three audiences for helpful criticisms. I would also like to record special thanks to Margaret Mullett for her early encouragement, and to Averil Cameron for infinite patience as well as encouragement over a very long period.

NOTES

1 Despite the theoretical differences between secular biography and panegyric (cf. Wardman 1974: 11–16), none the less, Leo 1901: 320–1 and still more Momigliano 1971: 82–3, 102–3 and 110 rightly stress their lengthy coexistence and cross-fertilisation. Certainly, Isocrates' *Evagoras* and Xenophon's *Agesilaus* remained the fundamental models for *encomia*, although the influence of the latter on Plutarch's *Agesilaus* should be stressed. Yet there is much common ground between the examination of *ethos* in a favourable biography or

in panegyric and the presentation of an individual as an ideal character. This is clear in some of Plutarch's more theoretical passages, e.g. *Alexander* 1, especially *Cimon* 2 and, by inversion, *Demetrius* 1. In discussing panegyric here, theoretical examples will be drawn for the most part from Russell and Wilson's edition of Men. Rhet. 2.368–377, both because Menander Rhetor uses that as the basis of his own prescription for the *epitaphios logos* (2.419–422), and because in the highly celebratory works under consideration the element of lament recommended throughout by Menander is frequently confined to the opening and to the final funeral sequence, but above all because the fourth-century writers are as unwilling to allow any criticism of their heroes as is Menander to permit such of an emperor (Men. Rhet. 2.368.5–6).

2 The dangers inherent in the search for a single overriding generic model, whether it be in Plutarchean biography, in aretalogies or in the ideal philosophical *bios*, are well illustrated in the otherwise profound study of Holl 1912. For a more profitable synthetic approach, albeit largely disregarding panegyric, see Cox 1983: 3–16, 45–66.

3 See Barnes 1981: 146–7.

4 This is not to say that full-scale separation would ever again be entirely possible. Eventual Cappadocian supremacy itself depended in large measure on the favour of Theodosius 1. However, the problematical nature of the issue is clear in all the texts after the *VC*.

5 The two most notable exceptions are Gregory of Nazianzus on Athanasius and Gregory of Nyssa on Basil. See below pp. 121ff., and for the double sequence of Gregory of Nyssa's *V. Moys.*, pp. 120, 125.

6 Sulpicius Severus' *Vita Martini* is the famous fourth-century exception, but a very special case. Its consequences for subsequent western biography, for example in Einhard's *Life of Charlemagne* and Asser's *Life of Alfred*, are largely irrelevant to the east, but do serve to underline the accessibility of a panegyrical reading of the *Vita Antonii*.

7 For Origen, see e.g. *Hom. in Ex.* 2.4; 3.2–3 and n. 92 below. See also Daniélou 1960: 197; for other aspects, Glasson 1963: 23, 70, 85; Hanson 1959: 66–7, 145; Cameron 1991: 55–6.

8 Bruns 1977: 117–25. See also below pp. 113ff. for Moses in Eus., *HE*.

9 For biography, Plutarch remains the most obvious example, both within individual lives and in the curiously arithmetical ethical comparisons or *synkriseis* which close each pair of Greek and Roman lives. See Wardman 1974: 33–4, 234–44; Erbse 1956: 398–424. For early variety of approach on the organisation of this aspect, see Momigliano 1971: 49–51 on Evagoras and Xenophon. Menander recommends *synkrisis* under each separate heading within the encomium: Men. Rhet. 2.370.6–8, 23–5; 371.5–11, 22–5; 372.1–2; 374.2–19; 375.13–18 and especially 377.1–9.

10 Below, pp. 124ff.

11 On Isocrates, above, note 1. In Menander Rhetor, e.g. Hercules: 2.370.23, 372.2; Achilles: 2.371.24, 372.2, 374.10; Alexander: 2.377.9.

12 On Constantine and Athanasius, below pp. 121ff.; for the Cappadocians, Harl 1967.

13 For Eus., *VC* below, pp. 112ff..

14 See for example implicitly Athan., *V. Ant.* proem. 2.94; more explicitly Greg. Nyss., *V. Moys.* 1.13–15, 2.319–20, and *Proem. in HL*. It
is illuminating that (at *Tric. Or.* 3.5–8) Eusebius had presented a
direct *synkrisis* between Constantine and the Word for his perceptions of what Christian kingship might entail. It is not a precedent
that would find many other fourth-century followers.

15 See especially pp. 124ff. below for what may almost be called
Cappadocian policy in this respect.

16 On miracles at this period, Karlin-Hayter 1991: 254–60; for the
sixth century, Cameron 1991: 208–13.

17 The image is found in the New Testament, Phil. 3.17, 1 Tim. 4.12,
1 Pet. 5.3, but has a long secular history, running back to Isocrates'
use of the word in the context of sculpture in general at *Evagoras* 74.
Palladius applies *encharaxas* to his own work, *Proem. in HL* 3.995 (5.1
Butler), see further Greg. Nyss. *V. Moys.* 2.47 (in combination with
the equally ubiquitous *eikon* and the image of the Platonic mirror in
a key passage), 231, 318–19 (*eikon* again, and, as in the preface an
outline drawing or template); Greg. Nyss *In xl mart.* 2 2 (of Basil);
Cyril of Scythopolis, *praef. in V. Euthym.* 6.10 (in *Kyrillos von Sky-
thopolis*, ed. E. Schwartz (TU 49.2) Leipzig 1939).

18 See the *VC*, with its stress on law-giving, and the respective teachings of Antony in Athan., *V. Ant.* to the monks (16–43) and to the
Greek philosophers (74–80).

19 See the closing passages of Isocrates' *Evagoras* (73–81).

20 Athanasius' *V. Ant.* and the series of *Vitae* of Pachomius and his
successors (see Halkin and Festugière 1982), along with the *Vita
Martini* of Sulpicius Severus in the West are the prime individual
cases, and their influence would be immeasurable; subsequent centuries would see the group accounts of the ascetics of Egypt, Syria
and Palestine in the work of Palladius, Theodoret, Cyril of Scythopolis and John Moschus.

21 Gregory of Nazianzus on Athanasius (*Oration* 21 = *PG* 35: 1081–
1128) and Basil (*Oration* 43 = *PG* 36: 493–605) and on his own
father Gregory (*Or.* 18 = *PG* 35: 985–1044); Greg. Nyss., *In Bas.
fratr.*, on Gregory Thaumaturgus (= *PG* 46: 893–958) and Meletios
of Antioch (*PG* 46: 851–64). The process was carried further in
Palladius' encomiastic *Dialogus* in defence of John Chrysostom as
well as in many subsequent Lives of the Constantinopolitan
patriarch.

22 Gregory of Nazianzus on Gorgonia: *Oration* 8 (*PG* 35: 789–817) in
his *epithalamion* for Olympias (*PG* 37: 1541–9).

23 For Gregory of Nazianzus on his mother Nonna, most strikingly in
his funeral oration for his father, see *Oration* 18.7–11 (*PG* 35: 992–
997); Greg. Nyss. on his mother Emmelia especially at *Vita Macrinae*
2–3, 5–7.

24 Greg. Nyss., *V. Macr.*; for asceticism within marriage, Gregory of
Nazianzus on Gorgonia, *Oration* 8, 13–14 (= *PG* 35: 804–5).

25 Eus., *VC* and *Tric. Or.*

26 *Tric. Or.* 1–5, 8–11 in particular.

27 *Tric. Or.* 6.

28 T. D. Barnes' learned and valiant attempt (Barnes 1989a) at a very detailed analysis of the work's constituents and construction, virtually paragraph by paragraph, seems to be over-mechanical, and to disregard its overwhelming literary impetus.

29 The most obvious example is *VC* 1.37–8 (= *HE* 9.9), on the Milvian Bridge. In general, see Barnes 1981: 267–8 and A. Cameron and S. Hall's forthcoming translation and commentary.

30 *VC* 3 54–55 = *Tric. Or.* 8.

31 See Barnes 1980b for an analysis of the genesis of the *HE*.

32 In this it will be clear that I differ somewhat from the view of Barnes 1989a: 98–110 that the *VC* was put together as it stands in response to Constantine's death from a funeral panegyric delivered at that time and a collection of pre-existing material perhaps already roughly shaped.

33 Barnes 1981: 150, cf. Barnes 1980b.

34 Barnes 1989a: 114 argues that the *VC* originated as a continuation of or sequel to *HE*, since three manuscripts of *HE* cite Constantine's letter to the Palestinian provincials of 324 as an appendix followed by Eusebius' promise to assemble together, making a fresh beginning, Constantine's letters and laws. Even this early, there seems to be the germ of an idea that something quite different is now required. There is also the question of the possible effect on Eusebius' own authority, of the reverses he suffered at the Council of Nicaea. This is awkward to calculate, in that we cannot be certain how widespread the prestige of the *Histories* had been hitherto either in fact, or in the perception of its author, and therefore how discouraging Nicaea might have been to his historical endeavours. See, Barnes 1981: 269–70.

35 On the comparative rarity of such occasions, Barnes 1981: 266.

36 See, however, Barnes 1989a: 110–14 on the very uneven chronological distribution of the documents in the *VC*, the preponderance dating from the mid-320s.

37 I use the word with some hesitation, and rather loosely, with regard to what Eusebius thought he was achieving even in *HE*, but regard that work itself as a major rewriting of genre.

38 Here I differ somewhat from Barnes 1989a: 110, for whom the work is 'a conflation' of a pre-existent but abandoned draft of an imperial 'panegyric and a documentary history of a hagiographical nature'. He goes on to stress the daring originality of the latter as something 'which hovers between ecclesiastical history and hagiography' (116), but his two drafts theory does not allow for wholesale generic fusion as fundamental either to the original concept or the final form.

39 See below, pp. 116ff. That the Moses *synkrisis* is found already at *HE* 9.9 may well be an indicator that Eusebius conceived of its wholesale use in *VC* very early on.

40 For the promise, *VC* 1.11.1. For criticism of apparently secular material, most recently Barnes 1989a: 99.

41 On the relationship of the Moses *synkrisis* to this, below p. 116.

42 Eus., *VC* 3.6–14, a passage which exercised no little influence on Eustratios' equally biased and tendentious account of the proceedings of the Fifth Ecumenical Council (*Vita Eutychii* 28–30, ed. C. Laga (Corpus Christianorum. Series Graeca, 25) 1992: 777–854).

43 At *VC* 3.14, the solution to the Easter question receives more emphasis than does that to the Arian issue. See also Barnes 1981: 270.

44 Suetonius' inclusion of verbatim documents within the earlier version of his *Lives of the Caesars*, is, however, surely much less significant than Eusebius' own earlier practice in *HE*.

45 So Barnes 1981: 271.

46 Barnes 1981: 138–9.

47 Exodus 20.2–31.18, 34.1–28, and see also the whole sequence from Leviticus to Deuteronomy.

48 *VC* 1.38–9, minimally expanded from *HE* 9.9. The repeated Septuagint quotations particularly from the songs of Moses and Miriam (Exodus 15) increase the impact of the passage but also mark it out stylistically from Eusebius' handling of the *synkrisis* elsewhere in the *VC*. I should make it clear that in the following discussion I am not concerned with the historicity or otherwise of any particular detail, merely with Eusebius' structuring of his account on the model of that in Exodus.

49 *VC* 1.12, and note the portrayal of his father Constantius as a Christian in 13–17, which reinforces the picture of Constantine as belonging from birth to the 'Hebrew' rather than the 'Egyptian' side. For the secular equivalents, I follow throughout the Menandrian categories.

50 *VC* 1.19–20, cf. Exodus 2.10–15. Naturally there is no mention of any slaying of an Egyptian at this juncture, nor of Moses' doings in Midian, although Moses' acquisition of a father-in-law whose flocks he herds (Exodus 3.1) is not altogether inapposite for Constantine's succession to his father's Western possessions and his driving out of some of the Rhine tribes like wild beasts (*VC* 1.24–5).

51 *VC* 1.23; Exodus 2.23. If Eusebius' brevity here may be partly explained by that of Exodus at this point, his postponement of the deaths of Galerius and Maximinus Daia to the final chapters of Book 1 also allows them to echo a different aspect of the Exodus story. See below pp. 118.

52 *VC* 1.26–7.

53 *VC* 1.28, cf. Exodus 3–4.

54 Men. Rhet. 2.377.1–3 on the delicate balance required here.

55 *VC* 1.17, 36, 37; Exodus 7.11–12. For Licinius, below pp. 117ff.

56 Although Eusebius makes this quite clear, referring to having seen the *labarum* himself and to the fact that it was done rather later (*VC* 1.30, and 32.1), he certainly fudges the chronology over the instructions for its making (*VC* 1.30).

57 *VC* 1.28–31.

58 Exodus 3.2–3; 3.4–22, especially 20 and 14; 4.2–4; 7.20. For the rod's change to a serpent and back as a type of Christ's incarnation,

Irenaeus, *Adv. Haer.*, 3.21.8; Greg. Nyss., *V. Moys.* 2.31–6; Cyril of Alexandria, *Glaphyra* 2.999 (*PG* 69.2: 469–72). For the rod as a frequent image of the crucifixion and the cross, Justin, *Dialogus* 86; 100.4; 126.1; Origen, *Hom. in Ex.* 5.5; 7.1–2; Cyril of Jerusalem, *Catecheses* 13.20 (= *PG* 33: 797); Greg. Nyss., *V. Moys.* 2.77–80; 132; 150–1; Thdt., *Quaest. in Ex.* 27 (*PG* 80: 257).

59 *VC* 1.37; 2.3; 6–7; 9; 16, although other aspects begin to intrude in the last two instances.

60 *VC* 1.29 etc, cf. Exodus 13.21–2; 14.19–20; 40.36.

61 See the story of the pillar of cloud above the Tabernacle (Exodus 40.34–8), but more significantly the doublet at Joshua 3.6–4.24 in the more explicitly military context, of the campaign against Jericho, where the Ark holds back the waters of the Jordan as Moses' rod had formerly held back those of the Red Sea (Exodus 14.15–29). Joshua's subsequent vision of the armed captain of the host of the Lord before Jericho (Joshua 5.13–15) provides an equally conveniently military doublette for Moses' vision of the burning bush, a point unlikely to have escaped Eusebius.

62 On which, see below p. 120.

63 Exodus 25–31; 35.4–40.33. The preparatory vision of God shared by Moses and his many companions (Exodus 24.9–10) begs comparison with Constantine's first shared vision with his whole army (*VC* 1.28), whilst his dream parallels Moses' meeting with God on the mount (Exodus 24.15ff). The tablets of the Law are generally viewed as Old Testament types for Christ. In particular, given the *Chi-Rho* inscribed by Constantine within the wreath at the top of the cross, see Gregory of Nyssa's application of the exegesis of Matthew 5.18 ('not one jot or tittle shall disappear from the Law') as relating the vertical and horizontal lines of the cross to the cross-like shape assumed by Moses, holding the 'rod of God' during the battle against the Amalekites (Exodus 17.9–12) at Greg. Nyss., *V. Moys.* 2.150–1, with Malherbe and Ferguson 1978 ad loc., and further, Rahner 1953. If Eusebius' description of the embroidery, gold interlace and precious stones on the traditional square banner hanging from the *labarum* is at all accurate, it so directly evokes Aaron's square breastplate (Exodus 39.8–14), that one is inclined to assume the hand of a theologian in its design. To link the *Chi-Rho* on the emperor's helmet to the writing on Aaron's crown (Exodus 39.30) may be to overstate the case, but that too is not altogether impossible. It should be noted that already in the Judaic tradition we find detailed exegesis of every aspect of the tabernacle and the high priest, for example, in the case of Josephus in terms of natural science (Hanson 1959: 53–54 and n. 7).

64 *VC* 1.30, cf. Exodus 35.30–36.2.

65 *VC* 1.32, cf. Exodus 4, especially 4.15.

66 *VC* 1.33–6, cf. Exodus 5. However, this transition back from the *labarum* as Ark of the Covenant, etc. to the theme of Pharaonic sorcery in 36–7 is eased by the fact that in Chapters 32–36 God-given teaching also links to Moses' receipt of the Law and that the anecdotal account of Maxentius' tyranny lays particular

stress on his transgression of several of the commandments, particularly those regarding honouring God, adultery and murder.

67 Men. Rhet. 2.372.27. Strictly speaking, this had begun with VC 1.25, with the substantial proem provided by this new heading (as recommended by Menander, 2.37.14–20) of 26–7 which stresses divine assistance and Constantine's piety as more praiseworthy than any of the conventional ruling virtues or military advantages.

68 Despite its concern with real warfare, the brief account at Exodus 17. 8–16 is too slight and too lacking in motivation to provide much material. However, VC 2.7–9, where the emperor directs his fifty strong standard-bearers to any weak point in the battle to instantaneous effect does seem to be modelled on Moses' raising and lowering of the rod, sustained with the assistance of Aaron and Hur during Joshua's battle against the Amalekites.

69 VC 1.38–9, cf. Exodus 14–15.

70 VC 1.48.

71 VC 1.49–56. Licinius' transgressions are rather closer to those of Exodus 5 than are those of Maxentius (above, p. 117). Particularly noteworthy is the comparison between his restrictions on the movement of bishops, on synods and on individual Christians (VC 1.51–2) and Pharoah's refusal to allow the children of Israel to go three days into the desert to sacrifice (Exodus 5.1–9).

72 VC 1.57–9. For the scourge, 56.2; for the fiery dart of sickness 58.4; for a divine stroke, 59.1, all three in terms of God's vengeance.

73 VC 1.56.1,2.

74 VC 1.59.2. σκοτομήνη, moonless night, or possibly eclipse, derives from Psalm 11.2, of the state of mind of the sinful who shoot at the righteous. Significantly, the same psalm speaks (v. 1) of the righteous fleeing to the mountains, and also (v. 6) of the punishments the Lord will visit upon the wicked: snares, fire, brimstone and the tempestuous wind.

75 VC 2.11.2, cf. Exodus 9.12, etc.

76 VC 2.3.2: 4,2.

77 VC 2.12.14, cf. Exodus 33.7–9. The fact that the pillar stands above the tabernacle there reinforces the linking of the two symbols. It should be noted that the secular prescription to dwell on the emperor's prowess in battle (Men. Rhet. 2.374.4–5) is largely handled in terms of the role of the cross in battle, of Constantine's prayerfulness, and of his clemency where appropriate.

78 VC 2.18, 19,3, cf. Exodus 14.23ff.; 15 and for Maxentius earlier, VC 1.38.

79 Menander Rhetor (2.375.5–376.23) prescribes their division under temperance, justice and wisdom, laying particular stress on the last two with regard to good government and legislative activity.

80 φθόνος is not mentioned in Menander's prescription. It is, however, a constant feature in Plutarchean biography, and particularly often applied to the peacetime experiences of those formerly successful in wars. See Russell (1973) 114, 124, 127.

81 VC 3.1,1. The phrase is a fixture in martyr hagiography, where it is closely related to the envy of the devil against Job; Athanasius will

use it also at *V. Ant.* 5. At *HE* 10.8.2, Eusebius uses very similar phraseology of Licinius' change of heart towards the Christians. The spirit of envy will recur as the villain at *VC* 4.40,1, necessitating the Council of Tyre, which Eusebius glosses over even more cursorily than he does Nicaea.

82 The most substantial passage in direct speech up to this point purports to be the speech of Licinius to his close associates whilst sacrificing before battle (*VC* 2.5.2–4), but Eusebius' evidence is hearsay (*VC* 2.5.5), and the speech as a whole gives the distinct impression that it has been written up appropriately although perhaps from a genuine summary. It is notable that although he several times cites Constantine as his source for information, at no point does he put words into his mouth.

83 This is the general Suetonian practice, by contrast with Plutarch, who tends to include such material early on as part of his introductory character description. At the same time, Menander Rhetor lays great emphasis on the topic of just law-giving as fundamental to the 'deeds of peace' at 2.375.24.

84 In Eusebius' defence, it should be noted that both *bios* and funerary encomium, except in the most skilled hands, can often show a slight bittiness, a tendency to mop up small items not hitherto covered in the final section before the author turns to the deathbed and funeral sequence.

85 Admittedly, there is some resumption of narrative in the book of Numbers, but even that account of the years in the wilderness is heavily punctuated by further reports of the Lord's commands to Moses.

86 *VC* 2.20–60, cf. Exodus 20–31.

87 Eusebius' emphasis on the Easter dispute as the trigger for Nicaea is revealing. One need only contemplate how he might have written up this Council had his own creed (cf. Socrates, *HE* 1.10) gained acceptance there to suspect that possible development of the Moses *synkrisis* from its original basis in the *HE* may have already been in his mind even then. Had he won, someone else, if not Eusebius himself, might have portrayed Constantine playing Aaron to Eusebius' own Moses – note the stress on the splendour of Constantine's clothing at *VC* 3.10, and both personal and literary frustration that such was not the outcome may still colour Eusebius' eventual version.

88 *VC* 2.61–3,5, cf. Exodus 3.21–6.

89 *VC* 3.10–13.

90 *VC* 3.25–53, within which the high spots are the description of the Church of the Holy Sepulchre, doubtless drawing in some respects on Eusebius' orations and treatise at the time of its dedication (cf. *VC* 4.45.3; 46), and the tribute accorded to Helena's building activities in Bethlehem (*VC* 3), for which Constantine alone had received the credit in his earlier speech (*Tric. Or.* 9.17).

91 *VC* 4.45,3. Even if Drake 1975 is correct in arguing that the second part of the *Tric. Or.* is indeed that on the Holy Sepulchre (although I

still have lingering doubts about this), such details as Eusebius gives in the *VC* will derive from the other missing works.

92 *Hom. In Ex.* 9.3–4.

93 *V. Moys.* 2.170–83, especially 170, with *Vie de Moïse*, ed. Daniélou ad loc. Gregory refers to the columns of the tabernacle itself here (Exodus 26.21, 25, 29; 37.15; 38.20), since he goes on to mention the silver and brass columns of the court (cf. Exodus 27.10; cf. 38.10).

94 *V. Moys.* 2.184–5, with Daniélou ad loc.

95 Cyril of Jerusalem, *Catacheses* 3.5.

96 κρατήρσι, *VC* 3.38

97 This is not to underestimate the role of Makarios, Bishop of Jerusalem, in the Constantinian projects in Jerusalem, but I am far from totally convinced by the general arguments of Walker 1990 about the extent to which Eusebius as metropolitan is likely to have distanced himself from the new churches. On this particular point, see the similar suggestion for the *labarum* above, n. 63. As in the *Oration* (9.17) so also at *VC* 3.26.2; 28; 41.1, Eusebius stresses the association of all three churches, that of the Sepulchre, and those of Helena at Bethlehem and on the Mount of Olives with caves, the possibility that Eusebius may have linked the idea of the cave in some way with that of the tabernacle also deserves raising.

98 For example, Numbers 21.1–4.

99 *VC* 4.43–7. In general, the sequence, Council of Tyre, dedication of church, reflects that in Book 3, probably deliberately.

100 *V. Ant.* proem. 94.

101 It will be apparent that I accept Athanasian authorship for the *V. Ant.*

102 For example, very strikingly in his legacy of one sheepskin and his cloak to Athanasius, and of the other sheepskin to Bishop Serapion, *V. Ant.* 92. See, further, Dörries 1949: 383.

103 *V. Ant.* 81.

104 Dörries 1949 passim on the contrast between the Athanasian account and the *apophthegmata* ascribed to Antony.

105 On the underlying theme of a Christ-like life in the work, but without the narrative details, Dörries 1949: 392–6.

106 *V. Ant.* 1.

107 Ibid. 5.

108 Ibid. 8–10.

109 Ibid. 11–12.

110 Ibid. 13.

111 Ibid. 16–43.

112 Ibid. 14.

113 Ibid. 3–4.

114 Ibid. 8–14.

115 Ibid. 10, although the primary model will be the angels ministering to Christ.

116 Ibid. 46, a passage which contains a primary defence of Antony against the charge of failing to be martyred, on the grounds that God preserved him to become a teacher of others.

117 Ibid. 14.
118 Ibid. 49–50.
119 Ibid. 72–80, although parallels with Christ's refutations of the Pharisees who test him may be uppermost here.
120 *V. Ant.* 92, cf. Deuteronomy 34.6; again this episode may also have New Testament links.
121 *V. Ant.* 91–2; cf. 2 Kings 2.13.
122 For references, above, nn. 134ff.
123 *Oration* 21.29–31 (= *PG* 35: 1116–20).
124 *Oration* 43.44–51, especially 49: cf. Eph. Graec. *Enc. Bas.* 293E–F.
125 Cf. Alexandre 1984.
126 M. Harl 1967, especially 409, citing the *Commentary on Isaiah* 7 attributed to Basil, for the clearest exposition of the threefold division.
127 For two striking formulations of this in terms of educational theory, see Basil, *De adulesc.* 3 and Greg. Nyss., *V. Moys.* 116.
128 *V. Ant.* 73.
129 Greg. Naz. *Or.* 43.11–24 (= *PG* 36: 508–29).
130 Greg. Naz. *Or.* 43.72 (= *PG* 36: 593).
131 Harl 1984, cf. Greg. Nyss., *In Bas. fratr.* 125–30.
132 Greg. Nyss., *In Bas. fratr.* 109–42.
133 See above, nn. 140ff.
134 For example, *V. Macr.* 9–10.
135 Ibid. 11.
136 Ibid. 17–39, especially 18.
137 Ibid. 2.
138 Ibid. 3.
139 Ibid. 7.
140 Ibid. 31.
141 *V. Ant,* 29; cf. *V. Macr.* 18.
142 *V. Macr.* 12.
143 See most strikingly, *V. Moys.* 2.96–9.
144 Ibid. 2.116.

8

FROM HISTORY TO LEGEND
AND LEGEND TO HISTORY

The medieval and Byzantine
transformation of Constantine's *Vita*

Samuel Lieu

THE SYLVESTER LEGEND AND THE
DONATION OF CONSTANTINE

In modern Constantinian studies, the name of Aldhelm is not likely to be on everyone's lips, even at a symposium on Constantine held on British soil. This Abbot of Malmesbury (d. 709), who later became the first Bishop of Sherborne in 705, was an outstanding representative of the so-called 'Canterbury school' of Archbishop Theodorus of Tarsus (*sedit* 669–90). He was also one of the earliest known British writers to have gathered material, possibly from Continental sources, on what was then seen as an important episode in the life of Constantine. As Jane Stevenson points out later in this volume, prior to the anecdotes related by Aldhelm, knowledge in post-Roman Britain of Constantine's life-history appears to have been both meagre and superficial. The first Christian Roman emperor was, till then, mentioned mainly in missionary contexts. To cite Constantine as an example of a ruler whose fortune decidedly turned for the better after his conversion offered clear advantages to the Roman Church in its attempt to convert pagan and barbarian rulers.

Constantine's pious mother Helena was exploited by Gregory the Great in his attempt to convert rulers through the female members of the royal family. In his letter to Bertha, Queen of the Angli, whose husband King Ethelbert of Kent was not yet a Christian, the pontiff says:

And we bless the Almighty God, who has been mercifully
pleased to apportion the conversion of the nation of the
Angli as your reward. For just as God kindled the hearts
of the Romans into Christian faith through Helena of
illustrious memory, the mother of the pious Emperor
Constantine, so we trust that He works in the nation of
the Angli through the zeal of your glory.

(Gregory the Great, *Epistles* XI.35, 9–15)[1]

Such references to Constantine for missionary purposes often contain the barest of information on the life-history of the emperor.
Aldhelm, however, offers something much more substantial for
those with a biographical interest in Constantine. In his collection
of accounts of the endeavours of Christian heroes of asceticism, the
De virginitate, a long entry is devoted to Pope Sylvester (*sedit* 314–
335) and a shorter one to Constantia, the daughter of Constantine.[2] Sylvester won a place among the heroes of asceticism not
because he distinguished himself in combating desires in lonely
places but because

relying on uncontaminated chastity of body and endowed
with the abstemiousness of continual abstinence, he is said
to have gone down inside, through the hundred steps of
its den, to the lethal dragon of Rome lurking in the secret
cavern of the crypt, which, fouling the air with its poi-
sonous maw and the pestilent exhalation of its breath, was
fiercely molesting the miserable populace.

(Ald., *De virg.* 25)[3]

Sylvester was able to restrict the nefarious activities of this pri-
meval beast in perpetuity with an inextricable collar. In so doing
he also 'reformed Rome, the worshipper of deceitful idolatry, from
the fatal practice of offering victims by his evangelical declarations
and by miracles of equal luminosity.'[4] The most famous of his
miracles of course was his curing Constantine – then a persecuting
emperor (!) – of elephantiac leprosy. Sylvester further distinguished himself in dispute with twelve instructors of the Jewish
faith ('rabbis of the Pharisees') who 'savagely hurled the dire shafts
of disputation against this soldier of Christ'.[5] Furthermore, he
played a crucial role in a dream which the emperor later had
when he was at the city of Byzantium – a subject to which we

shall return when discussing the Byzantine hagiographical sources on Constantine.

Aldhelm's incidental accounts of the baptism of Constantine by Sylvester and the foundation of Constantinople were probably the most detailed then available to the British reading public and different from those used for missionary purposes. The account of the foundation of Constantinople became standard in British medieval historiography, being cited by William of Malmesbury (*c.* 1090–*c.* 1143),[6] who incidentally ascribes to Constantine the British settlement in France which the then English kings were actively defending.[7] Through William, it passed into the *Abbreviationes Chronicarum* of Radulf (Ralph) de Diceto (d. 1202).[8]

We know that Aldhelm visited Rome at least once, probably before he was made bishop. The visit is most likely to have taken place during the pontificate of Sergius (*sedit* 687–701), who, as the *Liber Pontificalis* shows, was engaged in the task of reviving or maintaining interest in Constantine.[10] There can be little doubt that Aldhelm drew from a literary rather than an oral source for his versions of the exploits of Sylvester which were 'bruited through all the corners of the world'.[11] There are strong verbal resemblances between both Aldhelm's prose and poetic versions and a text known as the *Vita* (or *Actus*) *Sylvestri*, first critically studied in modern times by Boninus Mombritius in 1479.[12] In this we are told that Constantine, although he had been led to victory by the sign of the Cross, was cajoled by his wife Maximiana, the daughter of Diocletian (*sic*), to instigate a persecution of the Christians. (Constantine's wife after 307 was of course Flavia Maxima Fausta, the younger daughter of Maximianus Herculius.) Sylvester betook himself to a place called Serapte (which was afterwards identified with Soracte). The persecutor was soon afflicted by elephantiac leprosy and his pagan priests advised bathing in a pool of blood of infants, i.e., a pagan caricature of Christian baptism with overtones of the Mithraic *taurobolium*. Children were duly rounded up, but Constantine, troubled by their wailing, relented and sent them home. That same night the saints Peter and Paul appeared to him like a Christian version of the Dioscuri, promising as recompense for his humane gesture cure from his hideous illness, if he would seek out Sylvester and follow his commands. When summoned to the emperor's presence, Sylvester showed him images of Peter and Paul and these were duly recognised by Constantine as those who had appeared to him. He was then given Christian instruction and after a solemn fast he was baptised in the Lateran palace. A bright light was seen when he entered the water and he was instantly healed. This was followed by a flood of legislation against paganism and in favour of Christianity. A week after his baptism, Constantine also began the construction of a church in the Lateran palace. Helena, his mother, then living in Bithynia, wrote approvingly of his conversion from paganism but urged him to adopt Judaism instead. To satisfy her, a public disputation between twelve rabbis and Pope Sylvester took place on 13 August 315 before the emperor and his mother, with two pagans as judges. The high point of the debate was when the rabbis caused a bull to die by whispering the name Jehovah into its ear, but Sylvester was able to restore it to life by the uttering the name of Jesus Christ. Helena was so astonished by this that she instantly accepted the Christian faith. The account of the debate in the V. *Sylv.* is replete with quotations from the Old Testament, and Sylvester upheld the doctrines of the Trinity and the Incarnation against not so much the Jewish but the Monothelite critic. [13]

The legend of Constantine's baptism and cure from leprosy by Sylvester appears to have been well developed by the fifth century. The work became so popular in the Middle Ages that the large number of versions and of manuscripts has made it difficult to reconstruct an *Ur*-Text. At least two main versions (A and B) have circulated since the end of the fifth century. A – the longer version, in two books – was the most popular version in the West while B – the shorter version – enjoyed a wide circulation in the East. [14] Both were originally written in Latin although they may have contained material from oriental sources. B is likely to be a later derivative of A as it contains theological statements in the debate between Constantine and the Jews which are clearly post-Chalcedonian. [15] The pontificate of Caelestinus I (*sedit* 422–32) is a possible date for its developing into the form in which it would become widely diffused. Caelestinus was most interested in Sylvester; since he it was who decorated the Sylvester basilica in the Via Salaria with mural paintings, and was buried there. The legend was sufficiently developed for it to be summarised in the entry on Sylvester in the *Liber Pontificalis*:

He (*sc.* Sylvester) was Bishop in the time of Constantine and Volusianus from 1 February to 1 January in the consulship of Constantius and Volusianus. He was in exile on Mount Seracte <troubled by Constantine's persecution>;

afterwards he returned in glory and baptized the emperor
Constantine, whom the Lord cured from leprosy <by
baptism>, and from whose persecution he is known to
have previously fled into exile.

(*Liber Pontificalis* 34.1–2)[16]

In the image of Constantine presented by the *V. Sylv.* we can see
clearly reflected the Christianisation of the Roman idea of
emperor.[17] The image first and foremost had to be purged of
any hint of pagan criticism of the emperor. It is clear that criticism of Constantine was still being voiced in the fourth and early
fifth centuries. The best known example of this is the pagan (and
senatorial?)[18] legend hinted at by Julian and recounted by Eunapius (as preserved by Zosimus) that Constantine became a Christian because only Christianity could offer forgiveness to the
murderer of a wife and son.[19] But even in older Christian historiography the portrayal of the emperor was not without shadow.
The end of the reign offered serious cause for embarrassment to
the orthodox, as witnessed by Constantine's treatment of Athanasius and his death-bed baptism by the Arian Bishop Eusebius of
Nicomedia. Neither of these potential causes of future polemics
was mentioned by Eusebius of Caesarea in his panegyrical obituary
of Constantine[20] – a work which would remain as the only major
contemporary biographical account of the emperor for the Greek
East. The name of the priest responsible was given only by
Jerome, who did this in his continuation of Eusebius' chronicle.[21]
The Arian church historian Philostorgius (*c.* 425–33) named
Eusebius of Nicomedia as the person to whom Constantine
entrusted his testament.[22] On the other hand, Rufinus of Aquileia
(d. 410) completely left out the baptism of Constantine from his
continuation of Eusebius' church history. In this he probably
followed his source – the Greek continuation of Gelasius of
Caesarea. Orosius makes no mention of it either in his monumental *Historia contra paganos*. Eusebius' main continuators in Greek:
Socrates (*c.* 439), Sozomen (*c.* 443–50) and Theodoret (after 425)
all give accounts of the baptism in Nicomedia but without naming the initiating priest.[23] It is not impossible that by then the
heretical Bishop of Nicomedia had already been replaced in the
legend of the discovery of the true Cross by Eusebius of Rome as
attested in the Byzantine *visio Constantini*.[24] Since Eusebius of
Nicomedia later became Bishop of Constantinople, the New
Rome, it would have only been a short mental leap to replace

Eusebius of Nicomedia with Eusebius of Rome. When it was found that the pontificate of Eusebius (*sedit* 18 April 308, exiled September 30) did not fit the bill as he was pope in the time of Constantine's father,[25] he was substituted by Sylvester the confessor–pope.[26] By the time of the church historian Gelasius of Caesarea, it appears that the readers were prepared to accept that Constantine had been baptised by an orthodox priest and that his baptism was delayed because he had earnestly desired to be baptised in the waters of Jordan.[27] The need to purge the memory of Constantine of any taint of Arianism is found in a hymn of Severus, the Monophysite Bishop of Antioch, surviving in the Syriac translation of Paul of Edessa. Here Constantine is depicted as a champion of orthodoxy:

> Not from men nor through man came the calling to the elect Constantine, the believing king, but through Jesus Christ, even as to that great apostle Paul. For, having clearly seen in the sky the resplendent sign consisting of the form of the Cross, he believed that he who is God from the beginning, the Word of the Father, became flesh for our sake without being changed, and became truly man; and accordingly the king, having rejoiced in thy strength, and having greatly exulted in thy salvation, as the great prophet David sings, called and gathered together to himself the preachers of the orthodox faith from the four quarters, and expelled from the church the madness of Arius, who presumed to call the Word who is before the ages a creature; and further also he checked beforehand and annihilated the impiety of those who divide Emmanuel into two natures, in that he himself recognises him who became incarnate, who was crucified and suffered and died in the flesh for our salvation, to be one; and he further rebuilt and restored the holy churches; who is the beginning of all the believing kings who were after him; of whom David sings with us, 'The rulers of the peoples have been gathered together with the God of Abraham'. Praise to thee!
>
> (Severus of Antioch, *Hymns* 200-1-II)[28]

Constantine's commitment to the Arian cause towards the end of his life was clearly a major embarrassment for early medieval historians – both in the East and West. Take, for example, the

Venerable Bede (c. 673–735), the so-called 'Father of English History', who devoted far less space to the reign of the first Christian emperor in his *Historia ecclesiastica gentis Anglorum* than to Diocletian or Arcadius or Honorius. The reason must have been the implied association between Constantine and the heresy which came to divide the Church during his reign:

> At this time, Constantius died in Britain, a man of great clemency and courtesy, who had governed Gaul and Spain while Diocletian was alive. He left a son Constantine, who was made emperor of Gaul, being the child of his concubine Helena. Eutropius writes that Constantine was created emperor in Britain and succeeded to his father's kingdom. In his time arose the Arian heresy which was exposed and condemned by the Council of Nicaea. Nevertheless, the deadly poison of its evil doctrine, as has been said, tainted the churches of the whole world, including those of our own islands.
>
> (Bede, *HE* 1.8)

The brevity of the coverage and its use of a pagan source, Eutropius,[29] is particularly surprising when one considers the strong links between Britain and the Constantinian dynasty. Constantine himself had presented Britain as the starting-point of God's plan of salvation for him in an autobiographical statement found on a papyrus, now in the British Museum:

> It was He [i.e. the Christian God] who sought out my service, and judged it fitting for the achievement of His own purpose. Starting from the British Sea and the lands where the sun is ordained to set, He repulsed and scattered by his divine might the encompassing powers of evil, to the end that the human race might be recalled to the worship of the supreme law, schooled by my helping hand, and that the most blessed faith might be increased with the Almighty as Guide.
>
> (P. Lond. III 878 *descr.*, col. ii, 21–26)[30]

This is echoed in Eus., *VC* 2.28 where He (i.e. God) is sometimes interchanged with 'I' (i.e. Constantine).

The popularity of the *V. Sylv.* among Christians at Rome was acknowledged in the *Gelasian Decretals* (compiled early sixth

142

century)[31] but the work itself may have been in circulation as early as the late fourth century. Another early mention of the legend is found in the (Pseudo) *Gesta Liberii* in which Pope Liberius (*sedit* 17 May 352–24 September 366) is said to have countered those who derided the orthodoxy of Constantine with the account of the emperor's baptism in the name of the Trinity by Sylvester. The author of the *Gesta Liberii* also claims to have found the account in an 'old work' in order to give 'age' to the story.[32] Rome is still generally regarded as the document's most likely place of origin, since it shows considerable topographical knowledge of the city; however, the theme of a royal figure afflicted by a dreadful illness which could only be cured through the intercession of a holy man has an obvious parallel with the famous Abgar legend of Edessa.[33] Coincidentally, the earliest attested testimony in the East to the theme of Constantine being converted to Christianity through a miraculous cure is found in a homily of the Syrian poet, Jacob of Sarug (Batna), a small town near Edessa. Although Sylvester was not referred to by name in the homily, Constantine's miraculous cure from a fearful illness before (*not* after) his baptism as celebrated in one of his homilies (composed before 521) is clearly based on the same tradition as the Sylvester legend.[34] Some details of the latter were substituted with oriental features – it was Babylonian[35] or Chaldaean magicians who advised Constantine to bathe in the blood of children. Another detail is the placing of Constantine's baptism in the Lateran under the guise of Mount Sinai. However, even this metaphor was likely to have originated in Rome and not in Syria; and as Anna Wilson has already pointed out in this volume, it may well have sprung from the Eusebian image of Constantine which makes Moses an important member of the emperor's spiritual ancestry. Writing some time after 574, John Malalas was one of the first Byzantine historians to mention Constantine's baptism by Sylvester, but not his cure from leprosy.[36] Had the legend been known earlier, the orthodox-minded church historians like Gelasius of Cyzicus, Sozomen and Theodoret were likely to have used it, at least as an alternative to the death-bed baptism by an Arian bishop. But although we possess a number of versions of the *V. Sylv.* in Greek and Syriac, they all bear such strong similarity to the Latin version that they must be considered as derivative.[37] Theophanes, writing after 814, states categorically that Constantine was baptised by Sylvester as the baptistery in which the rite took place at Rome was preserved to his time.[38] In no uncertain

terms, he also refutes any suggestion that Constantine was baptised by an Arian while on his way East to be baptised in the
Jordan. How could Constantine have sat with the bishops and
celebrated communion with them at Nicaea if he was not already a
baptised Christian?[39] An Armenian version of the *V. Sylv.* circulated with the *Ecclesiastical History* of Socrates in the same language, which was used by (Pseudo-) Moses Khorenats'i.[40]

A hagiographical motif as alien to Eusebius' *VC* as Constantine
being afflicted by leprosy is most likely to have developed into a
full-blown legend in lands which were completely unacquainted
with that particular work of Eusebius. The version of *V. Sylv.*
presented by Mombritius says that the account of the exploits of
the pope was taken from the acts of the bishops of the principal
sees which, together with many acts of martyrs, were written by
Eusebius of Caesarea but not included in his Church History.[41]
Such a claim to the use of a Greek source would have been
impossible to verify in the Early Middle Ages, given the shortage
of manuscripts of the works of Eusebius in the West other than
those sections of his *Ecclesiastical History* which were available in
the Latin translation of Rufinus. The legend was known in Constantinople by the early sixth century. It was celebrated in a
mosaic in the church of Hagios Polyeuktos built by Anicia Juliana
between 512 and 527. A description of the mosaic in the *Palatine
Anthology* 1.10 42–47 mentions Constantine finding the 'light of
Trinity'- hardly an Arian formula – and the purification of his
limbs, which must be a reference to his miraculous cleansing from
leprosy.[42]

The church historians' belief in the legend of Constantine's
baptism by an orthodox pontiff at the very beginning rather
than the end of his reign presented the medieval historian with
an awkward chronological problem. Though the pontificate of
Sylvester is a long one (traditionally 31 January 314–31 December
355), it was not long enough to cover the period immediately
after the Battle of Milvian Bridge (28 October 312). The generally
held belief that Constantine gave the Lateran Palace to Sylvester as
his residence, and the fact that the Rome Synod of 313 on the
Donatist Schism was held in the Lateran Palace (then the house of
Fausta)[43] meant that the pontificate of Sylvester had to begin
earlier. It was pre-dated to 310 (!) in the *Chronicon* of Jerome[44]
which would allow the mythographer sufficient space to insert
Constantine's baptism into his stay in Rome, which historically
did not last even a year.[45]

The author of the *Liber Pontificalis* dates the beginning of the pontificate to the consulships of Constantius (*sic*) and Volusianus, which has a semblance of accuracy, as C. Ceionius Rufius Volusianus was Consul in 314, but this was his second consulship. He had been consul earlier in 311 at Rome with Aradius Rufinus.[46] As the *Liber Pontificalis* contains a brief account of the baptism of Constantine by Sylvester, the date it gives for the beginning of his pontificate is probably deliberately ambiguous. For the papacy, the image of Sylvester as a confessor was also vital counter-propaganda to the allegation made by the Donatists that Pope Miltiades (*sedit* 2 July 311–10 January 314), an African, was a *traditor*, with suspicion also later being cast on Marcellus and Sylvester.[47] This chronological shift is necessary given Sylvester's prominence as confessor in the Great Persecution, for which he would enjoy cultic veneration. The *V. Sylv.* takes great pains to stress the hospitality he offered, at considerable personal risk, to Timothy who was fleeing persecution from Antioch, and also the fact that his self-imposed exile at 'Syraptis' was for devotion in preparation for martyrdom rather than an attempt to escape the persecutions.[48] Once the starting date of his pontificate had been extended, no one would have known that this was in the time before his elevation to Bishop of Rome, and the Confessor–Pope will have been seen in Sylvester the Confessor. From this, the natural conclusion must be drawn that Sylvester had led the Roman Church before Constantine's defeat of Maxentius. The *V. Sylv.* goes one step further along the line of chronological inexactitude in placing the story of the aborted 'massacre of the innocents' after Constantine had acquired sole rule, after his second defeat of Licinius.[49] However, as long as the story of Constantine's baptism and cure by Sylvester were told in the context of the exploits of Sylvester rather than biographies of Constantine, what appear now as glaring chronological errors in relation to known political events of the reign would not have been at all obvious to the medieval reader.

At the turn of the ninth century,[50] the main theme of the *V. Sylv.* was put to good use in what must be regarded as one of the most controversial medieval forgeries with which the name of Constantine was to be associated. This *Constitutum Constantini*, or *Donation of Constantine* as it is more commonly known, is in the form of an official edict of the emperor issued shortly after his baptism. Its official tone is set by a list of the emperor's victory titles, which may amuse more than one modern specialist of imperial titulature:

> Imperator Caesar Flavius Constantinus in Christo Jesu, uno ex eadem sancta Trinitate salvatore domino Deo nostro, fidelis mansuetus, maximus, beneficus, Alamannicus, Gothicus, Sarmaticus, Germanicus, Britannicus, Hunicus, pius, felix, victor ac triumphator, semper augustus.
> (*Exemplar Constituti Domini Constantini Imperatoris* 1)[51]

The most important and controversial part of the document, however, is the decision by Constantine to grant special status to the See of Rome in gratitude for his life-saving baptism. In the emperor's own words:

> And so, on the first day after receiving the mystery of the holy baptism, and after the cure of my body from the squalor of leprosy, I acknowledged that there was no other God save the Father and the Son and the Holy Spirit, as preached by the most blessed Sylvester the pope; a trinity in one, a unity in three. [Editor's note: Constantine clearly had no need for an ecumenical council to meet in Nicaea a dozen or so years later to help him to formulate his personal Christology.] For all the gods of the pagans, whom I have worshipped up to this time, are proved to be demons, works made by the hands of men. For that venerable father Sylvester told us most clearly how much power in Heaven and on earth He, our Saviour, conferred on his apostle St Peter, when finding him faithful after questioning him He said: 'You are Peter, and upon this rock shall I build My Church, and the gates of hell shall not prevail against it.' Take heed all you powerful men, and incline the ear of your hearts to that which the good Lord and Master added, saying to His disciple: 'and I will give you the keys of the Kingdom of Heaven; whatever you bind on earth will be bound also in Heaven, and whatever you set free on earth will also be set free in Heaven'. This is most amazing and glorious, that what is bound or freed on earth is bound or freed also in Heaven.
>
> And when I perceived all this as the blessed Sylvester was preaching, I also learned that by the kindness of St Peter himself I had been entirely restored to health: I –

together with all our satraps and the whole senate and the
nobles and all the Roman people, who are subject to the
glory of our empire – considered it advisable that as on
earth Peter is seen to have been appointed representative
of the Son of God, so too the pontiffs, who fulfil the role
of that same chief of the Apostles, should obtain from us
and our empire the power of supremacy greater than that
which the earthly clemency of our imperial serenity is
seen to have been granted; we choose the same chief of
the Apostles, or his representatives, to be our constant
intercessors before God. And, just like our earthly imperial power, we have decreed that his holy Roman church
shall be honoured with veneration; and that, more than
our empire and our earthly throne, the most sacred seat of
St Peter shall be gloriously exalted; we grant to it power
and the dignity of glory, and the vigour and honour of
the empire.

And we ordain and decree that it shall have supremacy
as well over the four chief seats of Antioch, Alexandria,
Constantinople and Jerusalem, as over all the churches of
God in the whole world. And he who for the time being
shall be pontiff of that holy Roman church shall be more
exalted than, and chief over, all the priests of the whole
world; and, according to his judgment, everything shall
be administered which is to be provided for the service of
God or the stability of the faith of the Christians.
(*Exemplar Constituti Domini Constantini Imperatoris* 11–12)[52]

Though Rome is seen as a likely place of origin for the forgery
because its 'historical' sections are clearly drawn from the *V.
Sylv.*,[53] it was first cited by scholars outside Italy such as Ado
of Vienne, Hincmar of Reims and Aeneas of Paris who were all
writing in the Frankish Empire. As with the *V. Sylv.*, its falsity
could easily be exposed by those determined to do so by reference
to the *Chronicon* of Jerome or the *Historia Tripartita* of Cassiodorus,
both of which record the death-bed baptism of the emperor and
were readily available to scholars of the Middle Ages. In fact, the
authenticity of the *Constitutum* was challenged by Wetzel, a member of the party of Arnold of Brescia, as early as 1152 precisely on
those grounds.[54] Later, Otto III, in a grant to Sylvester II, had
stigmatised the *Constitutum* as a forgery.[55] That its genuineness
remained unchallenged for so long was indeed remarkable. The

answer is a complex one. In the Middle Ages, the fact that the majority of main and earlier sources did not mention a particular incident was no grounds for discounting the authenticity of an account or document. Morever, the purpose of the forgery, aimed no doubt at strengthening the position of the papacy *vis à vis* temporal powers, was not likely to be challenged by the Roman Church in the West which had the most to gain from it and also possessed the main research facilities for its exposure. The *Donatio* or *Constitutum Constantini* was adopted into the Pseudo-*Isidorean Decretals* when the latter was compiled in the middle of the ninth century (*c.* 847–53)[56] and was incorporated, two centuries later, into Gratian's *Decretum* by one of his pupils.[57] It proved useful to enemies of the papacy because the purport of the document could be understood to mean that the Pope's temporal powers, and especially his sovereignty over the lands under his direct rule in Italy, were derived from men and not from God. The earliest certain appeal to it as a source of legal power was made by Pope Leo X in the letter *In terra pax* (2 September 1053) to Michael Cerularius, then patriarch of Constantinople.[58] From then on it was much cited in disputes involving papal claims and was used by both papal parties for that purpose in the Avignon Schism. Surprising though it may seem at first sight, the Byzantine Church also came to accept its authority. Its exaltation of the Bishop of Rome was more than counter-balanced in the eyes of the Eastern churchmen by the fact that the second ecumenical council granted the Bishop of Constantinople privileges similar to those enjoyed by the Bishop of Rome. Thus they were not averse to increasing the latter. The famous Byzantine canonist Theodore Balsamon (*c.* 1140–after 1195) included it in his major collection of the canon laws of the East and his example was followed by Matthew Blastares (fl. 1335) of Thessalonica who composed an alphabetical handbook of canon law as well as treatises against the Latins (i.e. Catholics) and Jews. We have to wait until the Renaissance before we find systematic attacks on the authenticity of the *Donatio* led by such outstanding scholars as Lorenzo Valla (*c.* 1406–57),[59] Nicholas of Cusa (1401–64) and Reginald Pecocke (*c.* 1393–1461), the Bishop of Chichester. By the time of Alexander VI (*sedit* 1492–1503), the *Donatio* had become a joke in many quarters. A story runs that when that pope asked for a copy of the grant on the basis of which Venice claimed control of the Adriatic, the Venetian Girolamo Donato replied that he would find it written on the back of the *Donatio*

Constantini. Valla's treatise was secretly published and circulated by Ulrich von Hutten in Germany in 1517. Among its first, avid readers was, of course, Martin Luther. Writing to one of his pupils shortly after his famous debate with Eck at Leipzig, Luther said:

> I have at hand Lorenzo Valla's proof that the Donation of Constantine is a forgery. Good heavens! what darkness and wickedness is at Rome. You wonder at the judgement of God that such unauthentic crass, impudent lies not only lived, but were incorporated in the canon law, (and that no degree of horror might be wanting) that they became articles of faith. I am in such a fit that I scarcely doubt that the Pope is Antichrist expected by the world, so closely do their acts, lives, sayings and laws agree.
>
> (Luther, *ep.* 24 February 1520)[60]

A LATE MEDIEVAL CONSTANTINE ROMANCE

Without a Latin version of Eusebius' *VC*, the medieval West possessed in effect no major biographical source on Constantine beyond the various versions of the *V. Sylv.* and the role he played in ecclesiastical politics as recounted in the *Historia Tripartita*. Though legends on Helena abound, there was no full-scale biography of her in Latin comparable to those of her son in Greek.[61] Nor did Constantine fare better in hagiographical treatment in the West as the only substantial 'biography' of Constantine which was originally composed in Latin is a romance, published by Edward Heydenreich, a Gymnasialprofessor from Schneeberg, from a fourteenth-century manuscript.[62] In this we are told that Helena was a Christian pilgrim from Trier[63] who came to Rome to visit the churches of Peter and Paul when Constantius was emperor. The latter fell in love with her after catching a glimpse of her on a bridge over the Tiber. He then had the hostel in which she was staying watched, and bribed the warden to accuse her of theft so that she could not return to her native city with her companions. He then entered her room in the hostel and raped her, purely for self-gratification. After he had thus satisfied his lust, Constantius was surprised to discover that Helena did not rejoice in what he had done to her, instead bursting into tears. He learned then that she was a Christian and because he was a pagan, he left her two valuable gifts – a shoulder ornament then worn only by emperors and a ring. Helena did not return to Trier, but settled instead in Rome and told everyone there that the father of the child which she subsequently bore had died. Constantine grew under his mother's tutelage into a handsome young man with strong moral principles. Later, hostilities broke out between the King of Rome (i.e. Constantius) and the King of Constantinople (i.e. of the Greeks: *imperator Constantinopolitanus seu Graecorum*), who is unnamed. At that time there lived in Rome two merchants who enjoyed the exclusive right to trade between the two empires. They saw Constantine, then about 10 years old, and conceived a plan to kidnap the child, rear him and pass him off as a Roman prince to the King of the Greeks who had no son. Thus they presented the child before the King of the Greeks with the message that the King of the Romans had requested a marriage alliance with him. Not suspecting any ruse, the King of the Greeks duly sent them back with a ship laden with dowry. On the return journey, Constantine and the Greek princess were dumped on a desert island while the merchants went off with most of the rich presents. The couple were forced to sustain themselves by eating wild fruit and drinking sea water – a strong indication that the story originated somewhere in the heart of Europe. They were subsequently rescued by sailors and reunited joyously with Helena. The latter then used the gifts the princess had hidden to open an inn and thus became a *stabularia* – the profession with which Helena was traditionally associated.[64] Later, Constantius chanced upon his son who was distinguishing himself in tournaments, and was struck by his physical resemblance to him. He could not believe that he was someone without wealth and connection and therefore summoned his mother who duly produced the ring from the occasion of their union. Constantius was overjoyed, and hearing the story of the conspiracy of the merchants, had them executed and their property given to Constantine. The latter was proclaimed heir apparent and, as the Greek King did not have a son, Constantine eventually became emperor by treaty of both halves of the Empire and was baptised by Sylvester.[65]

The abduction theme in the romance closely resembles medieval tales about a legendary Kaiser Manfred, who as a young man also fell victim to unscrupulous merchants and was rescued by pirates.[66] Such tales of course have an existence of their own in which the use of historical personages as heroes is almost accidental.

But in this story it is worth noting how a number of features of the Greek *vitae* of Constantine such as the royal gift and the recognition theme have found their way to the Latin West from Byzantine *vitae*.[67] The lack of a Latin translation of Eus., *VC* prior to 1544 certainly gave free rein to fantasy in the Latin West over historico-biographical details. Even the most legendary of the Byzantine *vitae*, the so-called 'Halkin-*Vita*' (*BHG* 365n, see below) follows the traditional historical framework of the reign as laid down by Eusebius and the other Church historians. The purely fantastic nature of the 'Heydenreich-*Vita*', with its highly derogatory representation of Constantius, belongs to almost another literary genre.

THE MAIN BYZANTINE *VITAE* OF CONSTANTINE

To return to Aldhelm: in both his versions of the exploits of Sylvester, he also narrates the part the Bishop of Rome played in the foundation of the 'New Rome'. We are told that when Constantine was in Byzantium, given over to tiredness, he 'paid his debt to nature' by falling asleep. There then appeared to him the vision of a very decrepit woman, and at the command of Sylvester he engaged in prayer. The old woman then arose and became a beautiful young lady 'blushing with the glowing flower of exquisite youth'. The emperor covered her with his cloak and placed a diadem adorned with burnished gold and precious stones on her head. Helena, his mother, said to him the prophetic words: 'she shall be yours and shall not die except at the end of the world'. In a second dream which took place a week or so later, Sylvester appeared to him and explained that the old woman was the city of Byzantium, decrepit and in ruins from her various wars. But Constantine was to mount the horse on which at Rome he had ridden to the shrines of the apostles and martyrs in his white baptismal robes, and hold the *labarum* with the sign of Christ in his right hand. He was then to let the horse make its path and drag the shaft of the spear along the ground so as to make a furrow. Along this the walls of the new city were to be built, resuscitating the old city where he would build new shrines to the apostles, and which his sons would rule forever. Once awake, Constantine sought out Sisinnius, the Bishop of the city of Byzantium, and after recounting the vision to him and making offerings, he did exactly as instructed in his dream. The city which he thus refounded bears his name to Aldhelm's day (*civitas Constantini*) and in the Greek language Constantinopolis. Aldhelm of course never lived to see the fall of Constantine's city to the armies of the fourth crusade in 1203 or her famous defences crumbling under the artillery fire of Mehmet II in 1453. One interesting observation made by Vacher Burch on this text (in his remarkable but now hard-to-obtain work *Myth and Constantine the Great*), is the almost farcical comment made by the Latin author on the name of Constantine's city: *Appellata est ciuitas Constantini, quod greco sermone Kaide, et quod Latine interpretatur Constantinopolis usque hodiernum diem.*

Aldhelm, whose training at the 'School of Canterbury' under Theodore of Tarsus may have included Greek, apparently saw through the error by the 'author' of the *V. Sylv.* in composing the Greek name of Constantinople from the conjunctional link in the Greek sentence about the city's name, that is καὶ δή, upon which the compiler of his source has exercised his imagination, for Aldhelm simply says: *Appellata est ciuitas Constantini, quod greco sermone interpretatur Constantinopolis (De virg. 25).*

Burch has surmised that the *V. Sylv.* circulated in Greek as well as in Latin even though its western origin cannot be denied. Burch's monograph was published by Oxford University Press in 1927, by which time a number of Greek lives of Constantine composed mainly between the ninth and eleventh centuries had already been identified and published by continental scholars; yet these seem to have been unknown to Burch. As Canon Theologian of Liverpool Cathedral, he probably had little access to highly specialised journals published in Italy, Greece or Germany. The number of these Byzantine Greek *vitae* on Constantine unearthed from major monastic libraries has since then steadily increased, which is hardly surprising given the importance of Constantine and Helena as role models for later Byzantine emperors and empresses.[68] Constantine was commemorated as an *isapostolos*[69] or the thirteenth apostle whose joint feast-day with his mother Helena was (and still is) celebrated on 21 May. The cult of the saints in Byzantium demanded that the saint's ascetical achievements be celebrated in hagiography and summarised in *menologia*, collections of saints' or martyrs' lives arranged according to the date of their festival. Of the 35 or so *vitae* listed under Constantinus in *BHG*, the best-known ones were compiled between the ninth and the tenth centuries, and are commonly referred to by the names of their modern editors. For the dating of the main Greek *vitae* I have followed the generally accepted scheme of Winkelmann, which is summarised below:[70]

1 *BHG* 365z, 366 and 366a. (NB: these three texts are not listed in *BHG*.) This epitome of a *vita* is found in slightly variant forms in two partial and one full *menologion* of the eighth and ninth centuries.[71] It contains a number of features to be found in later and fuller *vitae*. The lack of any mention of the (legendary) baptism of Constantine at Rome by Pope Sylvester in the three extant versions which occurs in nearly all later *vitae* suggests a pre-sixth century date. It was used as a source by the compiler of the 'Guidi-*Vita*'. The excessive veneration of the Cross, which is so evident in the 'Guidi-*Vita*' and has led Kazhdan to suggest that the Byzantine *vitae* of Constantine arose in the Iconoclastic period because of the veneration of the Cross by the Iconoclasts,[72] is totally absent from this short 'proto-*vita*'.[73]

2 *BHG* 364 = The 'Guidi-*Vita*'.[74] With more than forty extant manuscripts of its two versions (one eleventh- and one twelfth-century), this is by far the most popular of the 'Pre-Metaphrastic' Byzantine lives of Constantine. Internal evidence and its apparent use of the *Chronicle* of Theophanes (completed *c.* 820) suggest a mid- to late ninth-century date[75] but it is possible that the long excursus on the building work of Helena in Palestine was a tenth- or even eleventh-century addition.[76]

3 *BHG* 365 = The 'Opitz-*Vita*'. The lives of Constantine and Helena are surprisingly omitted from the monumental hagiographical compilation of Symeon Metaphrastes completed at the end of the tenth century. However, other menologists did not make the same omission and self-standing *vitae* of Constantine also continued to be composed. The earliest of the post-Metaphrastic *vitae* of Constantine was one which was first edited by Pio Franchi de' Cavalieri[77] from MS Cod. Angelicus gr. 22 (tenth to eleventh century) foll. 1–54 in the Vatican, and re-edited with a more detailed historical commentary by H.-G. Opitz.[78] The text is acephalous and begins with Constantine's activities in Rome after his victory over Maxentius. Additional sections from its lost beginning which are likely to have been derived from the lost Arian church historian Philostorgius have been supplied by Bidez from MS Cod. Sabbaiticus gr. 366 (thirteenth century) foll. 9–22.[79] Further fragments from the lost beginning were supplied from the same Palestinian manuscript by Halkin together with the principal variants between the two manuscripts.[80] The work is

dated to between the end of the ninth and the eleventh century, and is characterised by its extensive use of Late Antique sources such as Eusebius, Socrates Scholasticus, Theodoret, Philostorgius, Georgius Monachus and even the pagan historian Zosimus (for the Battle of Milvian Bridge and the deaths of Fausta and Crispus).

4 *BHG* 365n = The 'Halkin (or Patmos)-*Vita*'. Edited by F. Halkin from MS Cod. Patm. gr. 179 (twelfth/thirteenth century) foll. 4b–25b,[81] it is the work of a monk from Berrhoea in the neighbourhood of Thessalonica and contains a number of fascinating local details as well as some geographical howlers. The style of the work is crude and it borrows material from the *Pass. Eusign.*, but it also contains much material not found in other Greek *vitae*.[82]

5 *BHG* 363 = The 'Gedeon-*Vita*'. This was edited by M. I. Gedeon from MS Cod. Kultumus. 23 (Lambros. 3092) (eleventh to twelfth century) foll. 286b–299b.[83] It is the oldest example of a group of texts known as the 'Imperial Menologion B' containing *vitae* which are not independent new works but are 'metaphrased' versions of older works. This is a highly mechanical compilation of material from earlier sources (especially *BHG* 364) and Eus., *VC*.[84]

6 *BHG* 362 = Life of Constantine Bishop Ignatius of Selymbria. The first of the many Byzantine lives of Constantine to be made available to modern scholars is also one of the last Byzantine *vitae* of Constantine to be compiled. The MS Cod. Ottob. gr. 441 which contains a version of it and no other hagiographical work, can be dated to 1481.[85] Ignatius' real name was John Chortasmenos, a man of letters and theologian who was born *c*. 1370 and held the office of notary in the patriarchal chancery till *c*. 1415. At an unknown date he became the monk (and then hieromonk) Ignatius and, by 1431, metropolitan of Selymbria, a town in Thrace.[86]

Besides these full-length hagiographies, much similar material can also be found in accounts of the discovery of the True Cross[87] and in the lives of saints, bishops and martyrs of this period as well as of those who were later *martyres sub Juliano*.[88]

From the historical-critical point of view, the Byzantine hagiographer was confronted with a major problem of sources in compiling any form of hagiographical commemoration of Constantine. The three sources on the reign most used by modern scholars (Lact., *De mort.*; Zos.; Eus., *VC*) would not have been the first port of call for the Byzantines. Lactantius' work was never translated into Greek and because of its early date (completed before

154

316), the author's attitude towards Constantine was probably regarded as being still too wary for his work to exert a meaningful influence on the development of hagiography both in Byzantium and the medieval West. Moreover, the work gives no detailed treatment on the period of Constantine's sole rule, especially of his attempt to establish Christianity at the expense of paganism.[89] Zosimus would have been ruled out on the grounds of his being a pagan and a polemicist against Christianity, but his work was used by at least one Byzantine hagiographer – the author of the so-called 'Opitz-*Vita*', for the account of the Battle of Milvian Bridge and for the death of Crispus. The *Breviarium* of Eutropius was the one fourth-century Latin source which was widely in use. It was translated into Greek *c.* 390 (by Paenius or Paianios)[90] and was the main source for the period for John of Antioch.[91] But Eutropius' brevity and his ambivalent attitude to Constantine's religious innovations reduced his value to the Byzantine hagiographer, except for his account of the rise of the Emperor. One would expect the panegyrical *VC* of Eusebius to be the model of Byzantine hagiographies, but there are two reasons why this was not the case. First, it was considered suspect in the Greek East (with the exception of Palestine–Syria) owing to the uncertainty over its author's loyalty to the Christian faith during the Diocletianic persecutions,[92] and the equivocal role he played in the Arian controversy.[93] This may explain why the work was utilised by Libanius whose *Or.* 59 on Constantius and Constans was delivered in Nicomedia and is a main and still largely unique source of information on the last years of the reign of Constantine.[94] The work was absent, therefore, from most Greek liturgical and hagiographical collections, though it was known and used by some later hagiographers and historians when the threat of an Arian takeover of the Byzantine church was remote. The fact that the *VC* was little read in the fourth century may explain John Chrysostom's lament that by his time (i.e. the end of the fourth century) the greater part of the emperor's deeds were already forgotten,[95] and Chrysostom's evidence is supported by other sources testifying to an early confusion between the various members of the Constantinian dynasty with similar sounding names. The difficult style of the *VC* certainly did not help the diffusion of the work in the Latin West, and there is no known Latin translation of it prior to the Renaissance.

The Greek *vitae* of Constantine follow a much more traditionally biographical format than the *VC*. They contain accounts of the

SAMUEL LIEU

parentage and birth of Constantine as well as his upbringing and exploits at the court of Galerius. There follows an account of his flight to rejoin his father, his war against the barbarians and Maxentius, his vision (or often visions) of the True Cross, his baptism in Rome, his military exploits especially against Persia – the other great and more importantly non-Christian power (a topic to which I shall return) – his 'crusade' against Licinius, his founding of the new capital on the site of former Byzantium, the discovery of the True Cross by Helena and her acts of philanthropy, his part in the formulation of an orthodox formula at the Council of Nicaea, and finally his death. Unsurprisingly, Constantine's attempt to arbitrate between the Catholics and the Donatists is omitted, as the schism never affected the Greek East. The story of his baptism by Sylvester features prominently in the 'Opitz-Vita' and the account is clearly based on the V. Sylv. The order of the events in the story is the same; even the story of the dragon (a typical piece of Roman mythology) is included, and the fact that the number of steps down to the beast is 365 instead of 150 betrays the use of the B-version of the Latin V. Sylv. as the source for the Greek.[96] Byzantine hagiographers were prepared to accept the legend of Sylvester as history, for they had few defences against those who detracted from Constantine's sainthood by pointing to his baptism on his death bed by the Arian Eusebius of Nicomedia. Two of the main Greek vitae contain lengthy citations from the Greek version of the V. Sylv., including the debate with the Jews.[97]

As in western hagiography, Constantine is depicted as a model Christian emperor in his Byzantine vitae. To him therefore were ascribed decidedly anti-pagan legislative activities and an intensive programme of church construction throughout the Empire in antithesis to the later failed efforts of Julian to restore paganism.[98] The contrast between the two reigns is so important for hagiographical purposes that they are often chronologically telescoped and much biographical material on Constantine can also be gleaned from the acta of the martyrs under Julian who had personally experienced the Christian policies of Constantine. Judas-Cyriacus, the Jew turned Christian Bishop who helped Helena to discover the True Cross (c. 326) was also said to have fallen victim to Julian. Eusignius, also martyred under Julian, claimed to have taken part in a 'Persian' campaign early in the reign of Constantine and had rescued the emperor from certain death, something which could not have happened unless

156

Eusignius was at least 100 years old when he was martyred. Similarly, the count Artemius, executed under Julian as a rapacious and unpopular Prefect of Egypt (he would later enjoy posthumous fame in seventh-century Constantinople as provider of miraculous cures for diseases of the genitalia), claimed to have been with Constantine when he saw his famous vision.[99] As this would have made him at least an octogenarian at the time of his martyrdom, he should have been forcibly retired from his prefecture on grounds of age, let alone his zealous exploitation of pagan temples. Moreover, Constantine, the first Christian emperor, was also the first orthodox emperor and thus regarded as the equal of a saint. Such a figure could not possibly have been tainted by heresy. The councils of the fifth century played their part in according canonical dignity to the emperor of the first universal council, as well as to the council itself. The fathers of the Council of Ephesus praised Constantine for his *recta fides* as well as the *clarior fides* of the ruling emperors. The parallel between the Constantinian past and the present in Byzantium was made apparent when Emperor Marcian, together with his wife Pulcheria, appeared personally in 451 at the Council of Chalcedon. Indeed, the emperor was then acclaimed as *Novus Constantinus, Novus Paulus, Novus David* and the empress as *Nova Helena*. Here the first Christian emperor appears beside the Old Testament king as bearer of the Christian concept of ruler. The comparison with Paul forms the New Testament counterpart to the identification with David, giving expression to the divine institution of emperorship, and here perhaps also casting a sideways glance at the Pope as Peter's successor. Comparisons and images which were first of all minted for Constantine, are applied in the carefully balanced acclamation of Chalcedon to the Christian concept of emperor. It is hardly a coincidence that at the same time the custom arose of the emperor being crowned by the Patriarch of Byzantium.[100]

The biographical details on Constantine provided by the Byzantine *vitae* are a fascinating combination and harmonisation of fact and fiction.[101] In the space available I shall focus attention on a number of aspects which I adjudge to be most interesting to scholars of the 'historical' Constantine.

The birth and childhood of Constantine

Constantine was born in Naissus, a garrison town in Dacia redolent with Claudian associations and a likely place for a soldier like

Constantius to have had his first serious liaison. The earliest source to record this is a chance remark in the *Mathesis* of Firmicus Maternus,[102] a work composed in the 330s before he was converted to Christianity and became the polemicist against paganism under Constantius II. It also has the *imprimatur* of the *Anon. Vales.* – generally regarded as a trustworthy source.[103] Though both of these are in Latin, Naissus as Constantine's birth-place was known to Byzantine antiquarians like Stephanus[104] and administrators in the reign of Constantine Porphyrogenitus.[105] However, the Byzantine hagiographer had to square this with one important and irreducible biographical detail: that Helena's birth-place was Drepanum in Bithynia (later to be named Helenopolis). How a woman of humble background from Bithynia could have married a man of some social standing in his native Dacia Ripensis has vexed more than one modern scholar. Piganiol,[106] for example, has suggested that she came from the same region as Constantius and the link with Drepanum was a legend born out of the association with the martyr Lucian, whose remains were buried there and whom Helena held in high regard. Modern research has suggested that Constantius could have met Helena in the East while serving as a *protector* in Aurelian's campaign against Zenobia of Palmyra, as the name of an officer with the rank of *protector Aureliani Augusti* was recorded on an inscription in Nicomedia *c.* 270.[107] The Byzantine hagiographers preceded modern research by employing the simple axiom that 'If Mohammed will not go to the mountain, then the mountain must come to Mohammed.' In the 'Guidi-*Vita*' we are told that the persecution of the Christians by Diocletian and Maximianus Herculius caused the Roman empire to be invaded by Persians, Parthians and Sarmatians. After consulting their pagan priests Theonas and Hymnaeus, Diocletian and Maximianus decided to send the *tribunus* Constantius Chlorus as envoy to the Parthian king Varachthes (presumably Vahram) to discuss a peace treaty.[108] This Constantius was a grandson of Claudius and had already been married to the daughter of Maximianus. Upon the successful conclusion of the mission, Constantius and his delegation of worthies returned to Rome in stages. At Drepanum they stayed overnight at a very 'distinctive' (ἐπίσημος) inn. That night Constantius fancied some female company and expressed his desire to the inn-keeper who, seeing that Constantius was a man of substance with good prospects, introduced his daughter Helena – a girl renowned for her beauty and a virgin.[109] The next morning Constantius gave her a purple chiton, a sure sign of royalty[110] and, in the 'Halkin-*Vita*', a golden necklace as well. Constantius, still a pagan, received a vision from Apollo, for the sun unexpectedly shone in the night on the inn while his union with Helena was taking place. By this he knew that Helena had conceived, and he ordered Helena's father to care for her as well as for the child who was to be born. Many years later, after Constantius had become emperor, another Roman embassy passed the same way to Persia. They stayed at the same inn and when they heard that the handsome young man they met there spoke of himself as the son of the reigning emperor, they burst out laughing. The lad went crying to his mother who reproached the officials and showed them the purple chiton. They duly reported to Constantius their discovery of a young man who was a 'copy' of him. Constantine was duly sent for and reunited with his father. In the 'Halkin-*Vita*' which parallels the *Pass. Eusign.* on this topic, Constantius had a mentally retarded son from his legitimate wife and desired to adopt a handsome and clever young man as heir.[111] A party of *protectores*, sent out for this mission, stayed at the same inn and the young Constantine played with their horses while they were eating. One indignant *protector* rushed out into the courtyard. He shouted, 'Behave yourself. You are not old enough to go riding!' and boxed him on the ear. Greatly upset by this, Constantine rushed in tears to his mother. As in the 'Guidi-*Vita*', the mother showed the royal gift and the *protectores* recognised its royal origin and escorted the young man to Constantius' court.[112]

One is entitled to wonder how a lowly *tribunus* could have possesed a purple chiton to give as a departing souvenir to his mistress of one night. It would have been different, of course, if Constantius was already an emperor – hence the development in the legend we see in the only *vita* of Constantine in the Latin West.

We know from the normally reliable sources that Constantine was sent as a hostage to the court of Galerius where he distinguished himself in a number of campaigns. In the 'Guidi-*Vita*' he went voluntarily after his reunion with Constantius, not wishing to embarrass his father who was legally married and had a large family. The *Anon. Vales.* tells us that when he was serving in the cavalry against the Sarmatians, he seized a fierce savage by the hair and threw him at the feet of the emperor.[113] Curiously, this episode which would have readily lent itself to embellishment, does not feature in the three main Byzantine *vitae*, but is recounted in a very similar way in Greek by the twelfth-century annalist Zonaras. It would be interesting to discover how Zonaras obtained this information, as the *Anon. Vales.* would not have been generally known to scholars of late Byzantium.[114] According to Lactantius, Galerius became so jealous of the military achievements of Constantine that he arranged for him to fight with animals, and we learn from Photius' summary of the now lost history of Constantine by Praxagoras that Galerius set him to fight with a savage lion. The 'Halkin-*Vita*' goes one step further in making Constantine a hero in the mode of Hercules. Instead of facing the normal opposition of a bear and a lion without claws or thirty men armed with dry sponges, Galerius sent him against a normal bear and lion as well as thirty men armed with rocks. Needless to say, Constantine was victorious.[115]

The Christian eunuch Euphratas

I first came across this legendary figure while in the process of collecting source-material on Romano-Persian relations. The *Annales* of Georgius Cedrenus (eleventh century) give an account of a Persian campaign of Constantine which has no parallel in any late Roman source, i.e. sources before and including the *Historia nova* of Zosimus:

> When he [i.e. Constantine] saw that a plague was impending, he left this city [i.e. Thessalonica] and went to Chalcedon in Bithynia. Finding that it had been desolated by the Persians, he began to rebuild it. Immediately eagles snatched up the stones[116] of the workmen and hurled them in the direction of Byzantium. When this had happened many times and everyone was perplexed, one of those serving the emperor by the name of Euphratas explained that it was God's wish that a city be established there for his mother. And so he immediately crossed over and, when he had looked over the site and given it his approval, he left Euphratas with a mighty power and much money to oversee the work. The emperor himself went off against the Persians. There he met with a defeat and by the foresight of God he escaped from their hands and returned back to Byzantium. Euphratas, however, built the underground water channels and opened up all the springs of water and made a start upon the walls. Again, the Persians moved against Roman territory.

The emperor gave instructions to Euphratas concerning the foundation of the temple, and himself took on the peopling of the city. Having received the rings of each of the leading citizens, he built magnificent houses and led their wives, children and all their households into the royal city. The emperor campaigned against the Persians once more, and when he had turned them to flight he returned again.

(Cedrenus 1, pp. 496,5–497,2 CSHB)[117]

Not surprisingly, the *Prosopography of the Later Roman Empire* could shed no light on the identity of this seemingly important personage. It was only after I had begun to work on the Byzantine *vitae* that I began to realise the legendary origin of the eunuch Euphratas and the role he played in the achievements of Constantine. He is encountered decisively, albeit briefly, in the otherwise well-researched 'Opitz-*Vita*', but in the opening sections which were not edited by Opitz as the beginning of *BHG* 365 is lost from the MS Cod. Angelicus gr. 22. The section in question was later edited by Halkin from the MS Cod. Sabbaiticus 366. Sadly, the beginning of the text is also fragmentary, but the context of the passage in which Euphratas appears is clear. After surveying the forces of Maxentius, Constantine returned to his camp, full of fear and anxiety about the numbers of the enemy forces, their preparations and good organisation. In his moment of self-doubt, a eunuch named Euphratas, whom he greatly admired, came to restore his courage and allayed his fears over the troops massed against him by giving him a homily on the punishment meted out by the Christian God against persecutors and on the victory offered to those rulers who respected Him:

'If you are willing, emperor,' he said, 'to take my advice which I know is well suited to your situation, I hope that you will prevail over all your enemies without difficulty.' Astonished, Constantine replied: 'How could this be achieved, my friend? What means could there be in this predicament to assure me of such a great victory?'

'Provided,' replied Euphratas 'that you reject the many gods and properly treat them with contempt, for they are not gods at all and it is madness to consider them as such, and that, turning to the only true God, you take his son, Christ, as your ally in this situation and throughout your life. Consider the superiority of his power: although by undergoing the Cross he was plunged into the deepest and most undeserved humiliation, by the strength of his works he obliged the majority of the human race to worship him and to recognise him as God. His glory advances unceasingly for all time: in public and in private, in all cities and nations and peoples, almost the whole of humanity seeks his favour. As for those who raised their hands against him, the Jews in particular, you see how they have perished, they and their city with them; those who escaped live scattered over all the world, they live a hard and wandering life, forced most harshly to serve their worst enemies as slaves.

'After them Nero, Domitian, Decius and many more in between and finally Maximinus in our day, have all come to a catastrophic end, receiving death as punishment for their acts of violence against the Church. Suppose I tell you from the beginning about the deserved misfortunes that were inflicted upon the impious ones. Diocletian became insane and abdicated his imperial status, he was forced to wear the garb of a private citizen; worn away by a long illness, he was cut off from the land of the living. Maximianus Herculius ended his life by hanging; Maximianus Galerius, struck down by an incurable ulcer, his body eroded by the putrefaction of his genitals and consumption by worms, sang a palinode and revoked persecution against the Christians by public decrees, but later, falling under the influence of Theotecnos, the magician of Antioch, he again worked terror against the Christians and was destroyed by the previous illness. Maximinus' fate was worse than all that, and the former Caesar Severus, who had been sent by Maximianus Galerius to arrest Maxentius, was put to death himself, his soldiers having betrayed him.

'If you consider, emperor, all this, you will abandon your many gods and bring yourself to join Christ and pray to him. Truly through his help you will conquer your enemies, then, trusting in him, you will be able henceforth to attend to affairs of State. If you follow my advice I promise you that the enemy will not even give battle, and that if they do so they will immediately be routed and turn tail without a confrontation. Thus the supreme power over all affairs will be yours.'

On hearing his words Constantine replied: 'Those are amazing and incredible facts. Nevertheless, I believe.' And, putting his words into actions, he called upon Christ and offered this prayer to him: 'If you are able, O Christ, to save those who invoke you, if what is said of you is true, if you are really God, now if ever is the time to prove it. You have won me as your servant, I will be more faithful to you than anyone else, my whole life will be devoted to you as a thank offering. Let my supplications meet success! If possible, give me a resounding victory over the enemy; or at least do not allow my life and my empire to be endangered as a result of my failure: let me be able to escape from this darkness which engulfs me.'[118]

The 'fabricator' of the story appears to be familiar with the *HE* and *VC* of Eusebius and probably with the *De mort.* of Lactantius. The story may have grown out of Eusebius' mention in the *VC* of Constantine's fear of the possible use of magical arts by Maxentius.[119] The addition of a human agent prefacing the divine apparition in the conversion of Constantine clearly helped to identify the Christian character of the subsequent supernatural happenings, but it also complicates the conversion story, as the 'Opitz-*Vita*' goes on to give a version of the standard Byzantine account of the conversion and baptism of Constantine by Pope Sylvester.[120] The 'Opitz-*Vita*' is unique among Byzantine lives of Constantine because of its substantial borrowings from the heretical church historian Philostorgius. There is no doubt, however, that this Euphratas episode was not derived from Philostorgius because of the late date of the introduction of Euphratas into the Constantine legend, and the story is crudely inserted: the phrase: 'the night having fallen' is almost immediately followed by 'after the night had overtaken him'.[121] From where the author of the 'Opitz-*Vita*' discovered the story of the conversion of Constantine by Euphratas is an intriguing question, since Euphratas does not appear elsewhere in the story – not even to play the role of principal architect of Constantinople's sewer systems and of Hagia Sophia, which was central to the achievements of Constantine as depicted in the 'Halkin-*Vita*' and outlined in Cedrenus. The dual role of Euphratas as the person who converted Constantine and constructed the sewers of Constantinople is briefly acknowledged in the Chronicle of Pseudo-Symeon (ninth century)[122] and the

Patria Konstantinopoleous of Pseudo-Codinus (compiled in the fifteenth century).[123]

The *locus classicus* of the *Gesta Euphratae* is found in the 'Halkin-*Vita*' which surprisingly does not mention his role in the conversion of Constantine. Here, as Cedrenus has already summarised, is a description of Euphratas' part not only in building the sewers and the church which was dedicated to the Mother of God, but also in 'tricking' the senatorial families from Rome to settle in the new capital. According to the 'Halkin-*Vita*', Constantine had received a command from the Lord in a dream near Rome to build a city for the Mother of God at a place which he would be shown. He went first to Thessalonica where, because of its wonderful situation, he built churches and baths, but because of an impending plague was forced to abandon the city he had adorned, in great distress. He travelled to Chalcedon in Bithynia and finding it long since fortified by the Persians, he immediately set about starting the work of rebuilding, but eagles took the workers' plumb-lines and carried them off to Byzantium. This happened more than once and when the emperor learned of it he was at a loss as to what to do. Then one of his trusted servants called Euphratas told him that this is the place where the Lord wanted the city for his mother, the holy Mother of God to be built. Constantine was pleased by the place which was then a bare hillside, and put Euphratas in charge of the work and provided him with the necessary labour and finance. First of all he created the inflow and outflow of the water channels according to the lie of the land, digging wells and laying underground cisterns from place to place. Because he was unable to carry out his tasks in public, some men denounced him before the emperor as having squandered the large sums of money entrusted to him without even clearing the trees from the hillside. Constantine, however, stayed loyal to his eunuch and when Euphratas came before him at Chalcedon, he said no hostile word towards him, but instead inquired in a friendly manner as to how the construction work was going. When Euphratas replied that work was progressing in line with his instructions, the emperor asked why they were not able to see any sign of it. Euphratas then took Constantine across the Bosphorus and led the emperor on horseback with a large retinue carrying torches from the colonnade of the area of Eugenius which neighbours the sea, and through the underground series of vaults as far as the foundation of the great column on which the statue of the emperor rests (i.e. the famous 'Burnt

Column'). There were to be found many and frequent subterranean vaults which completed the whole circuit of the circular structure which was visible above, each formed from a buttress and a column. From them great colonnades were laid in a straight line towards the sea on each side, through which all the refuse from the meat markets and the sewers could be discharged. When Constantine expressed his amazement at this, he was told by Euphratas that the structures were designed to take the overflow during heavy rains and that with them in place, building the walls would be a simple matter. Amazed, Constantine then entrusted Euphratas with the building of a great church and with bringing 'not only Romans but also people of all nations' to settle in the new capital. Euphratas consented to this but only on condition that the emperor take the signet rings from the leaders of the Senate and mark each of them and send them in a letter to him. This Constantine promised to do and carried out his promise at a convenient time. This was the fourteenth year of his emperorship. [124] Constantine then left to conduct his campaign against the Persians.

The narrative returns to Euphratas after the account of Constantine's Persian campaign in which he was first captured by the Persians and then rescued by his soldiers (see below). In the emperor's absence, Euphratas summoned men with knowledge of the leaders' houses at Rome and arranged for replicas of such houses to be built at the new capital paying attention to their original setting and position with regard to air and sea. He then sent the signet rings of the grandees by letters to their wives as if from their own husbands. The ladies were completely taken in by the deception. They took to the ships with all their most valuable possessions and with their whole households sailed for Byzantium. On arrival, each of them went to the house that had been built as exact replicas of their former residences in Rome. When Constantine returned triumphant to Chalcedon after the destruction of the Persian Empire, Euphratas was the first person to meet him as he came off his boat and greeted him with the request to guide each noble man in the emperor's retinue to his own home. Each of them stood astonished outside what was an exact impression of his house in the old capital and was greeted by his family, servants and wife, who informed him that she and their household had made the journey because of the letter and signet ring she had received. After a sleepless night of joyful reunion, the noblemen gathered before Constantine and expressed their amazement at the scheme. They were told by the emperor that it was the Mother of God who had summoned them and granted them three times the amount of land each had in Rome as well as large sums of money for the improvement of their new homes.

Though unhistorical, the legendary role of Euphratas in helping to create a new senatorial class in the New Rome reflects the resources Constantine had to lavish on those of the aristocracy in Rome and elsewhere to come to settle in Constantinople. This is clearly stated by the more contemporary *Anon. Vales.* 6 (30):

> Constantine, in memory of his famous victory, called Byzantium Constantinople, after himself. As if it were his native city, he enriched it with great assiduity, and wanted it to become the equal of Rome. He sought out citizens for it from everywhere, and lavished so much wealth on it that he almost exhausted the resources of the imperial treasury. There he founded a Senate of the second rank; the members were called *clari*.[125]

According to Zosimus, Constantine constructed houses for those senators who followed him to the new capital[126] and a later source, Hesychius of Miletus, claims that these were built at the emperor's own expense.[127] The legend underscores the difficulty which Constantine must have had in the creation of a senatorial class in Constantinople, especially if it was one which at the outset did not enjoy the same status as the senators in Rome as they were given the title of *clari* rather than the usual *clarissimi*.[128] Dagron has noted that this obviously did not apply to senators who came from Rome, who were mostly senior functionaries of the *comitatus*, but to important people from the former curial assembly supplemented by new members: their transfer from the curial system passed through this intermediate stage of a 'second-class' Senate. Euphratas' achievements did not end here. At the time of Constantine's death he had also surveyed the site for Hagia Sophia and had laid the foundations using strong timber, making the wood free from damp through specially dug channels in each section so that the moisture could escape. He also created a series of deep wells which were spaced throughout the church and in neighbouring areas. By the time of Constantine's death, the church had reached the level of the colonnade.[129] Euphratas continued the building work in the reign of Constantius II. By the time of his own death the church was beginning to be lavishly furnished, and he also bequeathed an almshouse which later became the church in which he was buried. The locals called the church which was situated near the Leomacellium 'the Euphratas'.[130]

The achievements of Euphratas both as converter and architect of Constantine are commemorated briefly in late Byzantine sources on the history of Constantinople. However, he received no mention in the highly polished *vita Constantini* of John Chortasmenos, written at about the same time as the locographical compilation containing the references to Euphratas was made. Clearly, he was too ahistorical to merit a mention, although he did find his way into the historical work of Cedrenus. The fact such a body of legend could have grown up round a totally fictitious person attests to the paucity of genuine 'bio-data' on Constantine available in Byzantium to the hagiographer.[131]

The Persian wars of Constantine

The third theme in Constantine's legendary Greek *vitae* which I would like to focus on is his Persian wars. The main enemies of Byzantium were its Eastern neighbours, first the armies of the Shahanshah and then the forces of Islam – Arabs and later Turks. Constantine was no Heraclius, although he might have been one had he lived long enough to carry out his last campaign to its successful conclusion. Legends, however, could be useful for political ends. In both the 'Guidi-' and 'Halkin-*Vitae*', as well as in the *Pass. Eusign.*, Constantine led an expedition against the Persians shortly after his conversion, but he was unfamiliar with the terrain and his army was ambushed and he himself captured. Overjoyed by this amazing windfall, the Persians decided to sacrifice Constantine at one of their religious festivals. Among those Romans who escaped capture, however, was Eusignius. He and a handful of comrades fell on a party of Persians out gathering wood. These 'Persians' happened to be slaves of Roman origin. They betrayed to the Roman soldiers the intention of the Persians to sacrifice their emperor at a religious ceremony, the layout of their camp and, most importantly, the fact that it was customary for the Persian officers participating in the festival to leave their arms stacked outside the sanctuary. With the help of the slaves, the Roman soldiers got themselves into the camp and, seizing the arms of the Persians, rescued the emperor who exclaimed 'You are great, Jesus Christ, who were crucified for us under Pontius Pilate and you alone are the performer of great miracles.' He had earlier refused to sacrifice to the idols in order to save his life. This incident has two different endings.[132] In the 'Guidi-*Vita*' the Persians agreed to a truce, while in the 'Halkin-*Vita*' the Romans massacred the Persians, thus bringing about a desire for a campaign of vengeance on the part of the Persians.[133] When this was launched, the Persians advanced unopposed as far as Chalcedon and laid waste to the city. Constantine raised an army in Macedon and marched through Bithynia to behind the Persian lines. He ordered the roads to be securely guarded, then, putting on Persian uniforms, the Romans rampaged through the countryside. Pregnant women were cut open in order for their foetuses to be eaten, and infants were sent to the threshing floor where they were decapitated by threshing machines as in time of harvest. All this barbarity was apparently necessary for the Romans to maintain their Persian disguise. Clearly adherence to the spirit of the modern Geneva Convention was not a prerequisite for sainthood in Byzantium. The Persian queen sent desperate messages for help to her husband encamped at Chalcedon without a fleet to cross the Bosphorus, but her messages were all intercepted. However, word of what happened in their homeland eventually filtered through to the Persian army and many began to desert; but as they travelled in small numbers along roads well guarded by the Romans, most of them perished. Echoes of the extraordinarily successful Persian campaigns of Heraclius in the seventh century are too numerous to mention. Between 610 and 616, the triumphant armies of the Shahanshah Chosroes Parwez carried everything before them until they reached Chalcedon. But beginning in 621, Heraclius led a series of seaborne campaigns against them by landing highly trained forces in Asia Minor and the Caucasus and thereby cutting the very extended Persian lines of communication into shreds. The horrendous description of the Roman war-crimes in the Constantinian legend probably reflects the realities of the Byzantine equivalent of General Sherman's 'march through Georgia' in the American Civil War.

CONCLUSION: FROM LEGEND TO HISTORY

Why should critical modern scholars concern themselves with these fictional legends on Constantine beyond what they can tell us about the aspirations and fears of the periods which produced them? For the Byzantinist, there is a very important reason: that the Byzantine legends became so popular that they were accepted as history and, as we have noted, many of the more regularly used Byzantine historical sources on the period of Constantine such as Cedrenus, Zonaras and the *Patria Constantinopoleos* (Pseudo-Codinus) drew material freely from these legends.[134] A knowledge of the main *vitae* is thus essential to help us distinguish fact from fiction in our Byzantine sources on Constantine. For the late Roman historian, the medieval and Byzantine legends are a reminder that the reign of Constantine is not just the beginning of the final chapter of Roman history. The study of the legends leads one to examine some of the key foundations of Christian Europe and of Byzantium, and one only needs to witness the tragic events in what was formerly Yugoslavia to realise that the medieval and Byzantine legacies of the tetrarchy and of Constantine are still very much with us.

ACKNOWLEDGEMENTS

The author is grateful to Frank Beetham and Mark Vermes, his research colleagues at the Centre for Research in East Roman Studies, for much useful help and advice. He would also like to thank Dr Ligotta and the other librarians of the Warburg Institute (London) for maintaining an outstanding collection of texts, monographs and bound off-prints on the *Nachleben* of Constantine, and arranging the material in a manner which makes it readily accessible to the research scholar.

NOTES

1 Text from *S. Gregorii Magni Registrum Epistularum Libri VIII–XIV*, ed. D. Narberg (CCSL 40) 1982: trans. D. Montserrat.
2 On Aldhelm, see Stevenson in this volume, especially pp. 189–91 and 193–200.
3 For the literary antecedents of the dragon-motif see in particular Pohlkamp 1983, especially 11.
4 Ald., *De virg.* 25.8–10.
5 Ibid. 25.15–21.
6 William of Malmesbury, *De gestis Regum Anglorum* 4.354 (= *PL* 179: 1307–12). The account contains the vision for the founding of Constantinople as revealed to Sylvester (see below, pp. 151–2) but not the baptism of Constantine by Sylvester. William gives Ald., *De virg.* as his source.

7 William of Malmesbury, *De gestis Regum Anglorum* 1 (= *PL* 179: 959–60).

8 *Radulfi de Diceto Decani Lundoniensis Opera Historica* I, ed. W. Stubbs, *The Chronicles and Memorials of Great Britain and Ireland during the Middle Ages* 68 (London 1876), 74–5.

9 Anonymous letter to Aldhelm; Aldhelm in MGH Auct. Ant. 15: 494.

10 Liber Pontificalis 86.10: *Qui etiam ex die illo pro salute humani generis ab omni populo Christiano, die exaltationis sanctae crucis, in basilicam Salvatoris quae appellatur Constantinian osculatur ac adoratur.*

11 Ald., *De virg.* 25. Cf. Pohlkamp 1988: 423–4.

12 Mombritius' text of the *V. Sylv.* is derived from a heavily contaminated version of B(1), one of the two principal variant versions of the text. According to Eis 1933: 51–2, two manuscripts are known to contain versions of the text reproduced by B. Mombritius; the first is Codex 1402 in the Stadtbibliothek of Reims and the second is a tenth-century Bavarian manuscript now in the possession of the Historische Verein of Regensburg. For a very full and up-to-date bibliography on the *V. Sylv.*, see Aiello in Bonamente and Fusco 1992: 19–20, n. 5.

13 Cf. Coleman 1914: 163. To Sylvester is attributed, but with no apparent justification, an *adversus Judaeos* tract (*PL* 8: 814). Cf. Schreckenberg 1990: 255–7, who also gives a convenient summary of the main theological issues touched on by this blatantly fictitious debate. See also the many important observations in Ehrhardt 1959–60: 307, who suggests, *inter alia*, that the author of the *V. Sylv.* had Sylvester's anti-Jewish writings before him as models for the fabrication of the debate between the pontiff and the rabbis.

14 Cf. Levison 1924: 191–221. The longer version A(1) which is generally regarded as older and more authentic, is currently being critically edited for publication by W. Pohlkamp. Cf. Fowden 1994: 155, n. 58.

15 Cf. Ehrhardt 1959–60: 290.

16 Silvester, natione Romanus, ex patre Rufino, sedit ann. XXIII m. X d. XI. Fuit autem temporibus Constantini et Volusiani, ex die kal. febr. usque in die kal. ian., Constantio et Volusiano consulibus. Hic exilio fuit in monte Seracten et postmodum rediens cum gloria baptizavit Constantinum Augustum, quem curavit Dominus a lepra, cuius persecutionem primo fugiens exilio fuisse cognoscitur.
English translation from Davis 1989: 14.

17 Ewig 1956 [1975]: 134.

18 On Flavius Nicomachus, the senatorial historian, as a possible source for this see F. Paschoud's long note in the first volume of his Budé edition of Zosimus (1971) (84–7). For critique see Fowden 1994: 158.

19 Cf. Julian, *Caesars* 336B (LCL Julian II 345–415) and Zos. 2.29 (based undoubtedly on Eunapius).

20 Eusebius mentions the baptism (*VC* 4.62) but does not name the priest responsible.

21 Jerome, *Chron.*, 337 AD:

> Constantinus extremo vitae suae tempore ab Eusebio Nico-
> medensi episcopo baptisatus in Arrianum dogma declinat.
> A quo usque in praesens tempus ecclesiarum rapinae et
> totius orbis est secuta discordia. Constantinus cum bellum
> pararet in Persas in Ancyrone villa publica iuxta Nicome-
> diam moritur anno aetatis LXVI. Post quem tres liberi eius
> ex Caesaribus Augusti appellantur.

22 Philost., *HE* 2.16.

23 Socrates, *HE* 1.39.2; Sozomen, *HE* 2.34,1; Thdt., *HE* 1.32,1.

24 Cf. Nestle 1895; for Latin versions see Borgehammar 1991: 255–71 (versio A) and 282–8 (versio B).

25 In the Middle Ages, the belief circulated that it was not Constantine but his father with a similar sounding name (i.e. Constantius Chlorus) who was baptised by Eusebius. Cf. Jacobus de Voragine, *Legenda Aurea vulgo Historia Lombardica dicta LXVIII* (64), ed. T. Graesse, Bratislava 1890: 305. The same source also refuted the claim that Constantine was baptised by Eusebius of Nicomedia as stated by the Historia Tripartita of Cassiodorus – a work which is an amalgam of the main continuations of Eus., *HE*. The *V. Sylv.* ends with a variant on Ruf., *HE* 10.8 with a claim to be direct translation of Eusebius from the Greek: cf. Levison 1924: 176.

26 A view first put forward in Dölger 1913, especially 416–26. See further elaborations and additional support for the thesis, particularly from the Syriac Julian Romance, in Fowden 1994: 158–60.

27 Phot., *Bibl.*, cod. 88 [67a]. Cf. Dölger 1913: 395.

28 Hymn 'On Constantine the King', ed. and trans. Brook 1911: 663–5.

29 Cf. Eutropius, *Breviarium* 10.4–8, which incidentally does not mention the rise of Arianism under Constantine.

30 On this papyrus, see Jones 1954: 199.

31   item actus beati Silvestri apostolicae sedis praesulis, licet
        eius qui conscripserit nomen ignoretur, a multis tamen in
        urbe Roma catholicis legi cognovimus et pro antiquo usu
        multae hoc imitantur ecclesiae.
   Text in *Decretum Gelasianum de libris recipiendis et non recipiendis*, ed. E.
   von Dobschütz (TU 38.4), Leipzig 1912: 42–3 (lines 222–4).

32   Hoc cum legisset ex libro antiquo, edoctus a libro Silvestri
        episcopi Romanorum, eo quod et publice praedicaret, quia
        in nomine Jesu-Christi a lepra mundatum fuisse per Sil-
        vestrum Constantinum patruum Constantis, erat enim
        Constans non integre Christianus, sed quasi tentator, bap-
        tizatus tamen in Trinitate, non tamen integre confitebatur
        Trinitatem. Baptizatus autem ab Eusebio Nicomediensi in
        Nicomedia in Aquilone villa. Hic vero dicebat, alios filios
        habuisse de Maria Joseph. Hoc cum audisset Liberius epis-
        copus Romae, coepit deridere eum, et clara voce accusare, et
        dicere ex omni virtute. Non erit tuum regnum, quia non
        times Dominum Deum tuum.

Text from *Gesta Liberii* 2, ed. P. Coustant, *Epistolae Romanorum pontificum, et quae ad eos scriptae sunt a S. Clemente usque ad Innocentium* III, I, Rome 1721: 90B. Cf. Coleman 1914: 166 and Pohlkamp 1988: 425–6.

33 Greek version in Eus., *HE* 1.13. For the Syriac version (later than the Greek), see Howard 1981; cf. Bauer 1964: 6–48.

34 See Frothingham 1883.

35 Ibid.; 221 (line 177 of Syriac text).

36 Malalas, *Chronographia* 13. See Scott in Magdalino 1994: 62, and also Pohlkamp 1988: 420, n. 25.

37 Greek version (translated from the Latin): F. Combefis, *Illustrium Christi Martyrum lecti triumphali,* Paris 1659: 258–336 and *BHG* 365, for which see Winkelmann 1987, and other references cited by Coleman 1914: 161, n. 1. For the Syriac version (very close to the Latin), see J. N. P. Land, *Anecdota Syriaca* III, Leiden 1870: 46–76, with German translation in Ryssel 1895.

38 Thphn., *Chron.* A. M. 5814.

39 Ibid. A. M. 5814. The argument is re-used by the author of the so-called 'Guidi-*Vita*' (see *FCJ* 123), and would resurface in the defence of the Sylvester legend in the *Donatio Constantini* by Steuchus, the librarian of the Vatican (where a number of the principal MSS of the Greek *vitae* are housed) at the time of the Reformation: see Coleman 1914: 205.

40 Moses Khorenats'i 2.83; translation in Thomson 1978: 234–5: see commentary *ad loc.* On the Sylvester legend in Armenian see van Esbroeck 1982, especially p. 93 on the texts appended to the Armenian version of Socrates Scholasticus.

41 [Editors' note: in this and following discussions of the *V. Sylv.*, references are given first by the volume and page of the Mombritius edition of 1910, followed by pages of the re-numbered De Leo edition of 1974: see abbreviations (p. xix above) for details.] *V. Sylv.* I: 508, 8–12 [De Leo: 153, 2–8]. The text's fabricator is conversant with Eus., *HE* in Rufinus' Latin translation, and Lact., *De mort.*: see Ehrhardt 1959–60: 299.

42 See Milner 1994: 79.

43 Optatus Milevitanus, *de schismate Donatistarum* 1.23: *conuenerunt in domum Faustae in Laterano Constantino quater et Licinio ter consulibus sexto Nonas Octobris die, sexta eria, cum consedissent Miltiades episcopus urbis Romae.*

44 Jerome, *Chron.*, AD 310.

45 Constantine was in Sirmium on 16 Feb. 313 according to *CTh* 7.22,1: cf. Barnes 1982: 71.

46 *PLRE*: 1043 under Fasti consulares.

47 Augustine, *De unico baptismo* 16.27: *Marcellinus et presbyteri eius Miltiades, Marcellus et Siluester traditionis codicum diuinorum et turificationis ab eo crimine arguuntur.* Cf. Frend 1971: 22 and Pohlkamp 1984: 368.

48 *V. Sylv.* I 508, 27–509,6 [De Leo: 156–57] and 511, 33–37 [De Leo: 163]. Cf. Pohlkamp 1984: 369–71.

49 *V. Sylv.* I 510, 34 [De Leo: 161].

50 Cf. Levison 1924: 159. The pontificate of Stephen III has been suggested as the date of the *Donation*: see Plöchl 1960 I: 309.

51 Text here from the edition of H. Fuhrmann, *Das Constitutum Constantini (Konstanische Schenkung)*, (Fontes Iuris Germanici Antiqui), Hanover 1968: 56, 2–6. See also the older edition by K. Zeumer, in C. Mirbt and K. Aland, *Quellen zur Geschichte des Papstums und des römischen Katholizismus* I, Tübingen 1967: 251, and Coleman 1914: 228. For Constantine's genuine titulature, see e.g. his letter to the Senate of Rome (337), quoted in Barnes 1982: 23.

52 See Coleman 1914: 233.

53 Cf. Levison 1924: 240–2 and Pohlkamp 1988: 416–17. The *Exemplar Constituti Domini Constantini Imperatoris* appears to have utilised both the A1 and B1 versions of the *V. Sylv.*

54 See Coleman 1914: 186.

55 Cited in Coleman 1914: 186, quoting Baronius, *Annales Ecclesiastici*, Lucca 1938–46: 1191, no. 57.

56 *Decretales pseudo-Isidorianae et Capitula Angilramni*, ed. P. Hinschius, Leipzig 1863: 249–54. On the reception of the Constitutum into collections of Canon Law and its influence on Church and State relations under the Ottonians, see Fuhrmann 1973: 354–407.

57 This is found among the 'Palea' to *Decreti prima pars Distinctio* CXVI (cf. c. XIV), *Corpus Iuris Canonici* I, ed. A. L. Richter and revised by A. Friedberg, Leipzig 1879: 342–3. See also *PL* 187: 460–6.

58 Cf. Loernertz 1974: 200.

59 On the historical background of Valla's *De falso credita et ementita Constantini Donatione* see especially Setz 1975: 3–50, which contains a text of the treatise. See also De Leo's edition of the *V. Sylv.*: 249–316. For an edition with English translation of this famous treatise, see Coleman 1922: 10–183.

60 Cited in ibid. 2: 205.

61 The *Vita de S. Helena, vidua, imperatrice* presented in *Acta Sanctorum, Aug.* III, Paris and Rome 1867: 548–99 is compiled by the Bollandists from Latin (both Late Antique and medieval) sources. On the 'historical' sources for her life, see Drijvers 1992: 3ff.

62 On the text and its contents see Heydenreich 1893: 5–11.

63 Helena's association with Trier is of long standing in medieval hagiography and has historical roots when one considers the importance of Trier as an imperial residence under the Tetrarchy: see Drijvers 1992: 22–30 and Leadbetter in this volume, n. 29. The centre of the medieval cult of Helena from the Ottonian period onwards was the monastery of Hautvillers, which acquired her relics from Rome and established a special service: cf. Linder 1975: 87.

64 This was acknowledged as early as the end of the fourth century. In the *oratio de obitu Theodosiani* 42 (*PL* 16: 1463A), Ambrose regarded this lowly occupation with favour because Jesus was born in the stables of an inn.

65 *Incerti auctoris de Constantino Magno eiusque Matre Helena Libellus* 2–5, ed. E. Heydenreich, Leipzig 1879, *passim*.

66 Heydenreich 1893: 17–18.

67 Cf. Linder 1975: 49.

68 See Whitby in Magdalino 1994: 83–93 and Linder 1975: 59.
69 On the use of the epithet in Greek *vitae* of Constantine see e. g. *BHG* 365n title, *BHG* 362 title (joint with Helena). The epithet, though closely associated with Constantine, was applied to other saints such as Mary Magdalene and Abercius: see Grégoire 1955/57: 365.
70 Winkelmann 1973.
71 See compiled text in Winkelmann 1987: 632–8.
72 Kazhdan 1987: 242ff; see also Bleckmann 1992: 152.
73 See the perceptive comments of Cameron 1992: 261–2.
74 Guidi 1907: 304–40 and 637–60; English translation in *FCJ*: 106–46.
75 See Heseler 1935.
76 Schneider 1934: 36–7 and Schneider 1941b.
77 Franchi de' Cavalieri 1896–97.
78 Opitz 1934.
79 Bidez 1935: 421–6, and reprinted in the revised edition of his GCS edition of Philostorgius, pp. 377–81.
80 Halkin 1960.
81 See Halkin 1959a and Halkin 1959b.
82 See Winkelmann 1973: 271.
83 Gedeon 1900: 253–4, 262–3, 279–80, 303–4.
84 Cf. Winkelmann 1962: 102–3.
85 Text in Ioannes 1884.
86 See Hunger 1969: 18.
87 See Alexander Monachus, *De inventione sanctae crucis* (*PG* 87: 4016–88).
88 See especially the *vitae* of Metrophanis et Alexander (edition in Winkelmann 1982); see also Phot., *Bibl.*, cod. 256; the Greek version of the *Pass. Eusign.*, and the *Artemii passio*, edition in Kotter 1988: 185–245.
89 Indeed, with the exception of a reference to it in Jerome's *De viris illustribus* 80.3, the *De mort.* remained otherwise barely known in antiquity. In the Latin west, it only survived in a single eleventh-century manuscript, rediscovered in the library of the Abbey of Moissac in 1678: see the introduction to J. L. Creed's edition of Lactantius, *De mort.*, xlv–xlvi.
90 See parallel edition of both by H. Droysen in MGH Auct. Ant. II 1879: 8–182.
91 See especially frags. 168 (= Eutropius, *Breviarum* 10.1), 169 (= Eutropius, *Breviarum* 10.2), 170 (= Eutropius, *Breviarum* 10.4), 172 (= Eutropius, *Breviarum* 10.5); *FHG* IV: 602–03.
92 Epiphanius, *Panarion haeresium* (*GCS* Epiphanius III) 68,8,4.
93 See material gathered by Winkelmann 1964: 93–5.
94 For a translation of Libanius, *Or.* 59 see *FCJ* 164–205. The parallels (mainly concerning the merits of Constantius Chlorus) are juxtaposed and analysed by Petit 1950. See also Moreau 1955, who suggests that Praxagoras rather than Eusebius was the source for Libanius. See now especially Wiemer 1994: 512–14, who argues that Libanius used the *VC*. Also, we cannot ignore the now lost panegyrical life of Constantine by Bemarchius, given Libanius' personal knowledge of (and rivalry with) the author.
95 *PG* 49: 216.

96 *BHG* 365.3–7 (Opitz 1934: 546–51). Cf. *V. Sylv.* I 530.3–9 [De Leo: 217]. On this see especially Levison 1924: 197.

97 *BHG* 365.3–6 (Opitz 1934: 546–51) and *BHG* 362.19–30 (Ioannes 1884: 192–4). A resumé is given in *BHG* 364 (Guidi 1907: 327–30) dependent on Thphn. *Chron.* A. M. 5814.

98 See especially *BHG* 362 (Ioannes 1884: 186), *BHG* 365, 5 and 8 (Opitz 1934: 548 and 551–2). On this see Linder 1975: 46. On Constantine as a model 'Christian' legislator in the West see Linder 1992: 494–7.

99 *Artemii passio* 45, ed. Kotter 1988: 227–8; cf. Brennecke 1988: 127–31.

100 Cf. Ewig 1956 [1975]: 140–3.

101 The main themes of the legends are outlined in Winkelmann 1978: 184–5.

102 Firmicus Maternus, *Mathesis* 1.10, 13.

103 *Anon. Vales.* 2.2. Cf. Syme 1974: 273 and Leadbetter in this volume, pp. 74–8.

104 Stephanus, *Ethnicorum quae supersunt, ex recensione A. Meinekii*, 1849: 467.3–4 (reprinted Graz 1958).

105 Constantine Porphyrogenitus, *De Thematibus Occidentis, Thema IX, Dyrrhachium* (*PG* 113: 128).

106 Piganiol 1932: 32–3.

107 *ILS* 2775. Cf. Barnes 1982: 36, n. 37.

108 *BHG* 365n, 2.1–2 (Halkin 1959a: 74) interestingly sets the story in the context of a treaty with the Sarmatians and he began his journey from Britain!

109 The *Lex Julia de adulteriis* as exemplified by Constantine in an edict of 3 February 326 (*CTh* 9.7.1) exempts servant girls working in taverns from the charge of adultery as they often had to serve the 'wines of intemperance' (*intemperantiae vina*) as part of their servile duty. Wives of taverners, however, were not exempt, even though they performed the duties of a servant girl.

110 *BHG* 364 (Guidi 1907: 308,1–24; trans. in *FCJ*: 108), *BHG* 365n 2.3–8 (Halkin 1959a: 74). Cf. Kazhdan 1987: 212–13.

111 *BHG* 365n 2.12–14 (Halkin 1959a: 74–5).

112 *BHG* 365, 2.28–47. A similar story is also found in *BHG* 365n but the relevant section is badly preserved. Cf. Halkin 1960: 11–12.

113 *Anon. Vales.* 2 (3), trans. in *FCJ*: 43.

114 Zon. 12.33. Both Zonaras and Leo the Grammarian used distinctively pagan sources for their respective accounts of Constantine. Cf. Bleckmann 1991 *passim* and Bleckmann 1992: 158–9.

115 *BHG* 365n, 3.17–44 (Halkin 1959a: 77).

116 Or 'plumb-lines' (reading λίνους instead of λίθους, cf. *BHG* 365n 8.17 (see below p. 164) and Ps.-Symeon 10 [for text see Halkin 1959–60: 18]).

117 Translation in Dodgeon and Lieu 1991: 146–7.

118 Cf. Halkin 1960: 7–8.

119 Eus., *VC* 1.27,1:

Constantine also considered the fact that he would need

more powerful aid than military might could give him, since the tyrant was making great efforts to obtain evil arts and deceitful magic spells. He sought a god to be his helper and depended on the armaments and size of the army only in second place. For he thought that that was of no use any way without the help of a god. He considered divine aid to be invincible and unconquerable.

120 Cf. Bidez 1935: 425. Cf. Philostorg., *HE* 1.6.

121 Bidez 1935: 424.6 and Halkin 1960: 6. See Bidez's commentary *ad loc.*

122 Halkin 1959–60: 11–27. Cf. Kazhdan 1987: 237.

123 Pseudo-Codinus, *Patria Konstantinoupoleos* I 58 (as architect) and I 65 (as chamberlain who converted Constantine). Both these sections in which the *parakoimomenos* Euphratas appears are considered to be part of a tenth-century revision of the work: Dagron 1974: 36, n. 1 and Dagron 1984: 87 n. 89.

124 *BHG* 365n, 10: cf. Halkin 1959a: 86–7.

125 Translation in *FCJ*: 47–8. Cf. Dagron 1974: 123.

126 Zos. 2.31,3.

127 Hesychius, Πάτρια Κωνσταντινουπόλεως 40 and 41 (= *FHG* IV: 154).

128 Cf. Dagron 1974: 123.

129 *BHG* 365n, 18. Cf. Halkin 1959a: 100–1.

130 Halkin 1959a: 102.

131 Dagron (1974: 36 n. 1 and 1984: 87 n. 89) suggests a possible connection between the eunuch and the district of Euphrata in Constantinople.

132 *BHG* 364, 316.2–319.5 and *BHG* 365n, 9 (Halkin 1959a: 84–5). The story is not found in the more 'historical' 'Opitz-*Vita*' (*BHG* 365: see Opitz 1934).

133 *BHG* 365n, 9.47–53 (Halkin 1959a: 85) and *BHG* 365n, 11.1–4 (Halkin 1959a: 87).

134 For a comprehensive list of occurrences of major legendary motifs such as the baptism of Constantine by Sylvester in Byzantine chronicles, see Di Maio 1977: 175–6, n. 6. For an earlier study of these Byzantine sources without the knowledge of the influence of the various *vitae*, see Heydenreich 1894.

9

CONSTANTINE IN COPTIC

Egyptian constructions of Constantine the Great

Terry Wilfong

Coptic texts would seem to be unlikely sources for information on Constantine the Great. Constantine certainly did not read or speak Coptic and, although he had considerable impact on the administrative and religious life of Egypt, he was not particularly associated with the land in which Coptic was used. Nevertheless, there are a number of original Coptic sources for the life and reign of Constantine. It is true that Coptic historical texts relating to Constantine are few, and his role in these is generally minimal: Constantine was more often used as an historical character in Coptic literature. Although overshadowed by his predecessor Diocletian, Constantine fulfilled a number of set functions in Coptic literary texts, mostly in his role as the first Christian emperor. Even in these, the focus is usually on Constantine as a facilitator of the pious acts of his family, rather than as an initiator of his own. An exception to these inactive portrayals is Constantine's unexpected role in Coptic texts as military victor over the 'Persians'. Such depictions of Constantine not only attest the Egyptians' opinions of the military abilities of Constantine, but also the anxieties in the minds of the writers over the Sassanian Persians. Examination of the Coptic sources on Constantine the Great may not give us new historical information about him, but they are important for understanding how he was perceived by the Egyptians.

Sources in Coptic represent a certain milieu in Egypt: that of the Christians who spoke and wrote the native Egyptian language. The people who wrote and spoke Coptic represent a broad cross-section of Egyptian society and culture: many Egyptians also knew

Greek with varying degrees of proficiency, and some Egyptians (who lived in Greek-speaking milieux) probably knew no Coptic at all.[1] What can be said for certain is that sources composed in Coptic were directed at an exclusively Egyptian audience: with only a very few and very late exceptions, Coptic was not used outside of Egypt. Thus, the original Coptic sources for Constantine (as opposed to sources translated into Coptic) were intended for Egyptians and show a specifically Egyptian point of view.

Coptic sources for Constantine are limited to historical and literary texts. Although surviving historical sources in Coptic are few, there was some sort of tradition of historical writing among Coptic authors. The most extensive historical work composed in Coptic (containing the most accurate account of Constantine) is known only from an Ethiopic translation of a lost Arabic version of a lost Coptic original. This is the *Chronicle of John of Nikiou*,[2] best known for its detailed account of the Muslim conquest of Egypt. John of Nikiou's history concentrated on Egypt and went back to the times of the Pharaohs, but for periods earlier than the seventh century, he is selective about what he includes and his sources are considerably less accurate. For the later periods, John's biases as a Monophysite living under Muslim rule are clear from his work.

John of Nikiou introduces Constantine with an extensive treatment of the reign of Diocletian, focusing on Diocletian's paganism and martyrdom of Christians. In this version, Diocletian repents and converts to Christianity towards the end of his reign, only to fall back into the persecution of Christians, which leads to his death. Constantine emerges as his successor, a pious Christian who attempts to right the wrongs done by Diocletian. His first struggles are with Maxentius and Maximinus; his battles with them are described throughout the section, battle with the former being the occasion for Constantine's vision of the Cross. Constantine's Christianity and goodness are extensively discussed following the battle accounts, where Constantine is described as going to war against the Persians. After conquering them and establishing them in peace he is said to have given them presents and a trumpet. John goes on to record the building of churches by Constantine and the discovery of the True Cross by an official. The Council of Nicaea is ostensibly called by Constantine so that the bishops assembled there could honour him and his mother Helena for their piety. The latter part of John's account is taken up by stories of Constantine's recalcitrant pagan relatives, Constantine's death and the succession of his two sons Constantius and Constans. Inaccurate in many details, John of Nikiou gives the only full treatment of Constantine's reign from Coptic sources; it also highlights some of the common themes and approaches to Constantine found in other Coptic writings.

Apart from the account in John of Nikiou's *Chronicle*, the only surviving Coptic historical writing about Constantine appears in the fragmentary Coptic *History of the Church*.[3] Although partially dependent on Eusebius' *Historia Ecclesiastica* in some sections, the Coptic *History* was essentially an original composition drawn from now-lost Coptic sources. The Coptic *History* formed one of the sources for the much better known Arabic *History of the Patriarchs of Alexandria*, traditionally ascribed to the Severus ibn al-Muqaffa but written and revised into its final form by Mawhûb ibn Mansûr ibn Mufarrig in the eleventh century. Being, essentially, a series of biographies of the Patriarchs of Alexandria, the *History* focuses on activity in Egypt and the amount of space devoted to Constantine is relatively small. Indeed, the only mentions of Constantine concern his death or events afterwards. In connection with Athanasius, the author wrote: 'and after this, Liberius brought Athanasius and took him with him to Rome until Constantine died and Constans became emperor'.[4]

A few folios later, the author of the Coptic *History* describes the accession of Emperor Julian:

> When Constans died, Julian became king in his place, he being a lawless pagan and one come from the sister of Constantine the Great, for her husband was a pagan. The children[5] of Constantine saw that this young man was impudent and they were afraid that he would take the kingship of their father from them. So they took him when (he was) young and gave him to the church. They made him a *lector*. But men of his father brought him up in paganism. . . . He dwelt in the palace at Antioch, because he was not worthy to live in the palace of Constantine.

Thus the anonymous author mentions Constantine's death, Constantine's sister and nephew, Constantine's children and Constantine's palace, but nothing of Constantine himself.

To find further attestations of Constantine in Coptic, it is necessary to turn to Coptic literature: although Constantine appears with some regularity here, he is overshadowed by his predecessor Diocletian. It would be difficult to underestimate the impact that Diocletian had on the Egyptian mind. Certainly Diocletian's administrative reforms had a major effect on Egypt, but it was Diocletian's persecution of Christians in Egypt that impressed Egyptians to the point that they dated their existence in terms of the beginning of Diocletian's reign; indeed, the Coptic church to this day dates from Diocletian's accession, the so-called 'Era of the Martyrs'. Coptic literature is full of portraits of Diocletian as mad king and Antichrist; these vary, but in all, he is, *par excellence*, persecutor of Christians.[6] Clearly, Diocletian left an indelible mark on the Egyptian consciousness, in contrast to Constantine.

This overshadowing of Constantine by Diocletian is especially noticeable in martyrdoms. In such stories, Diocletian is a figure of drama and interest but Constantine is not; when he is mentioned at all, it is usually as Diocletian's successor. Constantine's freeing of the Christian prisoners at his accession is prominent in several stories, although it is usually mentioned in passing and Constantine himself is not described. An interesting exception to the usual passing reference in Coptic martyrdoms is found in the martyrdom of Ter and his sister Irai.[7] Ter was a captain of Diocletian, who converted to Christianity during the persecution. His sister Irai also converted and together they went to Alexandria. In their absence, 'a young and valiant tribune named Constantine, whom the king loved very much', went to Diocletian and asked to marry Kalonia, the younger sister of Ter and Irai. Their mother refused permission and Constantine was very unhappy, as was Diocletian on his behalf. The emperor appealed to Romanos, another of his captains and Kalonia's uncle, who persuaded Kalonia's mother. He took Kalonia's hand and gave it in marriage to Constantine. 'Kalonia became the wife of Constantine until the day that the Lord smote down Diocletian and Constantine ruled in his place.' The implication at the end of this episode is that Kalonia ceased to be Constantine's wife after his succession. This text is an interesting attempt by its anonymous author to link his hero to Constantine, establishing an historical context for his story.

Elsewhere in Coptic literature, Constantine appears most often in connection with the finding of the True Cross in Jerusalem. Typical is this brief mention in an alphabetic acrostic hymn to St Mercurius:

When Decius died
Diocletian became Emperor in his place.
He slaughtered many martyrs.
After him Constantine became Emperor.
He was the one who revealed
The Cross of Jesus.
He built a multitude of martyr shrines,
In which great wonders occurred.[8]

(Pierpont Morgan Coptic MS M574)

But the most extensive version is in a homily on the True Cross by
an author known as Pseudo-Cyril of Jerusalem. The identification
of the works of Pseudo-Cyril was made fairly recently by Alberto
Campagno, previous editors of the texts assuming that they were
otherwise unknown works of Cyril himself.[9] The six known works
of Pseudo-Cyril were all composed in Coptic; they may have been
put together from various pre-existing Coptic sources. No date for
Pseudo-Cyril is certain, but it is likely that his works were written
in the form we have them today in the sixth or seventh century.

Pseudo-Cyril's homily on the True Cross is episodic, showing
the various events in the existence of the Cross. As in the martyrdoms, the account of Constantine begins with a description of the
wickedness of Diocletian. Pseudo-Cyril's description of Constantine's life before becoming emperor is much more extensively developed than the account of John of Nikiou; in Pseudo-Cyril,
Constantine and his parents are secret Christians during the persecution of Diocletian. Constantine is fighting against the Persians,
but becomes discouraged and attempts to sue for peace, which the
Persians take as a sign of weakness. Constantine goes to sleep full of
concern, but is awakened by the vision of the Cross and is told that
he will conquer under this sign. He does not know what the sign
means, since (being a secret Christian) he has never seen a cross. His
soldiers interpret it variously as symbols of different pagan gods, but
the soldier Eusignius comes to him and explains the true meaning.
Constantine fights under this sign of Christ and wins a decisive
battle; as a result he is made emperor. After spending freely on the
building of churches and the closing of pagan temples, Constantine
takes his family off to Jerusalem where they can find the True Cross.
He discovers that the location of the tomb in which it is contained
has been hidden for centuries by the Jews of the city; one of them is
able to tell him that it is hidden under the town dungheap. So
Constantine orders all Jews in the city to come clear away the

TERRY WILFONG

excrement. After protests, the tomb is cleared and the True Cross found. Constantine enters the tomb and looks at it. His mother Helena is the active agent of Constantine throughout the story, which ends with Constantine ordering the construction of an elaborate church on the site of the tomb. The Constantine episode of Pseudo-Cyril concludes with pious reflections on the finding of the True Cross. Although Constantine is more active in this story than in the martyrdoms, much of the activity in the story is done by others, especially Helena and a holy man named Apa Joseph. Only before he becomes emperor does Constantine act himself to any great degree. Again, as in the account of John of Nikiou, emphasis is put on Constantine's battles with the Persians, yet another instance of this motif.

Incidental references to Constantine and the finding of the Cross are numerous, but consecutive accounts in Coptic outside of Pseudo-Cyril are uncommon. The main text is the life of the martyr Eusignius, Constantine's soldier, but this is a translation of a Greek original.[10] A much shorter anonymous work on Constantine and the Cross from a Cairo Museum parchment was published by Henri Munier.[11] Although Munier entitled the work 'A Coptic Elegy on Emperor Constantine', the ancient title is, in fact, 'Concerning the Holy Cross'. The composition is apparently complete on the recto and verso of a single leaf from a codex, with only the beginnings and ends of some lines missing. As in other texts, Constantine is credited with releasing Christian prisoners after the death of Diocletian. This text also attributes to him the building of churches and the establishment of orthodox faith. The remainder of the text is in the form of a prayer, which includes a denunciation of the Jews for their role in concealing the Cross and a lament about the wicked teachings of Arius and Melitus. The editor of this text noted some parallels in a text in Strasbourg,[12] but the parallels are not particularly close; moreover, the Strasbourg text has been interpreted as something quite different. In his book on Coptic poetry of the tenth century, Hermann Junker treated the Strasbourg text as a poetic song (alongside other songs about historic events and holy subjects).[13] The tune of the song is given as 'Because of a woman'; the first line and refrain of the song is 'Look to the sky, great king Constantine!' Beyond this, however, Constantine is absent in name. The True Cross appears to the Christian soldier Eusignius, and the song is primarily concerned with Eusignius' description of the symbol and its amazing appearance and properties. This text is followed by yet another song on the finding of the Cross, but this work mentions neither Constantine nor his mother Helena directly.

A story about the finding of the Holy Sepulchre by Constantine's sister Eudoxia is one of the more extensive treatments of Constantine. This text is known from at least two manuscripts, one represented by a single fragment in the John Rylands Library and the other a complete manuscript in the Turin Museum. The text had been known from the Turin codex for about a hundred years from a rather poor publication, but it was only in 1980 that the text received a proper edition.[14] The text was composed in Coptic; the date of its final composition is uncertain, but the manuscripts have been dated to around 700 and the editors suggest a seventh-century date. The date of composition may have some connection to the subject matter.

The story is made up of three main parts, which may well have been separate compositions from which the final story was compiled. The first episode of the Eudoxia story concerns the downfall of Diocletian and the accession of Constantine, concluding with the release of all people jailed for their Christianity. The next section of the story opens with Constantine being baptised, never having been before. In the East, a group of five Persian kings are becoming unsettled at what they hear of Constantine's Christianity and declare war. Constantine goes to meet them, but when he and his men cross the Tigris and meet the Persians, the Roman troops are terrified by the huge numbers of Persians and run away. Constantine is left alone and the Persians descend upon him. An angel of God in a cloud, however, seizes Constantine, his chariot and his horse and whisks them away to the site of Constantinople. Constantine ordered that the walls of his new city be built here along with his palace; he also commanded that a painting of a horse and a cloud be set up as a memorial. The Persians, meanwhile, have concluded that Constantine was saved by the magic of the Christians and, after the year was out, took their troops to the Roman border. This time, Constantine was ready for them and the two sides remained opposite each other for three months, running out of water in the process. Both sides prayed to their respective gods for help. Constantine prayed that God bring water to show that He is the true God; he struck a rock with his rod and water gushed forth. After the Romans and their animals drank their fill, Constantine ordered them out of the way so that the Persians could drink too. The Persian kings saw the miracle and submitted to Constantine and his God, sending yearly tribute and keeping the peace from then on.

The final episode of the story is the longest and, indeed, the ostensible purpose for the composition: the account of the finding of the Holy Sepulchre by Constantine's virgin sister Eudoxia. The episode opens on Eudoxia sleeping in her lavishly appointed bedroom, in her gold and silver bed, under a richly embroidered cover presented to Constantine by a repentant Persian king. Christ appears to her in a dream and asks how she can sleep on a bed of gold and silver and fine linens and jewels when she has not sought the place of his resurrection. Christ proves his identity to her and describes the long history of neglect that his holy tomb has suffered. Eudoxia enlists her brother's help in a scene showing the close relationship between the two siblings, and Constantine sends her off to Jerusalem with attendants to find the Holy Sepulchre. From here on, the story closely resembles Pseudo-Cyril's homily on the True Cross. In the Eudoxia story, she finds the inscription from the True Cross and the bodies of the two thieves crucified with Christ. Constantine himself comes to Jerusalem to see the inscription. Constantine gives Eudoxia large sums to build the church on the site of the Holy Sepulchre, and it is with that event that the story concludes.

This story has been treated at great length by its recent editors and commentators and there is no point in recapitulating their work here. Harold Drake pointed out the general ahistorical nature of the text; the sister 'Eudoxia' of Constantine is clearly a conflation of Helena and the Theodosian empresses Eudocia and Eudoxia, although the Coptic author of this text has not taken any special pains to portray accurately the career of any of these women. Similarly, the account of Constantine's Persian wars cannot be matched to any known battles and, indeed, seems to have more parallels to Heraclius' fights against the Sassanians than anything else. This latter point may give a clue to the date of this text: internal evidence makes it likely that it was written sometime between the Sassanian domination of Egypt (618–628) and the beginning of the eighth century.

One text remains which has gone almost unnoticed in the scholarly discussion of Coptic literature on Constantine, but which sums up the Coptic preoccupations about the emperor quite well. This source is an ostrakon from the Theban monastery of Epiphanius, excavated by the Metropolitan Museum of Art and published by Walter Crum in 1926 as Ep 80 in his edition of the texts from that site.[15] In the addenda to the edition,[16] Crum noted parallels between this text and the early, faulty edition of the Eudoxia story, but the very location of Crum's note almost guaranteed the obscurity of his findings and it has been largely ignored. Because the text is so little known, so brief and of such interest, I give a new translation of it here. After a few broken lines, the import of which is unclear:

> Constantine, the righteous king, believed in God with all his heart. God guided him in all his ways and protected him from wars with de[mons and] wars . . . with heathens [. . .] because of his faith in God. He humbled his enemies under his feet. And when the Persians shot arrows at him, God sent a cloud and it took him out from among them, with his horse. And those barbarians were subject to him and gave him tribute for all of his time. And they did not make war at all during his time.

The text ends, apparently complete.

Among Coptic sources on Constantine, this text is unique for a number of reasons. It is the only such source with a known archaeological context – the Monastery of Epiphanius, a well-excavated and well-published site securely dated to the seventh century. It is also the only Coptic Constantine source written on a potsherd, rather than on papyrus or parchment. Ostraka were generally used for non-literary texts; literary texts found on ostraka are generally limited to the Bible or similar texts that could be used as amulets or texts for meditation and prayer. It is possible that this text was a school exercise, which might explain the use of a potsherd rather than a more prestigious writing material, but it demonstrates none of the usual signs of a school text. So the purpose of this ostrakon remains obscure; the Constantine text seems an unlikely candidate for either amuletic, educational or devotional purposes.

The broken beginning of the text is a general praise of Constantine, extolling his virtues as a good Christian. The reference to his battles with demons is tantalising; none of the Coptic Constantine texts mentions any such incident, although this may just be a general reference to pagan resistance. The story of a cloud carrying off Constantine during his battle with the Persians together with his horse is a general parallel to the Eudoxia story, but there are differences. In the Epiphanius ostrakon, the incident is climactic, ending the battle; in the Eudoxia story it does not finish the battle, but leads to the founding of Constantinople. The tribute and peace of the Persians are similarly paralleled, but again the ostrakon is more definite and abrupt in its descriptions.

Battles against 'the Persians' appear frequently in these Constantine texts.[17] Such battles are often found elsewhere in Coptic literature, particularly in the lives of saints, and they are also found in the so-called historical romances of Cambyses and Alexander.[18] It has been shown convincingly that the 'romance' about Cambyses was written in reaction to the Sassanian invasion of Egypt, possibly even as a disguised account of the Sassanians.[19] Other Coptic literary texts set in the fourth and fifth centuries, but written later, also refer to battles with 'the Persians' which cannot be matched to any known contemporary battles. There is, however, nowhere in Coptic literature an actual description of the Sassanian invasion and conquest of Egypt in the seventh century, despite the fact that this is the time when much Coptic literature was written down, and the time when some of it was composed. The only explicit references to it are later mentions of the devastation caused by the Sassanians, but there are never direct descriptions of the invasion itself in Coptic sources.

The exception that is usually cited is the *Chronicle* of John of Nikiou, despite the fact that he omits all mention of the Sassanian Persian domination of Egypt from 619 to 628. Traditionally, this omission has always been seen as the fault of the transmission of the manuscript through the Arabic and Ethiopic translation;[20] that is, scholars assume that John of Nikiou recounted these events in his (now lost) Sahidic Coptic original, but that they dropped out of subsequent versions. There is a chronological gap in John's narrative for this period, but there is no direct evidence that any of John's original text has disappeared here. In other words, there is no evidence that John actually wrote about the Sassanian domination at all, and there is no other account of the invasion in Coptic.

This reticence in writing about the Sassanian invasion is suggestive when examined in connection with the Coptic Constantine sources. Most of those referring to Constantine's battles with the Persians are thought to have been composed or written down in the seventh century. It is difficult not to make the obvious conclusion that the writers were influenced by the events of their time, but were unable or afraid to write about them directly and could only write about them set safely in the past. At a time when Christianity itself seemed threatened, the 'first Christian emperor' of Coptic tradition may have seemed an ideal hero against the Persians, especially considering that the reigning emperor Heraclius expended much effort, when not fighting the Persians, making life difficult for most of the Egyptian Christian population through persecution of the Monophysites. None of the contemporary literature from outside Egypt celebrating Heraclius as a second Constantine seems to have made it into Coptic; Egyptian writers seem to have preferred the original Constantine instead, as an heroic figure too remote to trouble them.

It is clear that the Egyptians were interested in Constantine as an historical person. They had access to historical traditions of varying degrees of accuracy and they used these according to their needs. As an historical figure, though, Constantine was somewhat overshadowed by his predecessor Diocletian, on the one hand, and his sister and other relatives, on the other. He was remembered as the first Christian emperor, but his activity is limited even in these accounts. The only role in which Constantine is portrayed with any degree of activity and vividness is as victor against the Persians; the details of these stories, however, are generally ahistorical and seem to reflect Egyptian anxieties about the Persians in the aftermath of the Sassanian invasion of Egypt in the seventh century. In the end, Constantine seems to have been used as a symbol more than anything else. To a Christian population brutally conquered by non-Christian Persians, delivered by the Byzantine reconquest into persecution on sectarian grounds, and then more or less cut off from the rest of Christendom by the Muslim conquest, Constantine represented hope: a Christian ruler to triumph over the Persians and free Egypt from persecution. In those uncertain times, the Egyptians needed an heroic figure. They looked back into their past and they chose Constantine.

ACKNOWLEDGEMENTS

I would like to thank Sam Lieu and Dominic Montserrat for inviting me to contribute this paper both to the original conference and to the present volume, and for their helpful comments and suggestions. I would also like to express my appreciation to the participants in the conference for their discussion of the paper and to Professor Tito Orlandi for drawing my attention to a Coptic source on Constantine.

NOTES

1 For a recent discussion of this topic, see Bagnall 1993: 230–60.
2 English translation and references in Charles 1916. Although there has been debate over the original language of this text (see Fraser 1991 for a summary), the text and the historical context of its composition make it virtually certain that this work was composed in Coptic.
3 Orlandi 1967–70; additional fragments of this work have turned up since Orlandi's edition, but do not relate to the present discussion. For full references and discussion of the complex history of this work, see den Heijer 1989.
4 This text and the following excerpts were originally edited with a Latin translation in Orlandi 1967–70, but are republished with revisions in den Heijer 1989: 160–2.
5 Reading *nešēre* instead of *nešpēre* in line 13 on page 36, clearly a typographical error; noted in den Heijer 1989: 160 n. 15.
6 For surveys of Coptic literary depictions of Diocletian, see van den Berg-Onstwedder 1990 and the earlier J. Schwartz 1958–1960.
7 Published in Hyvernat 1886, with additional fragments in Orlandi 1974; I owe this reference to the kind efforts of Tito Orlandi of the University of Rome.
8 Translation of Pierpont Morgan MS M574 after Kuhn and Tait 1996: 32–5.
9 Campagno 1980.
10 On St Eusignius, see Devos 1982 for an edition of the *Pass. Eusign.*, and Samuel Lieu in this volume, pp. 154, 156–7, 159 and 167–8.
11 Munier 1918: 65–71.
12 Spiegelberg 1901: 206–11.
13 Junker 1911: 175–81.
14 Orlandi *et al.* 1981.
15 Crum and Evelyn White 1926: 25 and 171–2.
16 Ibid. xv.
17 Noted in Simon 1935: 222–34, 227 n. 4, and Pearson *et al.* 1993: x, though without reference to the texts discussed below.
18 See Müller 1991 for bibliography on both.
19 MacCoull 1982, although many of the specifics in this article (the identity of the author and his precise location) are purely speculative. The suggestion of Cruz-Uribe 1986 that this work is, in fact, a reaction to the Arab conquest is ingenious, but unconvincing.
20 As suggested in, e.g., Butler 1978: xix and 219 n. 1. The full listing of chapter headings at the beginning of the Ethiopic text of John of Nikiou gives no indication of missing sections on the Sassanian domination.

10

CONSTANTINE, ST ALDHELM AND THE LOATHLY LADY

Jane Stevenson

Aldhelm's version of the legend of Sylvester and Constantine has been discussed elsewhere in this volume. What I am seeking to do in this chapter is to explore the issues which arise from one part of his account of Constantine, which appears to be a version of the story known to folklorists and English students as the 'Loathly Lady'. Was it an addition of Aldhelm's own to the accretion of stories about Constantine; how can we tell if so; and why would he do it?

Before tackling Aldhelm, it may be helpful very briefly to outline what he is likely to have gleaned about Constantine from other Insular writers. Let us begin with the Celtic evidence. As is well known, Constantius Chlorus died at York, with Constantine at his side, so it was from Roman Britain that Constantine began his long journey towards supreme power. We might therefore have expected that Constantine, the first Christian emperor, would have figured substantially in the collective lore of post-Roman Britain. This is very far from being the case. If we turn to the most important early source, the brief sketch of British history in Gildas' *De excidio Britanniae*, written some time in the sixth century,[1] we find that Constantine virtually disappears.[2] The persecutions under Diocletian are treated rather fully, but Gildas switches straight to the eruption of the Arian heresy without mentioning that it took place under a Christian emperor.[3] The really important figure in Romano-British history, to Gildas, is the usurper Magnus Maximus. The legendary version of Romano-British history which was available to Gildas, as a highly intelligent man with no specialist interest in history, is that Magnus caused the tragedy of Roman Britain by taking the entire flower of Britain's youth to Europe in pursuit of his dream of imperial glory, from whence they never returned, leaving Britain helplessly vulnerable to the encroachment of Scots, Picts and Saxons.[4] This myth of 'the men who marched away' is central to subsequent Welsh perceptions of their relationship to Roman history.[5] It is the failed challenger, Magnus, not the successful Constantine, who was remembered in the early Middle Ages. For instance, the so-called 'Pillar of Eliseg', erected in the first half of the ninth century to establish the genealogy of the royal line of Powys, traces their lineage back to a marriage between Vortigern and Severa, the daughter of Maximus.[6] Considerably later, the body of Welsh heroic legend assembled in the thirteenth century and known as the *Mabinogion* includes a free-standing short story called *Breudwyt Maxen* or 'The Dream of Macsen Wledig' (*gwledig*: 'ruler, prince') about Macsen's marriage to a British bride called Elen *luydawc* (Helen of the Hosts), who is elsewhere identified with Helen the mother of Constantine, suggesting that the figures of Maximus and Constantine have actually run together to some extent.[7] It is also interesting, and puzzling, that the name Macsen, though always associated with Magnus Maximus, looks more like a corruption of the name of Constantine's old enemy *Maxentius*.[8] Be that as it may, it is Magnus/Macsen who is 'the emperor' in the collective memories of the early Welsh. There is no comparable body of early lore associated with Constantine.

Bede, the first historical writer produced by Anglo-Saxon England (who was writing a few decades after Aldhelm), accepts Gildas' assessment of the relative importance of these figures, suggesting that there was no urge to revise Gildas' view of this part of the British past among Anglo-Saxon historiographers.[9] Magnus gets three chapters; Constantine gets three sentences. Like Gildas, Bede notes that the Arian heresy arose in Constantine's time, but not that he was the first Christian emperor.[10] The only place in the *Historia Ecclesiastica* where it is mentioned that Constantine was the first Christian Roman emperor is in a letter from Pope Gregory the Great to King Ethelbert of Kent which Bede quotes *in extenso*.[11]

However, another way of looking at the importance of Constantine in Insular culture is to see if the name was used, and if so, by whom. Though Gildas appears to have thought little of the Emperor Constantine, of the British kings who were his contemporaries, one bore the name.[12] Consantín occurs, though rarely, in early medieval Ireland.[13] The only place where the name is at all common is Scotland. It was used as a royal name by the Pictish kings,[14] and continued to be used by the kings of Scotland as late as the ninth and tenth centuries. Constantine himself appears (as Constantinus or Custennhin) in Welsh sources from the tenth century.[15] So his name was not forgotten (particularly not in Scotland), but there is no evidence from any of the Celtic countries that he was drawn into the repertory of heroic legend. Aldhelm, in introducing a number of stories about Constantine into his *De virginitate* late in the seventh century, was not describing a figure to whom his contemporaries and predecessors in the British Isles had assigned any distinct personality.

As Sam Lieu has shown elsewhere in this volume, Aldhelm draws on the *Vita*, or *Actus*, *Silvestri*. But as I hope to show, he also introduces a story which appears to be of Irish origin. The question of Irish influence on Anglo-Saxon culture is very much under examination at the moment from a variety of angles.[16] It is a matter of common knowledge that a number of stories current in medieval England appear to have an Irish background. Among the most notable are the Northern English romance *Gawain and the Green Knight* and Chaucer's *Wife of Bath's Tale* in his *Canterbury Tales*: the earliest analogues for both stories appear to be Irish.[17]

Aldhelm seems to have anticipated Chaucer's use of the 'Loathly Lady' tale by some 700 years. In its most familiar English form, as redacted by Chaucer in the *Wife of Bath's Tale*, it tells of a knight who is required to find out, within a year and a day, what women most desire. He is unsuccessful until he chances to meet an old woman, 'a fouler wight there may no man devyse' (l. 999), who tells him that 'wommen desiren to have sovereyntee' (l. 1038). The knight thus escapes with his neck, but the old lady inconveniently reappears and tells the court that in recompense for this wisdom, he has promised her marriage. He is then forced to marry her, and when she has reduced him, on their wedding night, to total abjection, she miraculously transforms into a lovely young bride and all ends happily. Chaucer's use of this story is replete with ironies – not least that it is of course being told by that masterful lady, the Wife of Bath – and of course it has lying behind it a historical context in which women, far from possessing 'maistrie' over their husbands, were subject to them even to the extent of corporal punishment.[18] But it is based on a probably much older Irish story, which also brings together women and sovereignty, though in a rather different way.

The broad outline of the Irish story which Chaucer was adapting is that the young man encounters the old woman, is induced to promise her marriage, forces himself to embrace her, and is then dazzled by the revelation that she is Sovereignty, which appears harsh and repulsive until it is embraced and accepted. It is told of Niall *noígiallach* ('of the nine hostages'), eponymous ancestor figure of the Uí Néill, the most powerful ruling dynasty in late seventh-century Ireland,[19] as well as of Lugaid Laigde, ancestor of the Érainn of Munster, and other heroes.[20] However, I shall be suggesting that its connection with Niall in particular is significant and relevant to its use by Aldhelm.

The version of which Niall is the hero, in the *Echtra mac n-Ecach Muigmedóin* (Adventures of the sons of Eochaid Mugmedón), combines it with another classic motif, that of siblings of whom the youngest is the most successful. Three sons of Eochaid's legitimate queen Mongfind, searching for water, refuse to give the hag who guards the well a kiss in exchange for water. The unregarded and illegitimate Niall offers her not merely a kiss, but sex, upon which she magically becomes beautiful.[21] In other cultures, this might appear to be an allegory; but it seems in fact to be a myth, which has its origin in the idea that the king is wedded to his *tuath* in a more or less literal sense.[22] The Irish 'Sovereignty' story has been intensively examined from various angles. It has attracted interest as a Chaucerian source, naturally, and it was also of obvious interest to the many scholars who have sought in Ireland the vestiges of a remote Indo-European antiquity:[23] it can be connected, for example, with the O'Neill inauguration ritual recorded by Giraldus Cambrensis in the twelfth century, in which the incoming ruler appears to 'marry' his kingdom (personified as a white mare),[24] and with the lusty and many-husbanded figure of Medb in the *Táin Bó Cuailgne*.[25]

Before turning to Aldhelm's use of this motif, it may be helpful to introduce the man and his work. He was the first Latin author of Anglo-Saxon England, and as far as he was aware, the first person learning Latin as a foreign language ever to write metrical verse. His *magnum opus* is a treatise on virginity, illustrated by the histories of numerous exemplary virgins, male and female. It is in the form of an *opus geminatum*: having written his treatise in prose, he paraphrased his own work in hexameter verse. The model for this 'double work' was the greatly admired Late Antique writer

Caelius Sedulius, whose *Opus paschale* similarly exists in both a poetic and a prose form. These paraphrases are witnesses to the Late Antique and early medieval fascination with form rather than content, which produced paraphrases, poetic versions, pattern poems (such as the extraordinary examples in praise of Constantine by Publilius Optatianus Porphyrius), and other curiosities of restrictive writing. Among Aldhelm's potted biographies of male virgins in the prose *De virg.*, written *c.* 680–700,[26] there appears an account of Pope Sylvester, based on the *V. Sylv.*. Sylvester (or Silvester) is the hero of a legend about Constantine the Great which appears in a fully developed form as early as the fifth century. The historical Sylvester was Pope from 314 to 335, and little is known of him. His legend, however, presents him as a wonder-worker who, among other feats, cured the Emperor Constantine of leprosy; a story which was, in its turn, the basis for that most famous of all medieval forgeries, the Donation of Constantine, already discussed by Sam Lieu in the present volume. In addition to this cure, Aldhelm notes a further, important interaction between Sylvester and Constantine, which appears to be a variant of the 'Loathly Lady' tale.

> When the emperor, (being) in the city which was called Byzantium, had given his limbs over to sleep and was paying the debt of nature, there appeared to him in a nocturnal vision a certain old woman, very decrepit – in fact near to death – whom he is ordered at Sylvester's command to resuscitate by praying. (When) Constantine prayed, that old woman arose and became an extremely beautiful young lady, blushing with the glowing flower of exquisite youth. When she had pleased the royal inspection in chaste contemplation (of her), he covered her with his cloak and placed a diadem adorned with burnished gold and shining gems on her head. But Helena his mother said to him: 'She shall be yours and shall not die except at the end of the world.' Thereupon, when he awakened, the emperor was bitterly constrained by his ignorance of future events until, after the simple space of a week – his body (having become) lean with the abstemiousness of temperance – he is again given over to sleep. Sylvester, the man of venerable life, is present before him on the seventh day of his fast, saying to him once again in his vision: 'The decrepit old woman is this city in which

you are staying, called Byzantium, whose walls are now
wasted away because of their age, and nearly all its fortifications have collapsed. Mount, therefore that horse of
yours, on which you sat when you were baptized, in white
linen . . . and sitting on him take up your ensign which
is decorated with the sign of Christ in gold and jewels.
Holding this ensign in your right hand, release the reins
of your horse so that he may go wherever the angel of God
shall lead him; and you drag the point of your ensign
fixed in the earth in such a way that it makes a path by its
passage; along this path you shall have walls constructed
and (so) shall resuscitate this veteran and nearly dead city
into (the likeness of) a young lady; and you shall name her
with your own name so that you make her the queen of
all cities.

(De virg. 25)

Sam Lieu's detailed study of the developing legend of Constantine
gives this as an episode from the *V. Sylv.*, which exists in two
principal, variant versions, both in existence by the end of the fifth
century. B(1) was first printed in 1479 by Boninus Mombritius.[27]
A, the long version in two books, was more popular in the West,
while the shorter version B circulated more widely in the East.
Both were originally written in Latin. A(1), generally regarded as
the older and more authentic, is now being edited by W. Pohlkamp.[28] It is probable, then, that A is the version used by Aldhelm. He may perhaps have come across it when he visited Rome,
which he did at least once.[29]

The 'Irishness' of this story is immediately striking. The sexual/
bridal motif of the basic tale-type is conspicuously missing, perhaps understandably, since Aldhelm is writing a work in praise of
virginity. Yet there are many points of similarity. The hero
encounters a decrepit old woman, whom he resuscitates by praying
(a substitute for the sexual encounter central to other versions,
perhaps suggested by the many hagiographic accounts of individuals brought back from the dead at the prayers of a saint), upon
which she becomes an exquisite beauty. He covers her with his
cloak and places his diadem on her head – that is, he performs
ritual gestures appropriate to taking her in marriage, as his queen.
The lady is revealed as his capital city, and thus, is as much the
personification of his sovereignty as is the woman encountered by

Niall. Constantine in this story might literally be said to have married his capital.

The real question is, is this episode directly based on part of the *V. Sylv.*, or not? Constantine's vision occurs in the version called *Legenda s. Silvestri papae ab Eusebio Cesariensi Palestino greco sermone compilata.*[30] This is, to a great extent, word-for-word the same as Aldhelm's prose account, with an interesting variant: '*appellata est civitas Constantini, quod Greco sermone dicitur **Kaide**, et quod Latine interpretatur Constantinopolis usque ad hodiernum diem*'. As Burch immediately observed, the words in bold represent the Greek particles *kai de* (καὶ δὴ) as a Greek word, suggesting a complete lack of comprehension of the Greek language, which cannot reasonably be ascribed to Aldhelm: he received at least part of his education at the Greek-speaking school of Canterbury, under Hadrian,[31] and though he probably could not read an actual Greek text, he was at least capable of such a hybrid phrase as *ad doxam onomatis cyrii*,[32] suggesting a basic knowledge of the language greater than would allow him to mistake a particle for a noun, and probably sufficient to enable him to translate Constantinopolis as *ciuitas Constantini.*[33]

How are we to read this? Both Burch and Lieu appear to assume a pre-existing text in Greek translated into Latin by some individual so inept that he mistook *kai de* for a name (but could anyone so ill-informed translate Greek at all?). Lieu suggests that, 'Aldhelm . . . apparently saw through the error by the "author" of the *V. Sylv.* in composing the Greek name of Constantinople from the conjunctional link in the Greek sentence about the city's name' and therefore left out the clause in question. By implication, Lieu and Burch put the composition of this version of the *V. Sylv.* between the fourth and the seventh centuries, a period in which it is far easier to find translations from Greek by Greek-speakers which show a poor knowledge of Latin than translations of Greek by Latin-speakers showing a poor knowledge of Greek.[34] But since the surviving text of the *V. Sylv.* is far later than *De virg.*, it seems equally possible that it is making use of Aldhelm rather than the other way round, in which case the offending clause could reasonably be interpreted as a marginal gloss which was interpolated by a later, Greekless, redactor into the text. Such a redactor may have found *Kaide: Constantinopolis* in a glossary and added it in as a piece of useful and esoteric information: early medieval glossaries are replete with exotic words (including Greek, Hebrew, and in

the case of Insular glossaries, Old Irish and Old English), often
terribly garbled and presented in a completely contextless fashion.

The introduction of pseudo-information derived from glossaries
is a feature of Insular Latin texts. They result from the creation of
what Henry Bradshaw christened *glossae collectae*: collections of
interlinear or marginal glosses extracted from the text to which
they refer and arranged in A- or AB- order.[35] For example,
Aldhelm himself uses *fastus* as an equivalent of *liber*, an error
which almost certainly derives from a gloss which originally
read something like **fasti: libri caerimoniarum*,[36] but was redacted
in the copy actually available to him as **fasti: libri*.[37] A tenth-
century Latin–Latin glossary of Insular origin, BL Harley 3376,[38]
contains a variety of peculiar words which illustrate this capacity
of glosses from Greek to create pseudo-vocabulary in Latin. For
instance, we find the gloss *callioren: prostituta mulierum*. This
almost certainly represents *callirhoen*, accusative of the personal
name Callirhoe, probably with reference to Persius, *Satire* 1.134.[39]
It would be perfectly possible to find an Insular author, in a
context of hyper-inflated language such as the *arenga* of a late
Anglo-Saxon charter, using *callioren, -enis* as a third-declension
Latin equivalent for 'prostitute' (as far as I know, it is not in
fact so used).

The equation of Constantinople with *kaide* was almost certainly
arrived at by a misreading of an interlinear gloss on a Greek text
(where the reader would normally expect to find the gloss written
directly over its lemma) in which '*Constantinopolis*' or '*civitas Constantini*' ended up over the wrong word due to its length. We have
a clear example of this kind of thing happening in the Harley
glossary, which makes use of the remarkable Hiberno-Latin poem
Rubisca.[40] The use of *Rubisca* is proved by the lemma *bifaxo ales*
(B212), glossed 'binos oculos habes', among others. This lemma is
a metrical adonic verse from *Rubisca* (properly 'bifax O ales'), and
the gloss is nearly identical to one found with the poem itself in
the Cambridge manuscript (UL Gg. 5. 35), written over the
line.[41] Here, we can see unequivocally that the confusion of the
glossator springs directly from the length of the gloss relative to
that of the lemma, since the original writer intended it to refer
only to *bifaxo*.[42]

The collection of names for something in different languages is
also a regular feature of Insular Latin prose: Adomnán's *De locis
sanctis*, for example, gives us

Arculfus etiam Tirum Fenicis prouinciae metropolim
introiit, quae Ebreico et Siro sermone Soar
appellatur . . . Grandis illa ciuitas [Alexandria], quae quondam
metropolis Aegipti fuerat, Ebraicae olim No uocabitur.[43]

A little later, we have a reference to the mouth of the Nile, 'quod
Canopecon nominatur'.[44] This interest in accumulating a the-
saurus of alternatives is found throughout pre-Conquest Latin
literature in both England and Ireland, particularly in the context
of the *tres linguae sacrae*.[45] Thus, it is quite possible that a perfectly
correct gloss on the name Constantinopolis, or Byzantium, or
perhaps *to polis*, could be created by one commentator, be wrongly
redacted into a glossary by a Greekless compiler misled by its
position, be used by a third Greekless scribe as a marginal note to
the *V. Sylv.*, and finally, be copied into a later redaction by a
scribe who was under the impression that it belonged to the text
and had been omitted in error. These successive Greekless scholars
are, by the implications of this argument, located in the British
Isles between the eighth and the fourteenth centuries, at least the
first two probably before the Norman Conquest; a milieu in which
inability to correct even the simplest Greek is far from surprising.

There is another way of addressing the question of the primacy
of Aldhelm's version over that of the *V. Sylv.* or vice versa. Let us
look more carefully at the context of the prose *De virg.* (the poetic
version is of no help, since on Aldhelm's own showing, it is
undoubtedly a later reworking of Aldhelm's prose). Aldhelm's
Latin prose style, though praised by Bede as *sermo nitidus*,[46] has
had few admirers since the Norman Conquest. But however one
might choose to judge it aesthetically, it is highly wrought and
highly self-conscious.[47] While the episodes in *De virg.* are of
course drawn from a variety of sources (some known, some
unknown), the treatment is stylistically distinctive and fairly
homogeneous, though influenced to some extent by the style of
the authors he was adapting.[48] In general, the episodes in *De virg.*
have a story-line in common with their originals (where these are
known), and may retain some vocabulary, but the treatment is
expanded and, indeed, inflated. As Winterbottom says, 'the treatise is, in essence, no more than a series of instances of virginity,
polished up by Aldhelm to make a row of always different beads,
strung, highly coloured and clinking, on a long necklace'.[49] The
redundancy and *copia uerborum* of Aldhelm's style where he is

working close to a known original are readily illustrated by his reworking of a sentence from Paulinus of Milan's *Vita Ambrosii*:

(Paulinus)

Qui infans in area praetorii in cuna positus cum dormiret, aperto ore subito examen apum adueniens faciem eius atque ora complevit, ita ut ingrediendi in os egrediendi-que vices frequentaret.

(Aldhelm)

. . . infantulus cum in cunis supinis quiesceret, ex impro-viso examen apium ora labraque sine periculo pausantis complevit, quae ingrediendi et egrediendi per tenera puerili labella certatim vices frequentabant.[50]

Characteristic features include the use of diminutives (*infantulus* for *infans*), the introduction of alliteration (*periculo pausantis*), redundancy, and the separation of nouns from accompanying adjectives (*per **tenera** puerili **labella*** for Paulinus's *in os*). The episode of the dream of Constantine is recounted in Aldhelmian style; similarly, Aldhelm uses *anicula* where the *V. Sylv.* uses *anus*, redundancy, separation of noun and adjective, and alliteration in a phrase such as '*quae cum casta contemplatione **regalibus** placuisset **obtutibus**'*. This obviously exists in some kind of relationship with the more soberly phrased text of the *V. Sylv.* Towards the end of the Constantine episode, the mutual resemblance is fairly close. It is possible that Aldhelm is rewriting his original, as he can be seen to do with Paulinus' of Milan's *V. Amb.*, but this is far from being necessarily the case. It is contrary to Aldhelm's usual prac-tice to copy without extensive revision. If he could be shown to have done so, we might reasonably assume it was in order pre-cisely to follow the words of a source which he regarded as particularly authoritative. There seems no obvious reason why he should have so regarded the legend of Constantine.

Why, then, should both Vacher Burch and Sam Lieu have assumed the primacy of the *V. Sylv.*? One of the most interesting aspects of the discussion of this story is that it illustrates the assumptions which academics make about the act of storytelling. It is assumed that Aldhelm's account of Constantine and Sylvester, written *c.* 690, must depend for *all* its episodes on a previously existing version of the *V. Sylv. Vitae* are highly accretive texts; yet the assumption is made that accretion invariably happens, so to say, off stage. No actual author is seen at work, though it is perfectly clear that a number of individuals must have deliberately and in cold blood added episodes to the story. In order to understand and explain the presence of the Loathly Lady in Aldhelm's version, therefore, we should be asking the question whether Aldhelm's general treatment of his sources in *De virg.* (which unfortunately are for the most part unknown) suggests that he is likely to be one of them.

We know little of Aldhelm's compositional technique or intentions, nothing beyond what can be deduced from his own writings, but there is some evidence that he did not regard his sources as sacrosanct, and was capable of rewriting a narrative for purposes of his own. One useful test case is his treatment of Thecla and Eulalia, whom he takes together in a single episode in his account of female virgins. He had a clear motive for including a treatment of both saints, even though, as we shall see, both involved him in some difficulties. We may reasonably assume that he felt it was incumbent on him to compliment his audience by including in his list of virgins all the saints whose names had been taken by his dedicatees in the convent at Barking: certainly, he does so. They include a Thecla and an Eulalia.[51]

In the cases of both Thecla and Eulalia, there is an important virgin saint of that name, the East Mediterranean Thecla of Iconium, described as 'Apostle and Protomartyr of the army of virginity',[52] and Eulalia, virgin martyr of Merida, one of the important saints of the early Spanish Church. Aldhelm's account of Thecla (clearly the famous Thecla, since he states that she was converted by the teaching of St Paul)[53] ends, in the *Carmen de virginitate*, with the statement that she was martyred: the problem is that the Thecla of the *Acta Pauli et Theclae* survived the arena and went on to a notoriously heterodox career as a female apostle.[54] Of Eulalia, Aldhelm clearly knew nothing at all beyond that she was both a virgin and a martyr: his extreme vagueness in both versions suggests that his source might have been a hymn,[55] or perhaps the *Martyrologium hieronymianum*, which gives her a mention in early December (10th, 11th or 12th in different versions). It is perhaps the paucity of his information on Eulalia which causes him to take the two virgins together, since he could hardly leave her out.

If his problem with Eulalia was that he did not have enough information, his problem with Thecla was probably that he had too much. As I have indicated, the *Acta Pauli et Theclae* send

Thecla off as an independent preacher of the gospel. We know from Tertullian that it was used by groups who wished to assert the rights of Orthodox Christian women to spiritual autonomy,[56] and following Tertullian, considerable numbers of male theologians went to some lengths to discourage this reading of the story. Anglo-Saxon nuns were not lacking in assertiveness, and we find Thecla used as a name in religion – not only by a dedicatee of *De virg.*, but also by an eighth-century nun (Thecla of Kitzingen) who went on the invitation of Boniface to help him with his conversion of the pagans north of the Rhine. Aldhelm, while certainly wishing to encourage his friends at Barking in their religious zeal, probably did not wish to offer them a model for complete independence from male authority. So, while he could hardly leave Thecla out, since his immediate audience would certainly expect an account of her, he could certainly tinker with her story in the interests of propriety. Rather than invoking a lost, anomalous version of the *Acta Pauli et Theclae* which omits chapters 36–43 as Aldhelm's source, I would suggest that he was perfectly capable of reworking an extra-biblical narrative if there was reason to do so.

Returning to Constantine, therefore, I have suggested there is reason for questioning the primacy of the *V. Sylv.* text over that of Aldhelm, on a number of counts. The mistaken equation *Kaide: Constantinopolis* is more plausibly located in the early Middle Ages than in Late Antiquity. Aldhelm tended to rewrite rather than directly to copy source-material, and his text (which was very widely read in England until the Conquest) was certainly a source for later writers. It would have been just as possible for some individual interested in the Sylvester story to redact Aldhelm's verbosity into plain prose as it was for Aldhelm to 'write up' the work of writers such as Paulinus of Milan; such rewriting can go either way, and there are examples of both to be found in Insular Latin. With regard to Aldhelm's possible source for the story, if he did not find it in the *V. Sylv.*, it is relevant to observe that he was personally acquainted with a number of Irishmen,[57] and had some knowledge of Insular Latin literature, if not of Irish: the references in his letter to Wihtfrith to a variety of extra-curricular study in Ireland suggest that he was at least aware of the Irish monasteries' surprisingly broad toleration of non-Christian learning and may perhaps have had some acquaintance with Irish story-telling.[58] It should not be forgotten that the 'Loathly Lady' story was told of Niall *noígiallach*, ancestor-figure of the Uí Néill, the most powerful family in Ireland at the time Aldhelm was writing, and indeed, the ancestor of the abbots of Iona, Columba and his *coarbs*, including Adomnán, with whom Aldhelm was indirectly linked through his godson king Aldfrip of Northumbria (685–705), who knew both writers well.

Aldhelm's attitude to the source-material of *De virg.* was not always or inevitably respectful. He was a highly original and creative individual; the first Latin poet who was not a native Latin speaker, the first English writer to forge for himself a distinctive prose style; and even, according to William of Malmesbury, so distinguished a poet in Old English that Alfred the Great regarded him as second to none. His confidence in himself and in his abilities was justifiably high. It seems to me that the balance of probability is in favour of his deliberately adding to the story as he originally received it. If this is so, of course, the really interesting question is why he did it.

The foundation of Constantinople was an event around which much mythography had gathered by the later seventh century. There are two direct avenues through which Aldhelm could have known the sort of tales which circulated in the Eastern Mediterranean: the story which the shipwrecked Gaulish pilgrim Arculf picked up in Constantinople itself and told to Adomnán,[59] or the recollections of Archbishop Theodore, who as Michael Lapidge has shown, probably received part of his education in Constantinople.[60] Though the *disiecta membra* of Theodore's teaching mention some sights of Constantinople,[61] no actual story about its foundation is recorded from him. Arculf's information about the origins of the city, on the other hand, is directly comparable with that of fourth-century and subsequent writers, Western and Eastern, in focusing principally on its catastrophic costliness.[62] Aldhelm's version is entirely different. The substitution, or addition, of an Insular hero-tale suggests that he was thinking of Constantine as if he was indeed a barbarian hero. Perhaps we should not be surprised that a man who, as William of Malmesbury tells us, redacted stories from the Bible into heroic ballads to lure his flock to church should think in terms of creative synthesis.[63]

It is noticeable that a number of other stories about Constantine discussed by Sam Lieu relate in one way or another to what Otto Rank called the 'Myth of the Birth of the Hero' (notably the 'Guidi-*Vita*' and 'Halkin-*Vita*').[64] Constantine is not brought up as his father's legitimate son and acknowledged heir, but achieves recognition due to his innate nobility and royal attributes. This might suggest a reason why Aldhelm grafted a story told of Niall onto the legend of Constantine. The legend of Niall resembles that of Constantine in some important particulars. He was the illegitimate son of his father by the concubine Cairenn, subject (together with his mother) to the persecution of the legitimate wife Mongfind and her four legitimate sons, but able to reverse his position *vis-à-vis* his brothers by dint, again, of his innate nobility, royal attributes and unmistakable fitness to rule. In both cases, their stories conform to some extent to what appears to be an international pattern of heroic tale-telling – in both cases, this is unlikely to be fortuitous. Constantine was not merely an emperor; he was the founder of a dynasty which he intended to last: image manipulation was important both to him and to those who supported him. The same is true of Niall, whose line was by some way the most ambitious and the most glorious in the Insular world of the seventh century, and had achieved that position not merely by dint of military prowess, but through a sophisticated and effective command of the techniques of propaganda, myth-making and disinformation. The *parvenu* dynasty of the Uí Néill (as Kelleher memorably put it), emerged into history 'like a school of cuttlefish, from a large ink-cloud of their own manufacture'.[65] There was no comparable figure, or dynasty, among the Anglo-Saxon kings at the time Aldhelm was writing (nor was there to be for some centuries). It is interesting that Aldhelm should have seen fit to render Constantine in the guise of a legendary hero; and doubly interesting that he should have done so through the medium of a story associated with the most carefully constructed hero-figure in Insular history.

ACKNOWLEDGEMENTS

Particular thanks to Sam Lieu for inadvertently inspiring this chapter, and also for the gift of his 'From History to Legend', to Mark Vermes and to Winifred Stevenson.

NOTES

1 The dating of Gildas' composition within the sixth century (early or late?) is a subject fraught with controversy. Recent attempts to

sort it out include McCarthy and Ó Cróinín 1987–88: 238; Sims-Williams 1983: 25; Wood 1984: 22–3; Higham 1995.

2 Aldhelm was intimately familiar with the writings of Gildas, who was a major influence on his prose style, as Winterbottom 1977 has shown.

3 Gildas 1.9 and 1.12.

4 Gildas 1.13–14.

5 See *Trioedd* no. 35.

6 Nash-Williams 1950: 123–5 and pl. xxxv (no 182). Vortigern is remembered in Welsh legendary history as the overweening king who let the Saxons into the country. Two of the Harleian genealogies (BL MS Harley 3859 ii and iv), relating to the royal lines of Dyfed and Gwynedd respectively, start with Maximus (see Stevens 1938: 89).

7 Text in Williams (ed.) 1927, translated in Jones and Jones 1982: 84–91.

8 Stevens 1938: 87.

9 For a general treatment of Anglo-Saxon attitudes to their inheritance, British and otherwise, see Hunter 1974: 29–50.

10 Bede, *HE* 1.9,11,12.

11 Ibid. 1.32, translated on p. 137 above.

12 For Constantine of Dumnonia, see Gildas 1.28, and Anderson 1922 I: 92–3.

13 O'Brien 1973: 231.

14 Anderson 1922 I: cxxvii, cxxxv.

15 He is incorporated as an ancestor into the tenth-century Harleian Genealogy of the royal line of Dyfed, which traces the lineage back to 'Constans map Constantii magni map Constantii et Helen Luitdauc': *Trioedd*, pp. 314–17.

16 For example, Wright 1993.

17 See Brewer 1973.

18 Shahar 1983: 89–90, explores the legal status of wife-beating in various European countries.

19 Byrne 1969; Byrne 1973: 70–86.

20 There are numerous versions, on which see Cross 1952: 118 (D732).

21 Stokes 1903: 172–207. This version cannot be earlier than the eleventh century since it sketches the history of the kings of Ireland down to Brian Bóruma (d. 1014), but there seems every reason to believe that the story is an ancient one.

22 Byrne 1973: 16–20. See also the inauguration of Féilim Ó Chonchobhair, reported in the Annals of Connacht for 1310: 'when Fedhlimidh son of Aedh son of Eoghan had married the province of Connacht, his foster-father waited upon him in the manner remembered by old men and recorded in old books; and this was the most splendid kingship-marriage ever celebrated in Connacht down to that day' (Byrne 1973: 17). The word for marriage is *feis/banais* (the latter compounded with the feminine prefix *ban-*). *Feis*, used of public occasions such as the *Feis Temro*, 'Feast of Tara', is the verbal noun from *Oir. fo-aid*, 'to sleep with' (see Binchy 1958: 134–5).

23 For example: Dillon 1947: 245–64; Carney 1979: 334–9.

24 Giraldus Cambrensis III.xxv.

25 Byrne 1973: 51, 'the name Medb means "the drunken" or perhaps "she who makes drunk", and there can be little doubt that she was the goddess of the sovereignty of Tara, with whom the king was to be united after she had proffered him the drink of ale or wine which in Irish tradition symbolised sovereignty . . . the promiscuous character attributed to Medb in the *Táin* and other sagas is explained by her true nature as the goddess who slept with many kings'. See also O'Rahilly 1946: 14–28.

26 See also Manitius 1886: 535–634, especially 535–614 which constitute the seminal work on Aldhelm's sources.

27 There is a full bibliography on the *V. Sylv.* given by Aiello in Bonamente and Fusco 1992: 19–20 n.5.

28 See Lieu above and Fowden 1994: 155 n. 58.

29 Letter to Aldhelm from an unknown Irishman: Aldhelm in MGH Auct. Ant. 15: 494.

30 Burch 1927: 124–5, described Burch 1927: 51.

31 Aldhelm's letter to Hadrian: Aldhelm in MGH Auct. Ant. 15: 478.

32 Aldhelm's letter to Heahfrith: Aldhelm in MGH Auct. Ant. 15: 490.

33 Note that Aldhelm's Irish contemporary, Adomnán (679–704), who probably had less access to Greek teaching than did Aldhelm, correctly analysed the name Constantinople in his *De locis sanctis* (3.2.8): *ciuitatem condidit, quae conposito nomine Constantinopolis uocitatur, ut conditoris uocamen in priore talis inhereat conpositionis parte.*

34 See, for example, Stevenson 1995: 87–93.

35 Bradshaw 1889: 462.

36 Compare the so-called Corpus Glossary (Corpus Christi College, Cambridge 114), which contains material from the school of Canterbury, where Aldhelm received part of his education: F.20, *Fastis: libri sunt in quibus sunt nomina consulum* (Hessels 1890: 53). See Pheifer 1987: 33–5, and Lapidge 1986: 58 n. 67.

37 Ald., *Carm. de virg.* 21.

38 BL Harley 3376, is fragmentary – the main section goes only up to letter F, and there is a separate fragment of I. It is arranged in AB-order, and was once very large. The lemmas and glosses of this collection come from a wide variety of sources, and include quite a large number of Greek words (Oliphant 1966).

39 *His mane edictum, post prandia Callirhoen do.* Note that the name appears in the same case as in the Harley glossary. Persius is not one of the writers who disappeared between the Silver Age and the Renaissance. He was read by the early Latin fathers, by Ausonius and Sidonius Apollinaris, and his work was also known to Aldhelm (Manitius 1886: 564–7), therefore available in Anglo-Saxon England.

40 On which poem and its context see Stevenson 1992: 1–27.

41 *Rubisca*, line 9.

42 A similarly incorrect gloss, from the same glossary, is *catacrinas*, from another Hiberno-Latin poem, the *Lorica* of Laidcenn. This is glossed (in Old English) *hypban*: 'hip-bone': the gloss in its original context

properly referred to *crinas*, and *cata* is the Greek *kata*: 'with'. Just as with *Rubisca*, we can compare the version in Harley 3376 with an actual text with interlinear gloss: the *Lorica* appears in the medical text 'Lacnunga' (BL Harley 585), ff. 152a-157a, with a complete interlinear gloss in Old English. Over *catacrin*[e]s (l. 60) is ð hypban (Grattan and Singer 1952: 142).

43 Adomnán 2.29.1 and 30.1.
44 Ibid. 2.30.26.
45 McNally 1958: 395–403.
46 Bede, *HE* 5.18.
47 See Winterbottom 1977: 39–76.
48 Ibid. 39.
49 Ibid. 44.
50 Ehwald's edition of this passage of Aldhelm (MGH Auct. Ant. 15: 260) refers to Paul., *V. Amb.*, in a footnote.
51 There is no prosopography of the early Anglo-Saxon church, but a scan of the religious women mentioned by Bede and in the various literature connected with the German missions of Boniface makes it clear that very few Anglo-Saxon nuns took non-Germanic names. However, the dedicatees of *De virg.* were Hildelith, Justina, Cuthburg, Osburg, Aldgith, Scholastica, Hidburg, Berngith, Eulalia and Thecla. Accounts of all four saints whose names were thus taken appear in both versions of *De virg.*
52 A homily on Stephen the Protomartyr preserved in Armenian and dubiously attributed to Gregory Thaumaturgus gives the leaders of various classes of Christian hero: Abraham, 'the first patriarch', Moses, 'head of the prophets', David 'founder of the Israelite state', Peter 'leader of the Apostles', Dionysius 'first Bishop of Athens', and Thecla, as above: see Aubineau 1975 from Pitra 1883: 168, 412. See also Isidore of Pelusium, *Letters* 1.87 (= *PG* 88: 241–2) who describes Thecla in a letter of exhortation to a nun as 'the head of female victories and triumphs . . . who stands forth as a column of immortal chastity'.
53 Ald., *De virg.* 300 and *Carm. de virg.* 435.
54 Lipsius and Bonnet 1891 I: 235–72 (Greek text); translated in Elliott 1993: 364–74. For further bibliography see Charlesworth and Mueller 1987: 278–87.
55 Most probably Prudentius, *Peristephanon* 3, though two other hymns on Eulalia appear in the Mozarabic Hymnal, attributed to writers of the generation before that of Aldhelm – Quiricius, a seventh-century Bishop of Barcelona, and Isidore of Seville (*PL* 86: 1099 and 1284): see Messenger 1944–5. Manitius 1886: 571 demonstrates that Aldhelm knew both Prudentius' *Cathemerinon* and the *Peristephanon*.
56 Tertullian comments in his treatise on baptism (*de baptismo* 17.5) that the impertinence and viciousness of women drive them to the usurpation of the masculine right to teach, and also of the right to baptise, taking as their excuse Paul's commandment to Thecla: *quodsi quae Acta Pauli quae perperam scripta sunt* [exemplum Theclae] *ad licentiam mulierum docendi tinguendique defendunt*. He explains, therefore, that the Acts has nothing to do with St Paul, but were

written by a presbyter in 'Asia', and thus have no authoritative status.

57 William of Malmesbury asserts that he was the pupil of the Irishman Maeldubh, founder of Malmesbury. This is to some extent corroborated by the letter of an anonymous Irishman to Aldhelm, which states, *a quodam sancto uiro de nostro genere nutritus es*. This reading of the letter is defended by Orchard 1994: 4–5.

58 Aldhelm's letter to Wihtfrith: Aldhelm in MGH Auct. Ant. 15: 479–80.

59 Adomnán 3.1–2. Note that Bede (*HE* 5.15) says King Aldfrip of Northumbria had copies made and circulated: *Porrexit autem librum hunc Adamnan Aldfrido regi; ac per eius est largitionem etiam in minoribus ad legendum contraditus*.

60 Lapidge and Bischoff 1994: 41–64.

61 Ibid. 42.

62 Jerome, *Chron.*, 354 AD, at 678: *Constantinopolis dedicatur, pene omnium orbium nuditate*. See also *Anon. Vales.* 6.30; and Eunapius, *Vitae Sophistarum* 462.8.

63 William of Malmesbury, *De gestis Pontificum Anglorum* 5.1 (= *PL* 179: 1621); this chapter is also the source for Alfred the Great's opinion of Aldhelm's English verse.

64 See Raglan 1965: 142–57. For the 'Guidi-*Vita*' see *FCJ*: 101–2, 106–42; for the 'Halkin-*Vita*', see *FCJ*: 104.

65 Kelleher 1963: 125.

BIBLIOGRAPHY

Abbott, F. F. and Johnson, A. C. (1926) *Municipal Administration in the Roman Empire*, Princeton, NJ.

Adams, J. N. (1976) *The Text and Language of a Vulgar Latin Chronicle (Anonymus Valesianus II)* Institute of Classical Studies Bulletin Supplement 36, London.

Aiello, V. (1992) 'Constantino, la lebbra e il battesimo di Silvestro', in G. Bonamente and F. Fusco (eds) *Constantino il Grande. Dall'Antichità all'Umanesimo, Colloquio sul Cristanesimo nel mondo antico, Macerata 18–20 Dicembre, 1990*, Macerata: 17–58.

Aland, K. (1960) 'Kaiser und Kirche von Konstantin bis Byzanz', *Kirchengeschichtliche Entwürfe*, Gütersloh: 257–79.

Alexandre, M. (1984) 'Les nouveaux martyres. Motifs martyrologiques dans la vie des saints et thèmes hagiographiques dans l'éloge des martyrs chez Grégoire de Nysse', in A. Spira (ed.) *The Biographical Works of Gregory of Nyssa: Proceedings of the 5th International Colloquium on Gregory of Nyssa, Mainz 1982* (= Patristics Monographs Series 12), Cambridge, MA.

Ameling, W. (1985) *Die Inschriften von Prusias ad Hypium*, Bonn.

Anderson, A. O. (1922) *Early Sources of Scottish History*, 2 vols, Edinburgh, (reprinted Stamford 1990).

Arce, J. (1984) *Estudios sobre el Emperador Fl. Cl. Juliano (Fuentes literarias. Epigrafia. Numismática)*, (Anejos de Archivo Español de Arqueologia 7) Madrid.

Aubineau, M. (1975) 'Le panégyrique de Thècle, attribué à Jean Chrysostome (*BHG* 1720): la fin retrouvée d'un texte mutilé', *AB* 93: 348–62.

Aufhauser, J. B. (1911) *Konstantins Kreuzevision*, Bonn.

Bagnall, R. S. (1993) *Egypt in Late Antiquity*, Princeton, NJ.

Bagnall, R. S. *et al.* (1987) *Consuls of the Later Roman Empire*, Atlanta, GA.

Baldini, A. (1992) 'Claudio Gotico e Constantino in Aurelio Vittore ed Epitome de Caesaribus', in G. Bonamente and F. Fusco (eds) *Constantino il Grande. Dall'Antichità all'Umanesimo, Colloquio sul Cristanesimo nel mondo antico, Macerata 18–20 Dicembre, 1990*, Macerata: 73–89.

Ballance, M. H. (1964) 'Derbe and Faustinopolis', *Anat. Studs* 14: 139–45.

Barcelo, P. A. (1982) *Roms auswärtige Beziehungen unter der Constantinischen Dynastie (306–363)*, Regensburg.

Barnard, L. W. (1977) 'Athanasius and the Roman State', *Latomus* 36: 422–37.

Barnes, T. D. (1971) *Tertullian: A Historical and Literary Study*, Oxford.

Barnes, T. D. (1975) 'Publilius Optatianus Porfyrius', *AJP* 96: 173–86.

Barnes, T. D. (1976a) 'The victories of Constantine', *ZPE* 20: 149–55.

Barnes, T. D. (1976b) 'The *Epitome de Caesaribu*s and its sources', *CP* 71: 258–68.

Barnes, T. D. (1976c) 'Imperial campaigns A.D. 285–311', *Phoenix* 30: 174–93.

Barnes, T. D. (1980a) 'Imperial chronology, A.D. 337–350', *Phoenix* 34: 160–6.

Barnes, T. D. (1980b) 'The editions of Eusebius' ecclesiastical history', *GRBS* 21: 191–201.

Barnes, T. D. (1981) *Constantine and Eusebius*, Cambridge, MA.

Barnes, T. D. (1982) *The New Empire of Diocletian and Constantine*, Cambridge, MA.

Barnes, T. D. (1983) 'Two victory titles of Constantius', *ZPE* 52: 229–35.

Barnes, T. D. (1984) 'Constantine's prohibition of pagan sacrifice', *AJP* 105: 69–72.

Barnes, T. D. (1985) 'Constantine and the Christians of Persia', *JRS* 75: 126–36.

Barnes, T. D. (1986) *The Constantinian Reformation* (The Crake Lectures 1984), Sackville, New Brunswick, Canada.

Barnes, T. D. (1987) 'Himerius and the fourth century', *CP* 82: 206–25.

Barnes, T. D. (1989a) 'Panegyric, history and hagiography in Eusebius's Life of Constantine', in R. Williams (ed.) *The Making of Orthodoxy: Essays in Honour of Henry Chadwick*, Cambridge: 94–123.

Barnes, T. D. (1989b) 'Jerome and the *Origo Constantini Imperatoris*', *Phoenix* 43(1): 158–61.

Barnes, T. D. (1989c) 'Pagans and Christians in the reign of Constantius', in A. Dihle (ed.) *L'Église et l'empire au IVe siècle*, Vandœuvres-Génève: 301–37.

Barnes, T. D. (1989d) 'Emperors on the move', *JRA* 2: 247–61.

Barnes, T. D. (1990) 'Religion and society in the reign of Theodosius', in H. A. Meynell (ed.), *Grace, Politics and Desire: Essays on Augustine*, Calgary: 157–75.

Barnes, T. D. (1992a) 'Praetorian prefects 337–361', *ZPE* 94: 249–60.

Barnes, T. D. (1992b) 'The Constantinian settlement', in H. W. Attridge and G. Hata (eds) *Eusebius, Christianity, and Judaism*, Detroit: 635–57.

Barnes, T. D. (1993) *Athanasius and Constantius: Theology and Politics in the Constantinian Empire*, Cambridge, MA.

Barnes, T. D. (1994) 'The two drafts of Eusebius' *Life of Constantine*', in Barnes, T. D., *From Eusebius to Augustine: Selected Papers 1982–1993*, Aldershot: XII [first publication, pages numbered separately].

Barnish, S. J. B. (1989) 'The transformation of classical cities and the Pirenne debate', *JRA* 2: 385–400.

Battifol, P. (1889) 'Fragmente der Kirchengeschichte des Philostorgius', *RQA* 3: 252–89.

Battifol, P. (1891) *Quaestiones Philostorgianae*, Paris.

Bauer, W. (1964) *Rechtgläubigkeit und Ketzerei im ältesten Christentum*, 2nd edn with a supplement by G. Strecker, Tübingen.

Baus, K. (1973) *Handbuch der Kirchengeschichte* 2.1, Freiburg, Basle and Vienna.

Baynes, N. H. (1911) 'Topographica Constantinopolitana', *JHS* 31: 266–8.

Baynes, N. H. (1931) *Constantine the Great and the Christian Church*, London.

Baynes, N. H. (1937) 'The death of Julian the Apostate in a Christian legend', *JRS* 27: 22–9.

Baynes, N. H. (1955) 'Rome and Armenia in the fourth century', in *Byzantine Studies and Other Essays*, London: 186–208.

Beck, H.-G. (1959) *Kirche und Theologische Literatur im byzantinischen Reich* (Handbuch der Altertumswissenschaft, XII, 2, 1), Munich.

Bees, N. A. (1920) 'Weiteres zum Kult des hl. Artemios', *BNgJ* 1: 384–5.

Bidez, J. (1930) *La vie de l'Empereur Julien*, Paris.

Bidez, J. (1935) 'Fragments nouveaux de Philostorge sur la Vie de Constantin', *Byz.* 10: 403–37.

Binchy, D. A. (1958) 'The Fair of Tailtiu and the Feast of Tara', *Ériu* 18: 113–38.

Bird, H. W. (1984) *Sextus Aurelius Victor: A Historiographical Study* (ARCA Classical and Medieval Texts, Papers and Monographs 14), Liverpool.

Bird, H. W. (1993) *Eutropius: Breviarium*, (TTH 14), Liverpool.

Bird, H. W. (1994) *Aurelius Victor: De Caesaribus*, Liverpool.

Bleckmann, B. (1991) 'Die Chronik des Johannes Zonaras und eine pagane Quelle zur Geschichte Konstantins', *Historia* 40: 343–65.

Bleckmann, B. (1992) 'Pagane Visionen Konstantins in der Chronik des Johannes Zonaras', in G. Bonamente and F. Fusco (eds) *Constantino il Grande. Dall'Antichità all'Umanesimo, Colloquio sul Cristanesimo nel mondo antico, Macerata 18–20 Dicembre, 1990*, Macerata: 151–70.

Blockley, R. C. (1981–3) *The Fragmentary Classicising Historians of the Later Roman Empire*, 2 vols, Liverpool.

Bonamente, G. and Fusco, F. (1992) *Constantino il Grande. Dall'Antichità all'Umanesimo, Colloquio sul Cristanesimo nel mondo antico, Macerata 18–20 Dicembre, 1990*, Macerata.

Borgehammar, S. (1991) *How The Holy Cross Was Found* (Bibliotheca Theologiae Practicae 47), Stockholm.

Botermann, H. (1993) 'Griechisch-jüdische Epigrafik: Zur Datierung der Aphrodisias-Inschriften', *ZPE* 98: 184–94.

Bowder, D. (1978) *The Age of Constantine and Julian*, London.

Bowen, R. F. (1982) 'The Emperor Constantius II (A.D. 317–361): a critical study', PhD thesis, University of Leeds.

Bowersock, G. W. (1978) *Julian the Apostate*, London.

Bradshaw, H. (1889) *The Collected Papers of Henry Bradshaw*, ed. F. J. H. Jenkinson, Cambridge.

Braun, R. and Richer, J. (eds) (1978) *L'Empereur Julien: De l'histoire à la légende (331–1715)* I, Paris.

Brennecke, H. C. (1988) *Studien zur Geschichte der Homöer*, Tübingen.

Brewer, E. (trs.) (1973) *From Cuchulain to Gawain*, Totowa, NJ.

Brook, E. W. (1911) *Hymns of Severus* (Patrologia Orientalis 7), Louvain.

Brown, P. D. C. (1971) 'The Church at Richborough', *Britannia* 2: 225–31.

Brown, P. R. L. (1970) 'Sorcery, demons and the rise of Christianity: From Late Antiquity into the Middle Ages', in M. Douglas (ed.) *Witchcraft Confession and Accusations*, London: 17–45.

Brown, P. R. L. (1981) *The Cult of the Saints*, Chicago and London.

Brown, P. R. L. (1992) *Power and Persuasion in the Late Roman World*, Madison, WI.

Bruns, J. E. (1977) 'The "agreement" of Moses and Jesus in the *Demonstratio Evangelica* of Eusebius', *Vigiliae Christianae* 31: 117–25.

Bruun, P. (1953) *Constantinian Coinage of Arelate*, Helsinki.

Bruun, P. (1961) *Studies in Constantinian Chronology* (Numismatic Notes and Monographs 146), New York.

Bruun, P. (1962) 'The Christian signs on the coins of Constantine', *Arctos* n.s. 3: 5–35.

Buck, D. F. (1977) 'Eunapius of Sardis', PhD thesis, University of Oxford.

Buck, D. F. (1988) 'Eunapius of Sardis and Theodosius the Great', *Byz.* 58: 36–53.

Buckler, W. H. (1937) 'A charitable foundation of A.D. 237', *JHS* 57: 1–10.

Burch, V. (1927) *Myth and Constantine the Great*, Oxford.

Burckhardt, J. (1853) *Zeit Constantins des Grossen*, Basle.

Burckhardt, J. (1880) *Zeit Constantins des Grossen*, 2nd edn, Leipzig.

Burn, R. (1871) *Rome and Campagna*, Cambridge.

Bury, J. B. (1896) 'Date of the battle of Singara', *BZ* 5: 302–5.

Butler, A. J. (1978) *The Arab Conquest of Egypt and the Last Thirty Years of the Roman Domination*, 2nd, revised edition, ed. by P. M. Fraser, Oxford.

Byrne, F. J. (1969) *The Rise of the Uí Néill and the High-Kingship of Ireland* O'Donnell Lecture, National University of Ireland, Dublin.

Byrne, F. J. (1973) *Irish Kings and High-Kings*, London.

Callu, J.-P. (1992) 'Ortus Constantini: aspects historiques de la légende', in G. Bonamente and F. Fusco (eds) *Constantino il Grande. Dall'Antichità all'Umanesimo, Colloquio sul Cristanesimo nel mondo antico, Macerata 18–20 Dicembre, 1990*, Macerata: 253–82.

Cameron, Averil (1983) 'Constantinus Christianus', *JRS* 73: 184–90.

Cameron, Averil (1991) *Christianity and the Rhetoric of Empire*, Berkeley, CA.

Cameron, Averil (1992) 'Byzantium and the past in the seventh century: the search for redefinition', in J. Fontaine and J. N. Hillgarth (eds) *Le septième siècle: changements et continuités* (= The Seventh Century, Change and Continuity, Proceedings of a joint French and British Colloquium held at the Warburg Institute, 8–9 July 1988) (Studies of the Warburg Institute 42), London: 250–70.

Cameron, Averil (1997) 'Eusebius' *Vita Constantini*: the construction of a Christian Constantine', in S. Swain and M. Edwards (eds) *Portraits: The Biographical in the Literature of the Empire*, Oxford.

Cameron, Averil and Herrin, J. (eds) (1984) *Constantinople in the Early Eighth Century: The Parastaseis Syntomoi Chronikai*, Leiden.

Campagno, A. (1980) *Ps. Cirillo di Gerusalemme: Omelie copte sulla Passione sulla Croce e sulla Vergine*, Milan.

Carney, J. (1979) *Studies in Irish Literature and History*, Dublin.

Casey, P. J. (ed.) (1979) *The End of Roman Britain* (British Archaeological Reports 71), Oxford.

Chadwick, H. (1972) 'The origin of the title "Oecumenical Council"', *JTS* n.s. 23: 132–5.

Chalmers, W. R. (1953) 'The ΝΕΑ ΕΚΔΟΣΙΣ of Eunapius', *Classical Quarterly* 47: 165–70.

Charles, R. H. (1916) *The Chronicle of John, Bishop of Nikiou*, London.

Charlesworth, J. H. and Mueller, J. R. (1987) *The New Testament Apocrypha and Pseudepigrapha: A Guide to Publications*, Metuchen, NJ.

Chastagnol, A. (1962) *Les Fastes de le Préfecture de Rome au bas-Empire*, Paris.

Chastagnol, A. (1981) 'L'inscription constantinienne d'Orcistus', *MEFRA* 93: 381–416.

Chitty, D. J. (1966) *The Desert a City*, Oxford.

Ciggar, K. N. (1976) 'Un description de Constantinople traduite par un pèlerin anglais', *Revue des Études Byzantines* 34: 211–67.

Clark, G. (1989) *Iamblichus: On the Pythagorean Life* (TTH 8), Liverpool.

Coleman, C. B. (1914) *Constantine the Great and Christianity*, Columbia University Studies in History and Public Law 60/1: whole series No. 146, New York.

Coleman, C. B. (1922) *The Treatise of Lorenzo Valla on the Donation of Constantine*, New Haven, CT.

Coleman-Norton, R. P. (1966) *Roman State and Christian Church*, 3 vols, London.

Coquin, R. G. and Lucchesi, E. (1982) 'Une version copte de la passion de Saint Eusignios', *AB* 100: 186–208.

Corcoran, S. (1993) 'Hidden from history: the legislation of Licinius', in J. Harries and D. Wood (eds) *The Theodosian Code*, New York: 97–119.

Cox, P. (1983) *Biography in Late Antiquity*, Berkeley, CA.

Crescenti, G. (1966) *Obiettori di coscienza e martiri militari nei primi cinque secoli del Cristianesimo*, Palermo.

Cross, T. P. (1952) *Motif-Index of Early Irish Literature*, Bloomington, IN.

Crum, W. E. and Evelyn White, H. E. (1926) *The Monastery of Epiphanius at Thebes, Part II: Coptic Ostraca and Papyri, Greek Ostraca and Papyri*, New York.

Cruz-Uribe, E. (1986) 'Notes on the Coptic Cambyses Romance', *Enchoria* 14: 51–6.

Dagron, G. (1974) *Naissance d'une capitale, Constantinople et ses institutions de 330 à 451*, Paris.

Dagron, G. (1984) *Constantinople Imaginaire. Études sur le recueil des 'Patria'*, Paris.

Daniélou, J. (1960) *From Shadows to Reality*, London.

Davis, R. (1989) *The Book of Pontiffs (Liber Pontificalis)* (TTH 5), Liverpool.

de Gaiffier, B. (1956) 'Sub Juliano Apostata dans le martyrologie romaine', *AB* 74: 5–49.

de Gaiffier, B. (1970) 'Les martyrs Eugène et Macaire morts en exil en Maurétane', *AB* 78: 24–40.

Delbrueck, R. (1933) *Spätantike Kaiserporträts*, Berlin.

Delbrueck, R. (1952) *Probleme der Lipsanothek in Brescia* (Theophaneia – Beiträge zur Religions- und Kirchengeschichte des Altertums 7), Bonn.

Delehaye, H. (1895) 'Les Synaxaires de Sirmond', *AB* 14: 396–434.

Delehaye, H. (1925) 'Les recueils antiques de miracles des saints', *AB* 63: 1–85 and 305–25.

Demandt, A. (1989) *Die Spätantike: römische Geschichte von Diocletian bis Justinian 284–565 n. Chr.* (Handbuch der Altertumswissenschaft, III/6), Munich.

den Boer, W. (1972) *Some Minor Roman Historians*, Leiden.

den Heijer, J. (1989) *Mawhûb ibn Mansûr ibn Mufarrig et l'historiographie copto-arabe: Étude sur la composition de l'Histoire des Patriarches d'Alexandrie* (*CSEL* Subsida 83), Louvain.

Devos, P. (1982) 'Une recension nouvelle de la passion grecque BHG 639 de Saint Eusignios', *AB* 100: 209–28.

de Vries, W. (1971) 'Die Struktur der Kirche gemäß dem ersten Konzil von Nikaia und seiner Zeit', in *Wegzeichen. Festgabe zum 60. Geburtstag von Prof. Dr. Hermenegild M. Biedermann OSA*, Würzburg: 55–81.

Dihle, A. (ed.) (1989) *L'Église et l'empire au IVe siècle* (Entretiens sur l'Antiquité Classique 34), Vandœuvres-Génève.

Dillon, M. (1947) 'The archaism of Irish tradition', *Proceedings of the British Academy* 33: 245–64.

Di Maio, M. (1977) 'Zonaras' account of the Neo-Flavian Emperors', PhD thesis., University of Missouri.

Di Maio, M. (1988) 'Smoke in the wind: Zonaras' use of Philostorgius, Zosimus, John of Antioch and John of Rhodes in his narrative of the Neo-Flavian Emperors', *Byz.* 58: 230–55.

Di Maio, M. and Arnold, W. H. (1992) '*Per vim, per caedem, per bellum*: A study of murder and ecclesiastical politics in the year 337', *Byz.* 62: 158–211.

Dodgeon, M. H. and Lieu, S. N. C. (1991) *Rome's Eastern Frontier and the Persian Wars, 226–363: A Documentary History*, London.

Dölger, F. J. (1913) 'Die Taufe Konstantins und ihre Probleme', in F. J. Dölger (ed.) *Konstantin der Grosse und seine Zeit* (*RQA* Suppl. 19), Freiburg: 377–447.

Dörries, H. (1949) 'Die Vita Antonii als Geschichtsquelle', *NGWG* 14: 359–410.

Dörries, H. (1954) *Das Selbstzeugnis Kaiser Konstantins*, Göttingen.

Dostálová, R. (1990) 'Frühbyzantinische Profanhistoriker', in F. Winkelmann and W. Brandes (eds) *Quellen zur Geschichte des frühen Byzanz (4.-9. Jahrhundert), Bestand und Probleme*, Amsterdam: 156–79.

Downey, G. (1938) 'The shrines of St. Babylas at Antioch and Daphne', in R. Stillwell (ed.) *Antioch-on-the-Orontes II, The Excavations 1933–36*, Princeton, NJ: 45–8.

Downey, G. (1951) 'The economic crisis at Antioch under Julian the Apostate', in P. R. Coleman-Norton (ed.) *Studies in Roman Economic and Social History in Honor of Allan Chester Johnson*, Princeton, NJ: 312–21.

Downey, G. (1959) 'Libanius' oration on Antioch (Oration XI)', *Proceedings of the American Philosophical Society* 103: 652–86.

Downey, G. (1961) *A History of Antioch in Syria from Seleucus to the Arab Conquest*, Princeton, NJ.

Drake, H. A. (1975) *In Praise of Constantine: A Historical Study and New Translation of Eusebius' Tricennial Orations*, Berkeley, CA.

Drijvers, J. W. (1992) *Helena Augusta: The Mother of Constantine the Great and the Legend of Her Finding of the True Cross*, Leiden.

Dummer, J. (1971) 'Fl. Artemius dux Aegypti', *Archiv für Papyrusforschung* 21: 121–44.

Duncan-Jones, R. (1990) *Structure and Scale in the Roman Economy*, Cambridge.

Dvornik, F. (1958) *The Idea of Apostolicity in Byzantium and the Legend of the Apostle Andrew*, Cambridge, MA.

Eadie, J. W. (1967) *The Breviarium of Festus: A Critical Edition with Historical Commentary*, London.

Ehrhard, A. (1939) *Überlieferung und Bestand der hagiographischen und homiletischen Literatur der griechischen Kirche* I/3 (TU 52), Leipzig.

Ehrhardt, A. (1959–60) 'Constantine, Rome and the rabbis', *Bulletin of the John Rylands Library of Manchester* 42: 296–308.

Ehrhardt, C. (1980) 'Constantinian documents in Gelasius of Cyzicus' Ecclesiastical History', *Jahrbuch für Antike und Christentum* 23: 48–57.

Eis, G. (1933) *Die Quellen für das Sanctuarium des Mailänder Humanisten Boninus Mombritius, Eine Untersuchung zur Geschichte der großen Legendensammlungen des Mittelalters* (Germanische Studien 140), Berlin.

Elliott, T. G. (1987) 'Constantine's conversion: do we really need it?', *Phoenix* 41: 420–38.

Elliott, J. K. (trs.) (1993) *The Apocryphal New Testament*, Oxford.

Elm, S. (1989) 'An alleged book-theft in fourth-century Egypt: P. Lips. 43', *Studia Patristica* 18.2: 209–17.

Emmett Nobbs, A. (1990) 'Philostorgius' view of the past', in G. Clarke (ed.) *Reading the Past in Late Antiquity*, Canberra: 251–63.

Engelmann, H. and Knibbe, D. (1989) 'Das Sollgesetz der Provinz Asia, Eine neue Inschrift aus Ephesos', *Epigraphica Anatolica* 14 [entire issue].

Ensslin, W. (1922) 'Kaiser Julians Gesetzgebungswerk und Reichsverwaltung', *Klio* 18: 104–99.

Erbse, H. (1956) 'Die Bedeutung der Sunkrisis in den Parallelbiographien Plutarchs', *Hermes* 84: 398–424.

Errington, R. M. (1988) 'Constantine and the pagans', *GRBS* 29: 309–18.

Esbroek, M. van (1982) 'Legends about Constantine in Armenia', in Th. J. Samuelian (ed.) *Classical Armenian Culture: Influences and Creativity*, Chico, CA: 79–101.

Evans-Grubbs, J. (1993) 'Constantine and imperial legislation on the family', in J. Harries and D. Wood (eds) *The Theodosian Code*, New York: 120–42.

Ewig, E. [1956] (1975) 'Das Bild Constantins des Grossen in den ersten Jahrhunderten des abendländischen Mittelalters', *Historisches Jahrbuch* 75 (1956): pagination here from the reprinted version in H. Hunger (ed.), *Das byzantinische Herrscherbild* (Wege der Forschung 341), Darmstadt: 133–92.

Fälschungen (1988) *Fälschungen in Mittelalter. Internationaler Kongreß der Monumenta Germaniae Historica, München, 16–19. September 1986.* Teil 2, *Gefälschte Rechtstexte – der bestrafte Fälscher*, Monumenta Germaniae Historica Schriften 33/2, Hanover.

Fatouros, G. and Krischer, T. (1980) *Libanios, Briefe, Griechisch-deutsch*, Munich.

Festugière, A. J. (1959) *Antioche païenne et chrétienne, Libanius, Chrysostome et les moines de Syrie*, Paris.

Floëri, F. and Nautin, P. (eds) (1957) *Homélies pascales iii. Une homélie anatolienne sur le date du Pâques en l'an 387* (SC 48), Paris.

Fontaine, J. (1963) 'Sulpice Sévère a-t-il travesti Saint Martin de Tours en martyr militaire?', *AB* 81: 31–58.

Foss, C. (1976) *Byzantine and Turkish Sardis*, Cambridge, MA.

Foss, C. (1979) *Ephesus after Antiquity: A Late Antique, Byzantine, and Turkish City*, Cambridge.

Foss, C. (1985) 'Ankyra', *RAC*: 448–65.

Foss, C. (1987) 'Late Antique and Byzantine Ankara', *Dumbarton Oaks Papers* 31: 29–87.

Fowden, G. (1978) 'Bishops and temples in the Eastern Roman Empire, A.D. 320–445', *JTS* n.s. 29: 53–78.

Fowden, G. (1991) 'Constantine's porphyry column: the earliest literary allusion', *JRS* 81: 119–31.

Fowden, G. (1994) 'The last days of Constantine: oppositional versions and their influence', *JRS* 84: 146–76.

Franchi de' Cavalieri, P. (1896–97) 'Di un frammento d'una Vita di Constantino', *Studi e Documenti di Storia e Diritto* 17–18: 89–131.

Franchi de' Cavalieri, P. (1953) 'Dei SS. Gioventino e Massimino', *Studi e Testi* 175: 169–200.

Fraser, P. M. (1991) 'John of Nikiou', in A. S. Atiya, (ed.) *The Coptic Encyclopedia*, 12 vols, New York: vol. 5: 1367.

Fremersdorf, F. (1952) 'Christliche Leibwächter auf einem geschliffenen Kölner Glasbecher des 4. Jahrhunderts', in *Festschrift für Rudolf Egger: Beiträge zur älteren europäischen Kulturgeschichte*, Klagenfurt: 66–83.

Fremersdorf, F. (1967) *Die Denkmäler des römischen Köln*, 8 vols, Cologne.

Frend, W. H. C. (1971) *The Donatist Church*, 2nd edition, Oxford.

Frend, W. H. C. (1984) *The Rise of Christianity*, Philadelphia.

Frere, S. S. (1978) *Britannia: A History of Roman Britain*, London.

Frothingham, A. L., jr. (ed.) (1883) 'L'Omelia di Giacomo di Sarûg sul battesimo di Constantino imperatore, publicata, tradotta ed annotato', *Atti della R. Accademia dei Lincei* 280, ser. 3, *Memorie della classe di scienze morali, storiche e filologiche* 8: 167–242.

Fuhrmann, H. (1973) *Einfluß und Verbreitung der pseudoisidorischen Fälschungen von ihrem Auftauchen bis in die neuere Zeit*, II (Schriften der Monumenta Germaniae Historica), Stuttgart.

Gabba, E. (1974) 'I cristiani nell' esercito romano del quarto secolo d.C. in E. Gabba, *Per la storia dell'esercito romano in età imperiale*, Bologna: 75–109.

Gardner, J. F. (1986) *Women in Roman Law and Society*, London.

Gaudemet, J. (1957) *La formation du droit seculier et du droit de l'église au IVe et Ve siècles*, Paris.

Gedeon, M. I. (1900) Δύω παλαιὰ κείμενα περί τοῦ μεγάλου Κωνσταντίνου, *Ἐκκλησιαστικὴ Ἀλήθεια* 20: 253–4, 262–3, 279–80, 303–4.

Gentz, G. (1966) *Die Kirchengeschichte des Nicephorus Callistus Xanthopulus und ihre Quellen, Nachgelassene Untersuchungen von Günter Gentz, überarbeitet und erweitert von F. Winkelmann* (TU 98), Berlin.

Geppert, F. (1898) *Die Quellen des Kirchenhistorikers Socrates Scholasticus* (Studien zur Geschichte der Theologie und der Kirche 3/4), Leipzig.

Gerland, E. (1937) 'Konstantin der Grosse in Geschichte und Sage', *Texte und Forschungen zur Byzantinisch-Neugriechischen Philologie* 23: 11–18.

Gibbon, E. [1776] (1909) *The Decline and Fall of the Roman Empire*, revised by J. B. Bury, 7 vols, London.

Girardet, K. M. (1974) 'Trier 385. Der Prozeß gegen die Priszillianer', *Chiron* 4: 577–608.

Girardet, K. M. (1975) *Kaisergericht und Bischofsgericht. Studien zu den Anfängen des Donatistenstreites (313–315) und zum Prozeß Athanasius von Alexandrien (328–346)*, Bonn.

Girardet, K. M. (1989) 'Die petition der Donatisten an Kaiser Konstantin (Frühjahr 313) – historische Voraussetzungen und Folgen', *Chiron* 19: 185–206.

Glasson, T. F. (1963) *Moses in the Fourth Gospel*, London.

Goodburn, R. and Bartholomew, P. (eds) (1976) *Aspects of the Notitia Dignitatum* (British Archaeological Reports 76), Oxford.

Grant, R. M. (1977) *Early Christianity and Society*, London.

Grattan, J. H. G. and Singer, C. (eds and trans) (1952) *Anglo-Saxon Magic and Medicine, Illustrated Specially From the Semi-pagan Text 'Lacnunga'* (Publications of the Wellcome Historical Medical Museum, n.s. 3), London.

Green, T. M. (1974) 'Zosimus, Orosius and their traditions: comparative studies in pagan and Christian historiography', PhD thesis, University of New York.

Grégoire, H. (1930/31) 'La "Conversion" de Constantin', *Revue de l'Université de Bruxelles* 36: 231–72.

Grégoire, H. (1955–7) 'Bardesane et S. Abercius', *Byz.* 25–27: 363–8.

Grigg, R. (1979) 'Portrait-bearing Codicils in the Illustrations of the *Notitia Dignitatum*?', *JRS* 69: 107–24.

Groag, E. (1907) 'Notizien zur Geschichte kleinasiatischer Familien', *Jahreshefte des Österreichischen Archäologische Instituts* 10: 282–99.

Grünewaldt, T. (1990) *Constantinus Maximus Augustus, Heerschaftspropaganda in der zeitgenössischen Überlieferung*, (Historia Einzelschriften 64), Stuttgart.

Grünewaldt, T. (1992a) 'Der letzte Kampf des Heidentums in Rom? Zu posthumen Rehabilitierung des Virius Nichomachus Flavianus', *Historia* 41: 462–87.

Grünewaldt, T. (1992b) 'Constantinus novus: zum Constantin-Bild des Mittelalters', in G. Bonamente and F. Fusco (eds) *Constantino il*

Grande. Dall'Antichità all'Umanesimo, Colloquio sul Cristanesimo nel mondo antico, Macerata 18–20 Dicembre, 1990, Macerata: 461–86.

Guidi, I. (1907) 'Un ΒΙΟΣ di Constantino', *Rendiconti della Reale accademia dei Lincei, Classe di Scienze Morali, Storiche e Filologiche*, 5th ser., 16: 304–40 and 637–60.

Günther, R. (1990) 'Lateinische Historiographie vom 4. bis 6. Jahrhundert', in F. Winkelmann and W. Brandes (eds) *Quellen zur Geschichte des frühen Byzanz (4.-9. Jahrhundert), Bestand und Probleme*, Amsterdam: 213–23.

Guthrie, P. (1966) 'The execution of Crispus', *Phoenix* 20: 325–31.

Habicht, C. (1958) 'Zur Geschichte des Kaisers Konstantin', *Hermes* 86: 360–78.

Hagel, K. F. (1933) *Kirche und Kaisertum in Lehre und Leben des Athanasius*, Leipzig.

Halkin, F. (1958) 'La Passion grecque des Saintes Libyè, Eutropie et Léonis, martyres à Nisibe', *AB* 76: 293–301.

Halkin, F. (1959–60) 'La règne de Constantin d'après la Chronique inédite du Pseudo-Syméon', *Byz.* 29–30: 7–27.

Halkin, F. (1959a) 'Une nouvelle vie de Constantin dans un légendier de Patmos', *AB* 77: 63–207.

Halkin, F. (1959b) 'Les deux derniers chapitres de la nouvelle vie de Constantin', *AB* 77: 370–2.

Halkin, F. (1960a) 'L'empereur Constantin converti par Euphratas', *AB* 78: 5–10.

Halkin, F. (1960b) 'Les autres passages inédits de la vie acéphale de Constantin', *AB* 78: 11–15.

Halkin, F. and Festugière, A.-J. (eds) (1982) *Le corpus athénien de s. Pachome*, Geneva.

Hall, S. G. (1993) 'Eusebian and other sources in Vita Constantini I', in H. C. Brennecke *et al.* (eds) *Logos: Festschrift für Luise Abramowski, Beihefte zur Zeitschrift für die neutestamentliche Wissenschaft*, Berlin: 239–63.

Hanson, R. P. C. (1959) *Allegory and Event: A Study of the Sources and Significance of Origen's Interpretation of Scripture*, London.

Hanson, R. P. C. (1974) 'The circumstances attending the death of the Emperor Flavius Valerius Severus in 306 or 307', *Hermathena* 118: 59–68.

Harl, K. W. (1987) *Civic Coins and Civic Politics in the Roman East A.D. 180–275*, Berkeley, CA.

Harl, M. (1967) 'Les trois quarantaines de la vie de Moïse, schéma idéal de la vie du moine-évêque chez les Pères Cappadociens', *REG* 80: 407–12.

Harl, M. (1984) 'Moïse figure de l'évêque dans l'Éloge de Basile de Grégoire de Nysse (381). Un plaidoyer pour l'autorité épiscopale', in A. Spira (ed.) *The Biographical Works of Gregory of Nyssa: Proceedings of the 5th International Colloquium on Gregory of Nyssa, Mainz 1982* (Patristics Monographs Series 12), Cambridge, MA: 71–119.

Heather, P. J. (1991) *Goths and Romans, 332–489*, Oxford.

Heather, P. J. and Matthews, J. F. (1991) *The Goths in the Fourth Century* (TTH 11), Liverpool.

Hefele, C. J. and Leclercq, H. (1907) *Histoire des Conciles* 1.1, Paris.

Herren, M.W. (ed.) (1987) *The Hisperica Famina II: Related Poems*, Toronto.

Herrmann, P. (1990) *Hilferufe aus römischen Provinzen. Ein Aspekt der Krise des römischen Reiches im 3. Jhdt. n. Chr.*, Hamburg.

Herz, P. (1988) *Studien zur römischen Wirtschaftsgesetzgebung: Die Lebensmittelversorgung*, Stuttgart.

Heseler, P. (1935) 'Neues zur Vita Constantini des Codex Angelicus 22', *Byz.* 10: 399–402.

Hessels, J. H. (ed.) (1890) *An Eighth-Century Latin-Anglo-Saxon Glossary Preserved in the Library of Corpus Christi College, Cambridge*, Cambridge.

Heydenreich, E. (1893) 'Constantin der Grosse in den Sagen des Mittelalters', *Deutsche Zeitschrift für Geschichtswissenschaft* 10: 1–27.

Heydenreich, E. (1894) 'Griechische Berichte über die Jugend Constantins des Grossen', in *Griechische Studien Hermann Lipsius zum sechzigsten Geburtstag dargebracht*, Leipzig: 88–101.

Higham, N. J. (1995) *The English Conquest: Gildas and Britain in the Fifth Century*, Manchester.

Hoffmann, D. (1969) *Das spätrömische Bewegungsheer und die Notitia Dignitatum* (Epigraphische Studien 7), Düsseldorf.

Holl, K. (1912) 'Die schriftstellerische Form des griechischen Heiligenlebens', *Neue Jahrbücher für klassische Altertum* 29: 406–27.

Homes Dudden, F. (1935) *The Life and Times of St. Ambrose*, Oxford.

Hopkins, K. (1980) 'Taxation and trade in the Roman Empire', *JRS* 70: 101–25.

Howard, G. (1981) *The Teaching of Addai*, Chico, CA.

Howe, L. L. (1942) *The Pretorian Prefect from Commodus to Diocletian*, Chicago.

Hunger, H. (ed.) (1969) *Joannes Chortasmenos (ca. 1370 – ca. 1436–47), Briefe, Gedichte und kleine Schriften*, Vienna.

Hunger, H. (ed.) (1975) *Das byzantinische Herrscherbild* (Wege der Forschung 341), Darmstadt.

Hunter, M. (1974) 'Germanic and Roman Antiquity and the sense of the past in Anglo-Saxon England', *Anglo-Saxon England* 3: 29–50.

Huttmann, M. A. (1914) *The Establishment of Christianity and the Proscription of Paganism* (Columbia University Studies in History and Public Law 60/2), New York.

Hyvernat, H. (1886) *Les actes des martyrs de l'Égypte tirés des manuscrits coptes de la Bibliothèque Vaticanae et du Musée Borgia.* I, Paris.

Ioannes, T. (1884) Μνημεία ἁγιολογικὰ νῦν πρῶτον ἐκδιδόμενα,

Venice, reprinted with new introduction by J. Dummer, Leipzig, 1973.

Ireland, S. (1986) *Roman Britain: A Sourcebook*, London.

Janin, R. (1953) *La géographie ecclésiastique de l'empire Byzantin, première partie: Le Siège de Constantinople et le Patriarcat œcuménique, Tome III, Les églises et les monastères*, Paris.

Jeep, L. (1885) 'Quellenuntersuchungen zu den griechischen Kirchenhistorikern', *Neue Jahrbücher für Classischen Philologie*, Suppl. 14: 53–178.

Jeffreys, E. *et al.* (1990) *Studies in John Malalas* (Byz. Aus. 6), Sydney.

Jeločnik, A. and Kos, P. (1973) *The Čentur Hoard: Folles of Maxentius and of the Tetrarchy* (Situla 12), Ljubljana.

Jones, A. H. M. (1948) *Constantine and the Conversion of Europe*, Harmondsworth.

Jones, A. H. M. (1953) 'Military chaplains in the Roman army', *Harvard Theological Review* 46: 239–40.

Jones, A. H. M. (1954) 'Notes on the genuineness of the Constantinian documents in Eusebius' Life of Constantine', *JEH* 18: 257–62.

Jones, A. H. M. (1955) 'The career of Flavius Philippus', *Historia* 5: 229–33.

Jones, A. H. M. (1963) 'The social background of the struggle between paganism and Christianity', in A. D. Momigliano (ed.) *The Conflict between Paganism and Christianity in the Fourth Century*, Oxford: 17–37.

Jones, A. H. M. (1964) *The Later Roman Empire*, 3 vols, Oxford.

Jones, A. H. M. (1970) *A History of Rome through the Fifth Century: Vol. 2, The Empire*, London.

Jones, G. and Jones, T. (1982) [1949] *The Mabinogion*, London and New York.

Junker, H. (1911) *Koptische Poesie des 10. Jahrhunderts. II. Teil (Text und Übersetzung)*, Berlin.

Kaegi, W. E. (1975) 'The Emperor Julian at Naissus', *L'antiquité classique* 44: 161–71.

Karlin-Hayter, P. (1991) 'Passio of the XL Martyrs of Sebasteia. The Greek tradition: the earliest account', *AB* 109: 249–304.

Kazhdan, A. (1987) '"Constantin imaginaire". Byzantine legends of the ninth century about Constantine the Great', *Byz.* 57: 196–250.

Kazhdan, A. (1988) 'Hagiographical notes', *Erytheia* 9: 200–5.

Kazhdan, A. and Ševčenko, N. P. (1991) 'Artemios', *ODB* I: 194–5.

Keil, V. (1989) *Quellensammlung zur Religionspolitik Konstantins Großen* (Texte zur Forschung 54), Darmstadt.

Kelleher, J. V. (1963) 'Irish history and pseudo-history', *Studia Hibernica* 3: 113–27.

Kelly, J. N. D. (1972) *Early Christian Creeds*, 3rd edn, London.

Kelly, J. N. D. (1975) *Jerome: His Life, Writing, and Controversies*, London.

Kent, J. P. C. (1994) *The Roman Imperial Coinage*, vol. 10, London.

Kent, J. P. C. and Painter, K. S. (eds) (1977) *Wealth of the Roman World AD 300–700*, London.

Kinch, K.F. (1890) *L'Arc de Triomphe de Salonique*, Paris.

Klebs, E. (1889) 'Das Valesische Bruchstück zur Geschichte Constantins', *Philologus* 47: 53–80.

Klein, R. (1977) *Constantius II und die christliche Kirche* (Impulse der Forschung), Darmstadt.

Klein, R. (ed.) (1978) *Julian Apostata* (Wege der Forschung 509), Darmstadt.

Klein, R. (1982) 'Zur Glaubwürdigkeit historischer Aussagen des Bischofs Athanasius von Alexandria über die Religionspolitik des Kaisers Constantius II', *Studia Patristica* 17.3: 996–1017.

Klein, R. (1990) 'Das Kirchenbauverständnis Constantins des Grossen in Rom und in den östlichen Provinzen', in *Das Antike Rom und der Osten: Festschrift für Klaus Parlasca am 65 Geburtstag, herausgegeben von Christoph Börker und Michael Donderer* (Erlanger Forschungen 56), Erlangen: 77–101.

Kolb, F. (1987) *Diocletian und die Erste Tetrarchie*, Berlin.

König, I. (1987) *Origo Constantini, Anonymus Valesianus,* (Trierer historische Forschungen 11), Trier.

Kopecek, T. A. (1974) 'Curial displacements and flight in later fourth-century Cappadocia', *Historia* 23: 320–6.

Kotter, B. (1988) *Die Schriften des Johannes von Damaskos*, 5 vols, Berlin: vol. 5.

Kraft, H. (1955) *Kaiser Konstantins religiöse Entwicklung*, Tübingen.

Kraft, H. (1957) *Zur Taufe Kaiser Konstantins* (Studia Patristica 1 = TU 63), Berlin.

Kuhn, K. H. and Tait, W. J. (1996) *Thirteen Coptic Acrostic Hymns from Manuscript M574 of the Pierpont Morgan Library*, Oxford.

Kurmann, A. (1988) *Gregor von Nazianz Oratio 4 gegen Julian. Ein Kommentar* (Schweizerische Beiträge zur Altertumswissenschaft, Heft 19), Basel.

Lane Fox, R. (1986) *Pagans and Christians*, Harmondsworth.

Lapidge, M. (1986) 'The school of Theodore and Hadrian', *Anglo-Saxon England* 15: 45–72.

Lapidge, M. and Bischoff, B. (eds) (1994) *Biblical Commentaries from the Canterbury School of Theodore and Hadrian*, Cambridge.

Laubscher, H. P. (1975) *Der Reliefschmuck des Galeriusbogens in Thessaloniki*, Berlin.

Leeb, R. (1992) *Konstantin und Christus. Die Verchristlichung der imperialen Repräsentation unter Konstantin dem Grossen als Spiegel seiner Kirchenpolitik und seines Selbstverständnisses als christlicher Kaiser* (Arbeiten zur Kirchengeschichte 58), Berlin.

Lehmann, K. (1920) 'Ein Reliefbild des heiligen Artemios in Konstantinopel', *BNgJ* 1: 381–4.

Leo, F. (1901) *Die Griechisch-Römische Biographie nach ihrer literarischen Form*, Leipzig.

Levison, W. (1924) 'Konstantinische Schenkung und Silvester-Legende', in *Miscellanea Francesco Ehrle, Scritti di Storia e Palaeografia II Per la Storia di Roma* (Studi e Testi 38), Rome: 159–247.

Liebeschuetz, J. H. W. G. (1961) 'Money economy and taxation in kind in Syria in the fourth century A.D.', *Rh. Mus.* 104: 242–56.

Liebeschuetz, J. H. W. G. (1992) 'The end of the ancient city', in J. Rich (ed.) *The City in Late Antiquity*, London: 1–49.

Lieu, S. N. C. (ed.) (1989) *The Emperor Julian: Panegyric and Polemic*, 2nd edn. (TTH 2), Liverpool.

Lieu, S. N. C and Montserrat, D. (1996) *From Constantine to Julian: Pagan and Byzantine Views*, London.

Lightfoot, C. S. (1978) 'The Eastern frontier of the Roman Empire with special reference to the reign of Constantius II', DPhil thesis, University of Oxford.

Lightfoot, C. S. (1990) 'Trajan's Parthian War and the fourth-century perspective', *JRS* 80: 115–26.

Linder, A. (1975) 'The myth of Constantine the Great in the West: sources and hagiographic commemoration', *Studi Medievali*, 3rd ser. 16/1: 43–95.

Linder, A. (1992) 'Constantine's "Ten Laws" Series', in *Fälschungen in Mittelalter. Internationaler Kongreß der Monumenta Germaniae Historica, München, 16–19. September 1986. Teil 2, Gefälschte Rechtstexte – der bestrafte Fälscher* (Monumenta Germaniae Historica Schriften 33/2), Hanover: 491–506.

Lippold, A. (1981) 'Constantius Caesar, Sieger über die Germanen – Nachfahre des Claudius Gothicus? Der Panegyricus von 297 und die Vita Claudii der HA', *Chiron* 11: 347–69.

Lipsius, R. A., and Bonnet, M. (eds) (1891) *Acta Apostolorum apocrypha*, 2 vols, Leipzig.

Loernertz, R.-J. (1974) 'Constitutum Constantini – Destination, destinaires, auteur, date', *Aevum* 48: 199–245.

Maas, M. (1992) *John Lydus and the Roman Past: Antiquarianism and Politics in the Age of Justinian*, London.

Maas, M. P. (1920) 'Artemioskult in Constantinopel', *BNgJ* 1: 377–80.

McCarthy, D., and Ó Cróinín, D. (1987–88) 'The "lost" Irish 84-year Easter table rediscovered', *Peritia* 6–7: 227–42.

MacCormack, S. (1972) 'Change and continuity in Late Antiquity: the ceremony of Adventus', *Historia* 21: 721–52.

MacCormack, S. (1981) *Art and Ceremony in Late Antiquity*, Berkeley, CA.

McCormick, M. (1986) *Eternal Victory: Triumphal Rulership in Late Antiquity, Byzantium, and the Early Medieval West*, Cambridge.

MacCoull, L. S. B. (1982) 'The Coptic Cambyses narrative reconsidered', *GRBS* 23: 185–8.

MacMullen, R. (1968) 'Constantine and the miraculous', *GRBS* 9: 81–96.

MacMullen, R. (1969) *Constantine*, London.

MacMullen, R. (1984) *Christianizing the Roman Empire*, New Haven, CT.

MacMullen, R. (1988) *Corruption and the Decline of Rome*, New Haven, CT.

MacMullen, R. (1990) *Changes in the Roman Empire*, Princeton, NJ.

McNally, R.E. (1958) 'The *tres linguae sacrae* in early Irish biblical exegesis', *Theological Studies* 19: 395–403.

Magdalino, P. (ed.) (1994) *New Constantines: Rhythm of Imperial Renewal in Byzantium, 4th–13th Centuries*, Aldershot.

Magoulias, H. J. (1964) 'The lives of the saints as sources of data for the history of Byzantine medicine in the sixth and seventh centuries', *BZ* 57: 127–50.

Malay, H. (1988) 'Letters of Pertinax and the Proconsul Aemilius Juncus to the city of Tabala', *Epigraphica Anatolica* 12: 47–52.

Malherbe, A. J. and Ferguson, E. (1978) *Gregory of Nyssa: the Life of Moses*, New York.

Mango, C. (1979) 'On the history of the Templon and the Martyrion of St. Artemios at Constantinople', *Zograf* 10: 40–3.

Mango, C. (1985) *Le dévelopement urbain de Constantinople IVᵉ-VIIᵉ siècles* (Travaux et Mémoires du Centre de Recherche d'Histoire et Civilisation de Byzance, Collège de France, Monographies 2), Paris.

Mango, C. (1990) 'Constantine's mausoleum and the translation of the relics', *BZ* 83: 51–61.

Mango, C. (1994) 'The Empress Helena, Helenopolis, Pylae', *Travaux et Mémoires* 12: 143–58.

Manitius, Max (1886) 'Zu Aldhelm und Baeda', *Sitzungsberichte der kaiserlichen Akademie der Wissenschaften, phil.-hist. Kl.* 112: 535–634.

Maraval, P. (1985) *Lieux-saints et pèlerinages d'Orient*, Paris.

Markus, R. A. (1975) 'Church history and the early church historians', in D. Baker (ed.) *The Materials, Sources and Methods of Ecclesiastical History*, Oxford: 1–17.

Marot, H. (1960) 'Conciles anténicéens et conciles œcuméniques', in *Le Concile et les Conciles*, Chevetogne: 19–43.

Matthews, J. F. (1989) *The Roman Empire of Ammianus*, London.

Messenger, R. (1944–5) 'The legend of St Eulalia in Mozarabic hymns', *Classical World* 38: 12–13.

Millar, F. G. B. (1969) 'P. Herennius Dexippus: the Greek world and the third-century invasions', *JRS* 59: 12–29.

Millar, F. G. B. (1971) 'Paul of Samosata, Zenobia and Aurelian: the church, local culture and political allegiance in third-century Syria', *JRS* 61: 1–17.

Millar, F. G. B. (1977) *The Emperor in the Roman World*, London.

Millar, F. G. B. (1989) 'Empire, community and culture in the Roman

Near East: Greeks, Syrians, Jews and Arabs', *Journal of Jewish Studies* 38: 143–64.

Millar, F. G. B. (1992) 'The Jews of the Graeco-Roman diaspora between paganism and Christianity, AD 312–438', in J. Lieu, J. North and T. Rajak (eds) *The Jews among Pagans and Christians in the Roman Empire*, London and New York: 97–123.

Milner, C. (1994) 'Image of the rightful ruler: Anicia Juliana's Constantine mosaic in the church of Hagios Polyeuktos', in P. Magdalino (ed.), *New Constantines: Rhythm of Imperial Renewal in Byzantium, 4th–13th Centuries*, Aldershot: 73–82.

Mitchell, S. (1988) 'Maximinus and the Christians in A.D. 312: A New Latin Inscription', *JRS* 78: 104–24.

Mitchell, S. (1993) *Anatolia: Land, Men, and Gods in Asia Minor*, 2 vols, Oxford.

Momigliano, A. D. (1963) 'Pagan and Christian historiography in the fourth century A. D.', in A. D. Momigliano (ed.) *The Conflict between Paganism and Christianity in the Fourth Century*, Oxford: 79–99.

Momigliano, A. D. (1971) *The Development of Greek Biography*, Cambridge, MA.

Momigliano, A. D. (ed.) (1963) *The Conflict between Paganism and Christianity in the Fourth Century*, Oxford.

Mommsen, T. (1905–13) *Gesammelte Schriften*, 8 vols, Berlin.

Moreau, J. (1954) *Lactance, De la mort des persécuteurs* (SC 39), 2 vols, Paris.

Moreau, J. (1955) 'Zum Problem der Vita Constantini', *Historia* 4: 234–45.

Moreau, J. (1971) *Excerpta Valesiana*, Leipzig.

Müller, C. D. G. (1991) 'Romances', in A. S. Atiya, *Coptic Encyclopedia*, 12 vols, New York: vol. 7: 2059–61.

Müller, H. (1946) *Christians and Pagans from Constantine to Augustine, Part 1, The Religious Policies of the Roman Emperors*, Pretoria.

Müller-Rettig, B. (1990) *Der Panegyricus des Jahres 310 auf Konstantin den Grossen*, (Palingenesia 331), Stuttgart.

Munier, H. (1918) 'Un éloge copte de l'empereur Constantin', *Annales du Service des Antiquités de l'Égypte* 18: 65–71.

Musurillo, H. (ed.) (1972) *The Acts of the Christian Martyrs*, Oxford.

Nash-Williams, V. E. (1950) *The Early Christian Monuments of Wales*, Cardiff.

Nestle, E. (1895) 'Die Kreuzauffindungslegende. Nach einer Handshcrift von Sinai', *BZ* 4: 325.31.

Nicol, D. M. (1992) *The Immortal Emperor: The Life and Legend of Constantine Palaiologos, Last Emperor of the Romans*, Cambridge.

Nicolet, C. (1991) 'Le *monumentum ephesianum* et les dîmes d'Asie', *BCH* 115: 465–80.

Nixon, C. E. V. (1981) 'The panegyric of 307 and Maximian's visit to Rome', *Phoenix* 35: 70–6.

Nixon, C. E. V. (1987) 'Latin panegryic in the tetrarchic and Constantinian period', in B. Croke and A. Emmett Nobbs (eds) *History and Historians in Late Antiquity*, Sydney: 88–99.

Nixon, C. E. V. (1993) 'Constantinus Oriens Imperator, propaganda and panegyric: on reading panegyric 7 (307)', *Historia*: 42/2: 229–46.

Nixon, C. E. V. and Rodgers, B. S. (1994) *In Praise of Later Roman Emperors: The Panegyrici Latini*, Berkeley, Los Angeles and London.

Nock, A. D. (1952) 'The Roman Army and the Roman religious year', *Harvard Theological Review* 45: 187–252.

Noethlics, K. L. (1971) 'Die gesetzgeberischen Maßnahmen der christlichen Kaiser des vierten Jahrhunderts gegen Häretiker, Heiden und Juden', PhD thesis, University of Cologne.

Nollé, J. (1982) 'Epigraphica Varia', *ZPE* 48: 267–82.

Nollé, J. (1986) '"Oriens Augusti" Kaiserpanegyrik und Perserkriegspropaganda auf Münzen der Stadt Side in Pamphylien unter Valerian und Gallienus (253–268)', *Jahrbuch für Numismatik und Geldgeschichte* 36: 127–43.

Nollé, J. (1993) *Side im Altertum I*, Bonn.

Norman, A. F. (1965) *Libanius' Autobiography (Oration 1)*, Oxford.

Oates, D. (1968) *Studies in the Ancient History of Northern Iraq*, Oxford.

Obolensky, D. (1988) *Six Byzantine Portraits*, Oxford.

O'Brien, M. A. (1973) 'Old Irish personal names', *Celtica* 10: 211–36.

O'Rahilly, T. F. (1946) 'On the origin of the names Érainn and Ériu', *Ériu* 14: 7–28.

Odahl, C. M. (1976) 'Constantine and the militarization of Christianity. A contribution to the study of Christian attitudes towards war and military service', PhD thesis, University of California at San Diego.

Oliphant, R. T. (ed.) (1966) *The Harley Latin-Old English Glossary*, (Janua Linguarum Series Practica 20), The Hague and Paris.

Opitz, H.-G. (1934) 'Die Vita Constantini des codex Angelicus 22', *Byz.* 9: 540–90.

Orchard, A. (1994) *The Poetic Art of Aldhelm* (Cambridge Studies in Anglo-Saxon England 8), Cambridge.

Orlandi, T. (1967–70) *Storia della Chiesa de Alessandria, Testo copto, traduzione e commento. Vol. I: Da Pietro ad Atanasio, Vol. II: Da Teofilo ad Timoteo II*, Milan.

Orlandi, T. (1974) *Papiri Copti di Contenuto Teologico*, Vienna.

Orlandi, T., Pearson, B. A. and Drake, H. A. (1981) *Eudoxia and the Holy Sepulchre: A Constantinian Legend in Coptic*, Milan.

Pack, E. (1986) *Städte und Steuern in der Politik Julians: Untersuchungen zu den Quellen eines Kaiserbildes* (Collection Latomus 194), Brussels.

Paschoud, F. (1971) *Zosime, Histoire Nouvelle, I (Livres I et II)*, Paris.

Pasquali, G. (1910) 'Die Composition der Vita Constantini des Eusebius', *Hermes* 45: 369–86.

Pasqualini, A. (1979) *Massimiano Herculius: per un'interpretazione della figure e dell'opera*, Rome.

Pätzig, E. (1898) 'Über die Quelle des Anonymus Valesii', *BZ* 7: 572–85.

Pearson, B., Vivian, T. and Spanel, D. (1993) *Two Coptic Homilies Attributed to Saint Peter of Alexandria: On Riches, On the Epiphany*, Rome.

Petit, P. (1950) 'Libanius et la "Vita Constantini"', *Historia* 1: 562–82.

Petit, P. (1955) *Libanius et la vie municipale à Antioche au IVe siècle après J.-C.*, Paris.

Petrović, P. (1980) 'Les forteresses du Bas-Empire sur le limes Danubien en Serbie', in W. S. Hanson and L. J. F. Keppie (eds) *Roman Frontier Studies 1979: Papers Presented to the 12th International Congress of Roman Frontier Studies* (British Archaeological Reports, International Series 21), Oxford: 757–74.

Pheifer, J. D. (1987) 'Early Anglo-Saxon glossaries and the School of Canterbury', *Anglo-Saxon England* 16: 17–44.

Piétri, C. (1989) 'La politique de Constance II: Un premier "césaropapisme" ou l'imitatio Constantini?', in A. Dihle (ed.) *L'Église et l'empire au IVe siècle* (Entretiens sur l'Antiquité Classique 34), Vandœuvres-Génève: 113–72.

Piganiol, M. (1932) *L'Empereur Constantin*, Paris.

Pilloy, J. (1895) *Études sur d'anciens lieux de sépultures dans l'Aisne*, 2 vols, Saint-Quentin.

Pitra, J.-B. (1883) *Analecta sacra Spicilegio Solesmensi parata IV*, Paris.

Plöchl, W. M. (1960) *Geschichte des Kirchenrechts* I, 2nd edn, Vienna.

Pohlkamp, W. (1983) 'Tradition und Topographie: Papst Sylvester I. (314–335) und der Drache vom Forum Romanum', *RQA* 78: 1–100.

Pohlkamp, W. (1984) 'Kaiser Konstantin, der heidnische und der christliche Kult in den Actus Silvestri', *Frühe Mittelalterliche Studien* 18: 357–400.

Pohlkamp, W. (1988) 'Privilegium ecclesiae Romanae pontifici contulit: Zur Vorgeschichte der Konstantinischen Schenkung', in *Fälschungen* 1988: 413–90.

Pohlkamp, W. (1992) 'Textfassungen, literarische Formen und geschichtliche Funktionen der römischen Silvester-Akten', *Francia* 19: 115–96.

Portmann, W. (1988) *Geschichte in der spätantike Panegyrik*, Frankfurt.

Portmann, W. (1989) 'Die 59 Rede des Libanios und das Datum der Schlacht von Singara', *BZ* 82: 1–18.

Potter, D. S. P. (1990) *Prophecy and History in the Crisis of the Roman Empire: A Historical Commentary on the Thirteenth Sibylline Oracle*, Oxford.

Previale, L. (1949) 'Teoria e prassi del panegirico bizantino', *Emerita* 17: 72–105.

Price, S. R. F. (1984) *Rituals and Power: The Roman Imperial Cult in Asia Minor*, Cambridge.

Raglan, Lord (1965) 'The hero of tradition', in A. Dundes (ed.) *The Study of Folklore*, Englewood Cliffs, NJ: 142–57.

Rahner, K. (1953) 'Antenna Crucis,' 5 'Das mystische Tau', *Zeitschrift für Katholische Theologie* 75: 385–410.

Restle, M. (1968) 'Ephesos', *Reallexikon zur byzantinischen Kunst* II: 179.

Reynolds, J. and Tannenbaum, R. (1987) *Jews and Godfearers in Aphrodisias*, Cambridge.

Ridley, R. T. (1982) *Zosimus: New History* (Byzantina Australiensia 2), Melbourne.

Robert, L. (1949) 'Inscriptions de la région de Yalova en Bithynie', *Hellenika* 7: 30–44.

Robert, L. (1982) *A Travers l'Asie Mineure*, Paris.

Rochow, I. (1990) 'Chronographie', in F. Winkelmann and W. Brandes (eds) *Quellen zur Geschichte des frühen Byzanz (4.-9. Jahrhundert): Bestand und Probleme*, Amsterdam: 190–201.

Rodgers, B. S. (1980) 'Constantine's pagan vision', *Byz.* 50: 259–78.

Rostovtzeff, M. I. (1957) *Social and Economic History of the Roman Empire*, vol. 2, Oxford.

Roueché, C. (1981) 'Rome, Asia and Aphrodisias in the 3rd century', *JRS* 71: 103–20.

Roueché, C. (1989) *Aphrodisias in Late Antiquity*, London.

Rubin, Z. (1982) 'The Church of the Holy Sepulchre and the conflict between the Sees of Caesarea and Jerusalem', in L. I. Levine (ed.) *Jerusalem Cathedra II*, Jerusalem and Detroit: 79–105.

Russell, D. (1973) *Plutarch*, London.

Ryssel, V. (1895) 'Syrische Quellen abendländischer Erzählungsstoffe', *Archiv für das Studium der neueren Sprachen und Literaturen*, XLIX (95): 21–54.

Şahin, S. (1979–87) *Katalog der Antiken Inschriften des Museums von Iznik*, 2 vols, Bonn.

Salway, P. (1981) *Roman Britain*, Oxford.

Schlumberger, J. (1974) *Die Epitome de Caesaribus. Untersuchungen zur heidenischen Geschichtschreibung des 4. Jahrhunderts n. Chr.* (Vestigia XVIII), Munich.

Schlumberger, J. (1982) *Die verlorenen Annales des Nicomachus Flavianus: ein Werk über Geschichte der römischen Republik oder Kaiserzeit?* (Bonner Historia Augusta Colloquium 1982–83), Bonn: 302–29.

Schneemelcher, W. (1970) *Kirche und Staat im 4. Jahrhundert* (Bonner Akademische Reden 37), Bonn.

Schneider, A. M. (1934) *Die Brotvermehrungskirche von Et Tabgah am Genesareth-see* (Collectanea Hierosolymitana 4), Jerusalem.

Schneider, A. M. (1941a) 'Zur Baugeschichte der Geburtskirche in Bethlehem', *Zeitschrift des deutschen Palästina-Vereins* 64: 74–91.

Schneider, A. M. (1941b) 'Zur Datierung der Vita Constantini et Helenae', *Zeitschrift für neutestamentliche Wissenschaft und die Kunde der alteren Kirche* 40: 245–9.

Schreckenberg, H. (1990) *Die christlichen Adversus-Judaeos-Texte und ihr literarisches und historisches Umfeld (1.-11. Jh.)*, Frankfurt.

Schwartz, E. (1936) *Kaiser Constantin und die christliche Kirche*, 2nd edition, Leipzig.

Schwartz, E. (1959) *Zur Geschichte des Athanasius* (= Gesammelte Schriften 3), Berlin.

Schwartz, J. (1958–60) 'Dioclétien dans la littérature copte', *Bulletin de la Société d'Archéologie Copte* 15: 151–66.

Scott, R. (1994) 'The image of Constantine in Malalas and Theophanes', in P. Magdalino (ed.), *New Constantines: Rhythm of Imperial Renewal in Byzantium, 4th-13th Centuries*, Aldershot: 57–71.

Scott, W. and Ferguson, A. S. (1936) *Hermetica. The Ancient Greek and Latin Writings which Contain Religious and Philosophic Teachings Ascribed to Hermes Trismegistus, Vol. IV, Testimonia*, Oxford.

Seager, R. (1983) 'Some imperial virtues in the Latin Prose Panegyrics, the demands of propaganda and the dynamics of literary composition', in F. Cairns (ed.) *Papers of the Liverpool Latin Seminar IV*, Liverpool: 129–65.

Seeck, O. (1906) *Die Briefe des Libanius zeitlich geordnet*, Leipzig.

Seeck, O. (1911) *Geschichte des Untergangs der antiken Welt*, 4 vols, Stuttgart: vol. 4.

Seeck, O. (1919) *Regesten der Kaiser und Papste für die Jahre 311 bis 476 n. Chr.*, Stuttgart.

Seeck, O. (1921) *Geschichte des Untergangs der antiken Welt*, 4 vols, Stuttgart: vol. 2.

Seston, W. (1946) *Dioclétien et la Tétrarchie*, Paris.

Setz, W. (1975) *Lorenzo Vallas Schrift gegen die Konstantinische Schenkung*, Tübingen.

Ševčenko, N. P. (1991) 'Menologion of Basil II', *ODB* II: 1341–2.

Shahar, S. (1983) *The Fourth Estate: A History of Women in the Middle Ages*, London and New York.

Sievers, R. (1868) *Das Leben des Libanius*, Berlin.

Simon, J. (1924) 'Note sur l'original de la Passion de Sainte Fébronie', *AB* 42: 66–76.

Simon, J. (1935) 'Homélie copte inédite sur S. Michel et le Bon Larron, attribuée à S. Jean Chrysostome', *Orientalia* 4: 222–34.

Sims-Williams, P. P. (1983) 'Gildas and the Anglo-Saxons', *Cambridge Medieval Celtic Studies* 6: 1–30.

Smith, R. B. E. (1986) 'Studies in the religious and intellectual background of Julian the Apostate', DPhil thesis, University of Oxford.

Speidel, M. P. (1986) 'Maxentius and his *Equites Singulares* in the Battle at the Milvian Bridge', *Classical Antiquity* 5: 253–62.

Speidel, M. P. (1995) 'Die Garde des Maximus auf der Theodosiussaüle', *Istanbuler Mitteilungen* 45.

Spiegelberg, W. (1901) 'Koptische Kreuzlegenden: Ein neues Bruchstück der koptischen Volksliteratur', *Recueil des Travaux relatifs à la Philologie et à l'Archéologie égyptiennes et assyriennes* 23: 206–11.

Staniforth, M. (1987) *Early Christian Writings: The Apostolic Fathers*, trans. M. Staniforth with Introduction and new editorial material by Andrew Louth, Harmondsworth.

Stein, E. (1959) *Histoire du Bas-Empire*, tr. J.-R. Palanque, Paris.

Stevens, C. E. (1938) 'Magnus Maximus in British History', *Études Celtiques* 3: 86–94.

Stevenson, J. (1987) *A New Eusebins*, 2nd edition revised by W. H. C. Frend, London.

Stevenson, J. B. (1992) 'Rubisca, Hiberno-Latin and the hermeneutic tradition', *Nottingham Medieval Studies* 36: 1–27.

Stevenson, J. B. (1995) *Laterculus Malalianus and the School of Archbishop Theodore*, Cambridge.

Stillwell, R. (ed.) (1938) *Antioch-on-the-Orontes II: The Excavations 1933–36*, Princeton, NJ.

Stokes, W. (1903) 'The death of Crimthann and the adventures of Eochaid', *Revue Celtique* 24: 172–207.

Syme, R. (1974) *The Ancestry of Constantine* (Bonner Historia-Augusta-Colloquium 1971), Bonn: 237–53.

Taft, R. F. and Ševčenko, N. P. (1991) 'Synaxarion', *ODB* III: 1991.

Thompson, E. A. (1947) *The Historical Work of Ammianus Marcellinus*, Cambridge.

Thomson, R. W. (1978) *Moses Khorenats'i: History of the Armenians*, Cambridge, MA.

Tolstoi, J. (1926) 'Un poncif arétologique dans les miracles d'Asklepios et d'Artemios', *Byz.* 3: 53–63.

Trebilco, P. (1991) *Jewish Communities in Asia Minor*, Cambridge.

Treggiari, S. (1991) *Roman Marriage*, Oxford.

Vaes, J. (1984–6) 'Christliche Wiederverwendung antiker Bauten: ein Forschungsbericht', *Ancient Society* 15–17: 305–443.

van Berchem, D. (1937) *L'Annone militaire dans l'empire romain du IIIe siècle*, Paris.

van Dam, R. (1986) 'Emperors, bishops, and friends in Late Antique Cappadocia', *JTS* n.s. 37: 53–76.

van den Berg-Onstwedder, G. (1990) 'Diocletian in the Coptic tradition', *Bulletin de la Société d'Archéologie Copte* 29: 87–122.

van Esbroeck, M. (1982) 'Legends about Constantine in Armenian', in T. J. Samuelian (ed.) *Classical Armenian Culture: Influences and Creativity* (University of Pennsylvania Armenian Texts and Studies 4), Philadelphia, PA: 91–6.

Vogt, J. (1963) 'Pagans and Christians in the family of Constantine the Great', in A. D. Momigliano (ed.) *The Conflict between Paganism and Christianity in the Fourth Century*, Oxford: 38–54.

Vogt, J. (1973) *Constantin der Grosse und sein Jahrhundert*, Munich.

BIBLIOGRAPHY

von Domaszewski, A. (1895) *Die Religion des römischen Heeres*, Trier.

von Harnack, A. (1905) *Militia Christi: die Christliche Religion und der Soldatenstand in den ersten Drei Jahrhunderten*, Tübingen.

von Petrikovits, H. (1960) *Das römische Rheinland. Archäologische Forschungen seit 1945* (Arbeitsgemeinschaft für Forschung des Landes Nordrhein-Westfalen, Geisteswissenschaften 86), Cologne and Opladen.

von Petrikovits, H. (1971) 'Fortifications in the North-Western Roman Empire from the third to the fifth centuries A.D.' *JRS* 61: 178–219.

von Petrikovits, H. (1978) *Rheinische Geschichte, I. Altertum*, Düsseldorf.

Walker, P. W. L. (1990) *Holy City, Holy Places*, Oxford.

Wardman, A. (1974) *Plutarch's Lives*, London.

Warmington, B. H. (1974) 'Aspects of the Constantinian propaganda in the Panegyrici Latini', *TAPA* 104: 371–84.

Warmington, B. H. (1985) 'The sources of some Constantinian documents in Eusebius' Church History and Life of Constantine', *Studia Patristica* 18(1): 93–8.

Weis, B. K. (1973) *Julian, Briefe, Griechisch-deutsch*, Munich.

Weiss, P. (1992) 'Münzprägung in Pisidien', in E. Schwertheim (ed.) *Forschungen in Pisidien* (Asia-Minor-Studien 7), Bonn: 143–65.

Westerhuis, D. J. A. (1906) *Origo Constantini Imperatoris sive Anonymi Valesiani pars prior*, Groningen.

Whitby, M. (1994) 'Images for emperors in late antiquity: a search for New Constantine', in P. Magdalino (ed.) *New Constantines: Rhythm of Imperial Renewal in Byzantium, 4th–13th Centuries*, Aldershot: 83–94.

Whittaker, C. R. (1994) *Frontiers of the Roman Empire: A Social and Economic Study*, Baltimore, MD.

Whittow, M. (1990) 'Ruling the late Roman and early Byzantine city: a continuous history', *Past and Present* 129: 3–29.

Wiemer, H.-U. (1994) 'Libanius on Constantine', *Classical Quarterly* n.s. 44/2: 511–24.

Wilbur, D. N. (1938) 'The Plateau of Daphne, the springs and the water-system', in R. Stillwell (ed.) *Antioch-on-the-Orontes, II: The Excavations 1933–36*, Princeton, NJ: 49–56.

Wilken, R. (1983) *John Chrysostom and the Jews*, Berkeley, CA.

Wilkinson, J. (1971) *Egeria's Travels*, London.

Williams, I. (ed.) (1927) *Breudwyt Macsen*, Bangor.

Williams, M. H. (1992) 'The Jews and Godfearers Inscription from Aphrodisias – a case of patriarchal interference in early 3rd century Caria?', *Historia* 41: 297–310.

Williams, S. (1985) *Diocletian and the Roman Recovery*, London.

Windass, S. (1964) *Christianity versus Violence*, London.

Winkelmann, F. (1962) *Die Textbezeugung der Vita Constantini des Eusebius von Caesarea* (TU 84), Berlin.

Winkelmann, F. (1964) 'Die Beurteilung des Eusebius von Cäsarea und seiner Vita Constantini im griechischen Osten', in J. Irmscher (ed.), *Byzantinische Beiträge*, Berlin: 91–119.

Winkelmann, F. (1966) *Untersuchungen zur Kirchengeschichte des Gelasios von Kaisareia* (Sitzungsberichte der Deutschen Akademie der Wissenschaften, Klasse für Sprachen, Literatur und Kunst Jahrgang 1965, No. 3), Berlin.

Winkelmann, F. (1973) 'Ein Ordnungsversuch der griechischen hagiographischen Konstantinviten und ihrer Überlieferung', in J. Irmscher and P. Nagel (eds) *Studia Byzantina* II, Berlin: 267–84.

Winkelmann, F. (1978) 'Das hagiographische Bild Konstantins I. in mittelbyzantinischer Zeit', in V. Vavřínek (ed.) *Beiträge zur byzantinischen Geschichte im 9.-11. Jh.*, Prague: 179–203.

Winkelmann, F. (1982) 'Vita Metrophanis et Alexandri (*BHG* 1279)', *AB* 100: 147–83.

Winkelmann, F. (1987) 'Die älteste erhaltene griechische hagiographische Vita Konstantins und Helenas (*BHG* N. 365z, 366, 366a)', in J. Dummer (ed.), *Texte und Textkritik. Eine Aufsatzsammlung* (= TU 133), Berlin: 623–38.

Winkelmann, F. (1990) 'Kirchengeschichtswerke', in F. Winkelmann and W. Brandes (eds) *Quellen zur Geschichte des frühen Byzanz (4.-9. Jahrhundert): Bestand und Probleme*, Amsterdam: 202–12.

Winkelmann, F. (1993) *Studien zu Konstantin dem Grossen und zur byzantinischen Kirchengeschichte*, ed. W. Brandes and J. F. Haldon, Birmingham.

Winkelmann, F. and Brandes, W. (1990) *Quellen zur Geschichte des frühen Byzanz (4.-9. Jahrhundert): Bestand und Probleme*, Amsterdam.

Winterbottom, M. (1977) 'Aldhelm's prose style and its origins', *Anglo-Saxon England* 6: 39–76.

Wood, I. (1984) 'The end of Roman Britain: continental evidence and parallels', in M. Lapidge and D. N. Dumville (eds) *Gildas: New Approaches*, Woodbridge: 1–25.

Woods, D. (1991) 'The date of the translation of the relics of SS. Luke and Andrew to Constantinople', *Vigiliae Christianae* 45: 286–92.

Wright, C. D. (1993) *The Irish Tradition in Old English Literature*, Cambridge.

Young, F. M. (1983) *From Nicaea to Chalcedon: A Guide to the Literature and its Background*, London.

Zecchini, G. (1993) *Ricerche di storiografia latina tardoantica*, Rome.

Ziegler, R. (1985) *Städtisches Prestige und Kaiserliche Politik*, Düsseldorf.

INDEX OF ANCIENT SOURCES

GENERAL INDEX

heresies, heretics 9, 23, 31, 35, 36,
40, 67, 86, 88, 90, 117, 145, 178,
182, 187
Hesychius of Miletus 166
Hilary of Poitiers 15, 17
Hispellum 53
Honorius 21, 25, 35
Hopkins, Keith 63
Hyginus 63
hymns 118, 141, 180–1, 199

iconoclasts 3, 153
Ignatius, St, martyr 22
Irai, St, martyr 180
Ireland 192, 194, 196, 200, 202
Isauria 10, 59

Jacob of Sarug 142
Jerome, St 21, 26, 140, 147
Jerusalem 29, 96, 147, 180, 181–2;
Church of Holy Sepulchre 12, 120,
183–4; Council of 12
Jews 8, 67–8, 100–02, 118, 137, 139,
181–2
John Chrysostom, St 22, 33, 155
John the Evangelist, St 29
John of Lycopolis, hermit 29
John Malalas 52, 143
John of Nikiou 178–9, 181, 186
Jovian, Emperor 34–5
Julian, Emperor 12, 15, 28, 30, 31–5,
40, 64, 80, 108, 154, 156, 179
Jupiter 23, 36

Kelly, J. N. D. 9

labarum 26–8, 117, 131, 134, 151
Lactantius 25, 59, 76, 154–5, 163
Lane Fox, Robin 96
legislation, imperial 55, 59, 66, 81,
97, 99, 114, 119, 120
Leonas, comes 10
Libanius 30, 31, 60
Liber Pontificalis 139, 145
Liberius, Pope 15, 40–1, 143, 179
Licinius 11, 22, 23, 25, 27, 80, 86,
90, 91, 98, 117, 118, 145
Lucian, St 52, 158
Lucifer of Caralis 15, 17
Luther, Martin 149

Lycaonia 59
Lycopolis 29
Lydia 60

Macrina, St 2, 124, 125
Magnentius 28, 29, 31
Magnus Maxiumus 34, 190
Mamertinus 75
Manichaeans 23, 37
mansiones 53, 56, 64
Marcellus of Ancyra 12
Marcellus, bishop of Apamea 30
Marcellus, St, martyr 24
Marcian, Emperor 157
Marianus, imperial notarius 11, 95
Marinus, St, martyr 24
Marnas, temple of 30
Martin, St 25, 34, 39
martyrs 24, 33, 39, 52, 108, 123,
124, 144, 152, 156, 180, 181, 199
Mascezel 29
Mawhûb ibn Mansûr ibn Muffarig 179
Maxentius 25, 26, 76, 116, 117, 145,
153, 162, 163, 178, 190
Maximian 24, 74, 75–7
Maximianus Herculius 158, 162
Maximinus Daia 118, 178
Maximus, philosopher 32
Maximus, bishop of Turin 40
Mehmet II 4, 152
Meletius of Antioch 124
Melitians 87, 182
Mercurius, St, martyr 180
Milan 21; Council of 15; Edict of 67
Militiades, Pope 8, 145
Millar, Fergus 7
Milvian Bridge, battle of 7, 21, 24,
25, 116, 144, 154, 155, 182
Minervina 79
Mithras 23, 138
monks, monasteries 22, 23, 27, 122,
125, 184, 185
Monophysitism 178, 187
Moses 27, 107; as biographical
paradigm for Constantine 107–26,
143
Mursa, battle of 28

Nacolea 53, 66
Naissus 32, 157–8